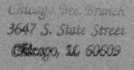

PLATE 1 Etowah Mound, Etowah, Georgia

PLATE 2 Burial site of Bartholomew Gosnold, Jamestown, Virginia

PLATE 3   Wooden crosses, San Juan Bautista Mission, California

PLATE 4 Death's-heads, Circular Churchyard, Charleston, South Carolina

PLATE 5 Soul effigy, Circular Churchyard, Charleston, South Carolina

PLATE 6 Heavenly Queen, Calvary Cemetery, St. Louis, Missouri

PLATE 7　Separation fence, Jewish section, Oak Woods Cemetery, Chicago

PLATE 8 Lin Yee Chung Chinese Cemetery, Oahu, Hawaii

PLATE 9 Mary Baker Eddy Memorial, Mount Auburn Cemetery, Cambridge, Massachusetts

PLATE 10   Forest Lawn Cemetery, Glendale, California

PLATE 11   King's Chapel Burying Ground, Boston

PLATE 12 Jonathan and George Bunker, Phipp's Street Burying Ground, Charlestown, Massachusetts

PLATE 13 Copp's Hill Burying Ground, Boston

PLATE 14   Lopez tombstone, Touro Jewish Cemetery, Newport, Rhode Island

PLATE 15 "Ann, A Negro Child," Common Burial Ground, Newport, Rhode Island

PLATE 16   Calvary Cemetery, Queens, New York, with nearly 3 million graves

PLATE 17 Dutch Reformed Churchyard seen from inside the church, Brooklyn, New York

PLATE 18 Trinity Churchyard, New York City

PLATE 19   Warner tomb, Laurel Hill Cemetery, Philadelphia

PLATE 20   Amish cemetery, Bird-in-Hand, Lancaster County, Pennsylvania

PLATE 21 Ecclesiastes XII, Beth Elohim, Charleston, South Carolina

PLATE 22   Coffin-shaped tombstone, Bethel United Methodist Church, Charleston, South Carolina

PLATE 23 Cannon and Civil War dead, Magnolia Cemetery, Charleston, South Carolina

PLATE 24 Rural burial ground, Nassau Island, South Carolina

PLATE 25 Slave headstones, Laurel Grove Cemetery, Savannah, Georgia

PLATE 26 "August," Laurel Grove Cemetery, Savannah, Georgia

PLATE 27   Statue under hanging moss, Bonaventure Cemetery, Savannah, Georgia

PLATE 28 Mausoleum lock, Bonaventure Cemetery, Savannah, Georgia

PLATE 29 Aboveground tombs, St. Louis II Cemetery, New Orleans, Louisiana

PLATE 30 Angels at night, Metairie Cemetery, New Orleans, Louisiana

PLATE 31 "So Sadly Misted," Holt Cemetery, New Orleans, Louisiana

PLATE 32 After Hurricane Katrina, half-buried Madonna, Holt Cemetery, New Orleans, Louisiana

PLATE 33   Carmelino Maciocia, Calvary Cemetery, St. Louis, Missouri

PLATE 34 Dred Scott, Calvary Cemetery, St. Louis, Missouri

PLATE 35   Charles Balmer, Bellefontaine Cemetery, St. Louis, Missouri

PLATE 36 Isaiah Sellers, Bellefontaine Cemetery, St. Louis, Missouri

PLATE 37 Anthropomorphic marker for Angelina Hardin, Jewell Family Cemetery, Columbia, Missouri

PLATE 38 Sleeping mother and child, Roseland Cemetery, Chicago

PLATE 39 Gypsy couple, Forest Home/German Waldheim Cemetery, Chicago

PLATE 40 Getty tomb, Graceland Cemetery, Chicago

PLATE 41 Schoenhofen mausoleum, Graceland Cemetery, Chicago

PLATE 42   Crucifix, All Saints Polish National Catholic Cemetery, Chicago

PLATE 43 Gravestones, Mount Olive Scandinavian Cemetery, Chicago

PLATE 44 Niche, Bohemian National Columbarium, Chicago

PLATE 45   Wrought-iron Alsatian cross, Castroville Catholic cemetery, Castroville, Texas

PLATE 46 Day of the Dead, San Fernando Cemetery, San Antonio, Texas

PLATE 47   Four candles, San Fernando Cemetery, San Antonio, Texas

PLATE 48 Junípero Serra among the tombstones, Mission Dolores, San Francisco

PLATE 49   Drytown City Cemetery, Amador County, California

PLATE 50 Remembrance stones, Jewish cemetery, Jackson, California

PLATE 51   Mausoleum, Hollywood Forever, Hollywood, California

PLATE 52   Spirit trail, Honokahua, Maui, Hawaii

PLATE 53   Catholic cemetery, Honolulu, Oahu, Hawaii

PLATE 54   Loo Lum Shee, Lin Yee Chung Chinese Cemetery, Oahu, Hawaii

PLATE 55 Fallen Chinese tombstones on beach, Lahaina, Maui, Hawaii

PLATE 56   Japanese cemetery above Red Sands Beach, Hana, Maui, Hawaii

PLATE 57 Arlington National Cemetery, Arlington, Virginia

PLATE 58   Markers, Gettysburg National Cemetery, Gettysburg, Pennsylvania

PLATE 59   "Punchbowl," National Memorial Cemetery of the Pacific, Oahu, Hawaii

PLATE 60   Pet cemetery, Presidio military base, San Francisco

PLATE 61   Native American veteran, Shivwit band of Paiute Indians, reservation cemetery, Gunlock, Utah

PLATE 62 Replacement military headstones, Magnolia Cemetery, Charleston, South Carolina

PLATE 63 "Beloved Mother," Japanese headstones on beach, Maui, Hawaii

PLATE 64 "Looking Forward," Kate Tracy and her mother, 1854, Walnut Grove Cemetery, Boonville, Missouri

THE AMERICAN RESTING PLACE

ALSO BY MARILYN YALOM

MATERNITY, MORTALITY, AND THE LITERATURE OF MADNESS

BLOOD SISTERS: THE FRENCH REVOLUTION IN WOMEN'S MEMORY

A HISTORY OF THE BREAST

A HISTORY OF THE WIFE

BIRTH OF THE CHESS QUEEN: A HISTORY

ALSO BY REID S. YALOM

COLONIAL NOIR: PHOTOGRAPHS FROM MEXICO

THE
AMERICAN
RESTING
PLACE

FOUR HUNDRED YEARS
OF HISTORY THROUGH
OUR CEMETERIES
AND BURIAL GROUNDS

MARILYN YALOM

PHOTOGRAPHS BY REID S. YALOM

HOUGHTON MIFFLIN COMPANY

BOSTON · NEW YORK   2008

www.houghtonmifflinbooks.com

Library of Congress Cataloging-in-Publication Data

Yalom, Marilyn.
The American resting place / Marilyn Yalom ; photographs by Reid S. Yalom.
p. cm.
Includes bibliographical references and index.
ISBN 978-0-618-62427-0
1. Cemeteries — United States. 2. Cemeteries — United States — Pictorial works. 3. United States — History, Local. 4. United States — History, Local — Pictorial works. 5. Sepulchral monuments — United States. 6. Funeral rites and ceremonies — United States. 7. United States — Social life and customs. I. Title.
e159.y35 2008 929'.50973 — dc22 2008001861

PRINTED IN THE UNITED STATES OF AMERICA

BOOK DESIGN BY ROBERT OVERHOLTZER

MP 10 9 8 7 6 5 4 3 2 1

PHOTOGRAPH ON PAGE viii:
Veiled Column, Loudon Park Cemetery, Baltimore, Maryland

FOR THE NEXT GENERATION:

Lily, Alana, Lenore, Jason, and Desmond

CONTENTS

PHOTO PORTFOLIO

PREFACE

Tombstones to Live By

Prefaces are always written at the end. When authors look back on their work, they often wonder how they managed to fashion a book out of so much (or so little) material; how they soldiered on despite doubts and fears and the knowledge that their publication would be thrown into the world with thousands of others. What are my feelings at the end of this book? Primarily amazement at my hubris. How did I dare write a history of American cemeteries encompassing four hundred years?

The project turned into an astonishing adventure for me and my photographer son, Reid, as we traveled together to more than 250 cemeteries. To borrow words from James Agee in his explanation of how he and Walker Evans produced their landmark book *Let Us Now Praise Famous Men:* "The photographs are not illustrative. They, and the text, are co-equal, mutually independent, and fully collaborative." My text and Reid's photos are essentially parallel narratives intended to convey the wonders found in the land of the dead.

The first English settlers in America did not commonly use the word "cemetery," which would have referred to ancient European sites such as the Roman catacombs. During the seventeenth and eighteenth centuries, English-speaking people on both sides of the Atlantic would have employed such terms as "burying ground," "burial ground," "graveyard," or "churchyard."

The word "cemetery" crept into popular language during the nineteenth century, along with a new concept of funereal landscape. After two centuries of grim, gray, urban graveyards, the new philosophy called for expansive rural vistas enhanced by carefully chosen flora and artful monuments. The dead could find peace in such settings, and mourners too could take comfort in nature's bounties. "Cemetery," derived from the Greek "koimeterium," meaning "a place to sleep," was the right term for fields of eternal rest.

By now, in the twenty-first century, "cemetery" is the generic word of choice for Americans describing burial grounds, evoking a vision of flat markers flush with well-watered lawns, or identical crosses standing erect in military rows, or bucolic assemblies of the dead shaded by white clapboard churches. Most people have a favorite cemetery. Before going further, ask yourself if there is one with special meaning for you, or one you might choose for yourself.

The cemetery I know best is the one where my mother is buried and where my husband and I shall join her, in due time. Long before she was laid to rest in Alta Mesa Memorial Park in Palo Alto, California, I used to walk there from my home a mile away. The eye-catching array of tombstones dating back one hundred years piqued my curiosity. Who were all these people brought together in this graveyard? How did this verdant swath of land become their last stop on earth?

What impressed me especially was the diversity of religions and ethnicities assembled in the newer sections: Protestants, Catholics, Mormons, Jews, Muslims, and Buddhists; Americans of European, Asian, Latino, African, and Middle Eastern origins. They or their ancestors had come from all points of the compass to lie next to one another, for eternity. Their coexistence after death represented peaceful multiculturalism, California at its best.

Over time, I began to reflect on their individual destinies and make up life stories suggested by their tombstones. What was the history behind the inscription "Two devoted Christians"? How was it that Moise Verblunsky, whose marker was crowned with a Jewish star, had taken a

Japanese wife named Noriko Saito? Why was Gus Mozart's life encapsulated in a headstone featuring the image of a Volkswagen?

In the patch of cemetery that I began to think of as mine, many of the deaths were recent — ten or twenty years ago at most. These graves bore the mark of regular visits: flowers and potted plants, wreaths and toys, oranges and bottled beverages. Often I would see people tending these graves: a mother leaving flowers for her son, a man watering the family plot. How had their lives been altered by the death of a child, spouse, mother, father, brother, or sister?

On the first day of 1998, when holiday gifts still lay on many of the graves — miniature Christmas trees bearing shiny balls, Santa Claus figures, and Styrofoam candy canes — I went to put flowers on my mother's site. As I stared down at her pink granite tombstone with the inscription "Celia Koenick Chernigow 1904–1997," I knew she was in the right place, surrounded by people like herself — immigrants who had started over again and again in that geographical and spiritual enterprise we call life.

Born in London, raised in Kraków, married in Chicago, my mother moved with my father to Washington, D.C., in the 1930s. There they raised three daughters, including me, the middle one. Widowed at the relatively young age of fifty, my mother was to marry again three more times and outlive all her husbands. At the age of eighty-eight, she moved from Miami to California, where she died halfway through her ninety-third year.

Two years before her death, when she could still walk, she came with me to Alta Mesa. Although she had planned to have her body sent to Washington to join my father, it didn't take long for her to decide to be buried in Palo Alto. "This way you will come to see me more often." And I have.

This book originated in my visits to her grave. At first, it was to be the study of only one site — a year in the life of "our" cemetery. I would note seasonal changes, various offerings left at different seasons, occasional gatherings in front of ethnically diverse plots, open graves for the newly deceased — everything that brings life to a landscape devoted to the dead.

In time, with a cultural historian's curiosity, I began to ask questions about the broader picture. When did European-style graveyards come to the Americas? What were the first ones like? How dissimilar were they from today's cemeteries? What differences existed among Protestant, Catholic, and Jewish burying grounds? How long did immigrants in a strange country hold on to the burial practices of their original homelands? Where were slaves buried? What regional variations would I find in the North, the South, the Midwest, and the West? How have Asians and Near Easterners with Taoist, Confucian, Buddhist, Hindu, and Muslim rituals entered the cemetery landscape?

The canvas got larger and larger. Every new person I met was enamored of a specific cemetery that had to be included. Reid and I were constantly on the run, in planes, cars, taxis, and buses. Finally, having spent days and weeks over a period of three years in various parts of the country, we decided it was time to stop, to garner from our notes and photos those that could help to tell a four-hundred-year-old story.

The first four chapters of this book lay out the broad historical themes: (1) how colonial settlers from foreign countries claimed the land from Native Americans and introduced European-style burial grounds; (2) how these immigrants and later Americans marked their graves with wood and stone; (3) how specific religious and ethnic groups remained together even in the graveyard; and (4) how funeral rituals and cemetery history during the past two hundred years reflected a national distancing of death from everyday life.

Chapters 5 through 15 trace a journey that is obviously regional, but also chronological, since it follows the paths of our immigrant ancestors — individuals and groups coming from Europe, Africa, Latin America, Asia, and the South Pacific. We start with burial grounds in New England, descend the coast to the South, move inland to the Mississippi region and the Midwest, then go across the country to the Southwest, the Pacific Coast, and Hawaii.

Chapter 16 focuses on military cemeteries, and chapter 17 rounds out the book with an appraisal of old and new fashions in death. From an estimated 250,000 cemeteries scattered across the country, we have chosen those that highlight America's diverse religions and ethnicities, as well as demonstrate major changes in cemetery mores since the founding of Jamestown, Virginia, in 1607.

Every cemetery is unique, each has its own aura, and each is there waiting for visitors. We like to think that visitors help rescue the dead from oblivion. Individually and collectively, our visits fulfill the hope expressed in a popular American epitaph:

TO LIVE IN HEARTS WE LEAVE BEHIND
IS NOT TO DIE

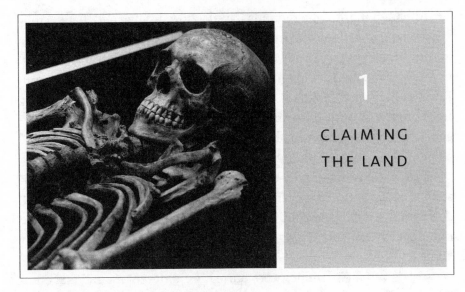

1

CLAIMING THE LAND

LONG BEFORE EUROPEANS crossed the Atlantic and set foot on New World soil, lofty burial mounds dotted the American landscape. Concentrated in the Mississippi region, as far south as today's Florida, as far west as Texas, and as far north as Illinois and Ohio, they were built by Native Americans who lived in settled communities and interred their dead near their homes in mounds that were meant to be permanent. In contrast, nomadic Indian societies in the Plains and Pacific Northwest, always on the move, exposed corpses to the elements using trees, scaffolds, canoes, and boxes on stilts — all of which were ephemeral.

Most of the mounds were conical, some roughly rectangular, and others shaped in the form of animals, reptiles, and birds. All were built from earth that had been carried in baskets from "borrow pits" and then piled over the dead, the mounds increasing in size as new bodies were added. Some were low, no more than three or four feet high, while others rose to eighty or ninety feet. These sacred mounds were still plentiful in the 1540s when the Spanish explorer Hernando de Soto made his extensive expeditions across the South, and they were still visible in 1832 when the poet William Cullen Bryant eloquently exclaimed, "Are they here — the dead of other days? . . . Let the mighty mounds . . . answer."

Above: Skeleton of Bartholomew Gosnold, Jamestown, Virginia

Although most of the mounds have by now disappeared, flattened by successive generations of farmers and urban developers, a few can still be found in the South and Midwest. The awesome Etowah mounds pictured in this book (plate 1) stand on a tract of fifty-four acres next to the Etowah River in northern Georgia. Constructed over a period of five centuries, from around 1000 to 1550 the mounds were central to the political organization of a community that at its peak numbered several thousand people.

The tallest mound, sixty-three feet high, was not used for burial; it supported the house of the chief and his family. From here, he could look down on the wattle-and-daub huts scattered across the village. The common folk living below simply buried their dead in the earth next to their homes.

Chiefs and their families were buried in a different mound that eventually held 350 bodies, a number known from excavations carried out in the twentieth century. Precious objects — jewelry made from copper, bone, shell, and pearl; pottery vessels and pipes carved with animal images; wooden and stone effigies — were often placed in the designated mounds to accompany the dead person's spirit on its journey to the afterworld. Among the many artifacts found in this mound were two marvelous painted marble statues of a man and a woman in a sitting position, each weighing 125 pounds. These were probably ancestor figures buried as symbolic members of the Etowah elite.

Atop the burial mound there would have been a mortuary temple housing the most exalted bones. The current chief's divine status was demonstrated by the bones of his ancestors stored at this elevated height. As in the case of other political and religious leaders from far distant civilizations — think of Egyptian pharaohs — preservation of ancestral remains not only honored the dead but also conferred authority on living rulers.

We are not certain why the Etowah mounds were suddenly abandoned in the mid-sixteenth century, but our best guess is that the tribes were destroyed by disease that had been brought their way by Europeans such as de Soto. It has been estimated that 80 percent of Mississippian Indians, including the Etowahans, died after the arrival of Hispanic explorers. In time, the Indian nations who resettled the Etowah River valley — the Creek and the Cherokee — lost all memory of the significance of the mounds.

Early Spanish Burials When the Spanish explorers arrived in the sixteenth century, they buried their dead as best they could in the wilderness. Hasty disposal of the body, a few ritual words from the Catholic liturgy, no coffin, and a wooden cross were the most one could expect. But with the founding of St. Augustine on the eastern coast of Florida in 1565 and the establishment of a colony in New Mexico in 1598, the Spanish began to build Catholic churches with adjacent churchyards. According to an oral narrative passed down from one generation to the next in a New Mexican village and recorded in 1933, this is how the burials took place:

> In the olden days the church was used for a graveyard and the planks were removed while the grave was dug. The body was wrapped in a rug and lowered into the grave, which was filled and the boards replaced. This custom prevailed until the entire space was filled with the dead.

Prominent Catholics would be placed under the floor close to the altar, but as no records were kept of the location and no markers set into the floor, it is impossible to know exactly where a specific individual lay. When the space under the church was filled, bodies were interred outside the church in an area known as the *campo santo* — the sacred field. In the Southwest, the *campo santo* became the final resting place for generations of converted Indians, whereas members of the Spanish community continued to be buried under the church.

Jamestown, Virginia Hard on the heels of the Hispanic Catholics, English Protestants found their way to the Americas in the early seventeenth century, and they, like the Spaniards, were quickly faced with the task of burying their dead in foreign soil. Most of the English settlers who founded Jamestown in the spring of 1607 were dead by the end of summer; of the original 104, only 38 remained alive the following January. One of them noted: "Our men were destroyed with cruell diseases, as

Swellings, Flixes, Burning Fevers, and by warres, . . . but for the most part they died of meere famine." Those who survived were, in the words of Captain John Smith, "scarce able to bury the dead."

Where were all these dead buried? Extensive archaeological work undertaken at Jamestown since 1994 has unearthed the remains of numerous bodies within the confines of the fort, buried there behind the palisade at night in an attempt to conceal the settlers' losses from the surrounding Indians. Twenty-two of the graves are now marked with wooden crosses. Most of the corpses were placed in the ground without coffins, many wrapped in shrouds, and a few buried fully clothed — probably because these had died of contagious diseases.

A larger, more substantial cross marks the spot where a single coffin — gable-lidded in the style of the affluent — was discovered just outside the fort palisade (plate 2). There is good reason to believe that the skeleton it contained is that of Bartholomew Gosnold, captain of the *Godspeed,* one of the first three ships sent to Jamestown by the Virginia Company. The *Godspeed* and the other vessels arrived in May after a grueling five-month voyage; Gosnold was dead by August, at the age of thirty-six — the same age determined for the skeleton at the time it was interred. Written records indicate that Gosnold's burial was accompanied by many volleys of gunshot.

A second piece of evidence for identification of the skeleton was the five-foot iron-tipped staff that had been laid on top of the coffin. This ceremonial weapon would have belonged to the captain of a company, to be used while leading his men through military exercises. Bartholomew Gosnold was an experienced captain, respected not only for his participation in the Jamestown enterprise but also for his previous expeditions on the northeast coast, where he had discovered the islands of Martha's Vineyard and Elisabeth Island, named for his daughters. A large cross has been erected at his burial site, but his skeleton now reclines in the nearby museum. If we are to judge from the size of his skeleton and the soundness of his teeth, he must have been a strapping fellow.

During its first two years, under the leadership of Captain John Smith and with help from the Powhatan Indians, the colony survived — but just barely. Only ninety of nearly three hundred colonists made it through the "starving time," the winter of 1609 and 1610. The by-now-famous story of the Indian princess Pocahontas, who reputedly saved the life of John Smith and definitely married the tobacco planter John Rolfe, contributed to a long period of peace between the English and the Powhatans. But eventually, in 1622, members of the Powhatan chiefdom attacked the English and killed off a third of the population.

By then, the settlement had an Anglican frame church and a proper English-type churchyard, both situated on one side of the fort. Today's visitor will find the remains of a later brick church, a church tower dating from the 1640s, and twenty-five tombstones from an estimated several hundred burials in the churchyard. Tombstones were uncommon throughout the seventeenth and eighteenth centuries in tidewater Virginia, since the area had very little natural stone, and headstones had to be imported, usually from England. Most people were laid to rest in unmarked graves or in graves with wooden markers that quickly disintegrated.

In addition to the churchyard burials, some parishioners of high status were buried within or underneath the church. Excavations conducted in the early twentieth century revealed at least twenty burials within the church chancel, including two marked graves, one the tomb of a British knight and the other the tomb of a minister.

It is a rare sensation to stand beside the church ruins on the banks of the James River and imagine yourself as one of the 104 men and boys who first came ashore in the spring of 1607 to claim the fertile lands they called Virginia; or as one of the first slaves whose forced passage from Africa to Jamestown in 1619 was the beginning of unspeakable suffering and dehumanization; or as one of the ninety unmarried women who arrived in 1620, ready to marry any man who would pay her unpaid passage. Or, reversing one's viewpoint, imagine the emotions of the Powhatans watching from a distance as strange fair-skinned people encamped upon territory that had belonged to their tribe. Did they feel in their bones that those pale-faced strangers would eventually dispossess them of their land and their entire way of life?

Plymouth, Massachusetts The settlers who arrived at Plymouth, Massachusetts, on the *Mayflower* in December 1620 — like those in Jamestown thirteen years earlier — were immediately assailed by overwhelming hardships. In the words of William Bradford, "In two or three months half of their company died, especially in January and February being the depth of winter. . . ." Bradford attributed their deaths specifically to "the scurvy and other diseases which this long voyage and lack of accommodation had brought upon them."

Though 52 of the original 102 settlers survived the winter, only "six or seven sound persons" were fully functional at the times of greatest distress. Among those healthy enough to help were the Puritan elder William Brewster and the military captain Miles Standish; Bradford praised their ministrations, noting that they cared for the sick and dying and "spared no pains night nor day but with abundance of toil and hazard of their own health, fetched them wood, made them fires, dressed them meat, made their beds, washed their loathsome clothes, clothed and unclothed them; in a word did all the homely and necessary offices for them which dainty and queasy stomachs cannot endure to hear named."

One of their most onerous duties was to bury the dead. The first burial site, eventually named Cole's Hill, was used until around 1637; thereafter, Burial Hill, with the colonial tombstones still there today, became the principal Pilgrim burying ground.

A sarcophagus commissioned by the Society of Mayflower Descendants contains the bones of Pilgrims found in or near Cole's Hill. A part of its inscription reads: "The Monument marks the First Burying Ground in Plymouth of the passengers of the Mayflower. Here under cover of darkness the fast dwindling company laid their dead, leveling the earth above them lest the Indians should know how many were the graves." As in Jamestown, it seems to have been common practice in Plymouth for the settlers to perform burials at night. They did such a good job in hiding the dead that some of the bones on Cole's Hill were not uncovered until more than a hundred years later during a violent rainstorm. Yet when their first governor, John Carver, died, in the spring of 1621, the Pilgrims laid him to rest with public ceremony befitting his station, including volleys of gunshot.

Native American and Christian Burial Practices Christians brought from Europe their manner of burial, but Native Americans had their own practices, which European settlers observed with curiosity. Upon their arrival at Plymouth, a Pilgrim scouting party came across a gravesite consisting of sand mounds covered with decaying reed mats. The Pilgrims poked into the mounds and, in one of them, found a bow with several rotting arrows. As narrated by William Bradford and Edward Winslow, "We supposed there were many other things, but because we deemed them graves, we put in the Bow againe and made it up as it was, and left the rest untouched, because we thought it would be odious unto them to ransacke their Sepulchers."

Continuing their exploration, the scouting party came upon other gravesites, including "a great burying place, one part whereof was incompassed with a large Palazado, like a churchyard . . . those Graves were more sumptuous then those at Corne-hill, yet we digged none of them up, but only viewed them, and went our way." Despite their curiosity and some grave pilfering when they first arrived, the Pilgrims tended to respect the sanctity of Indian graves.

Later in the seventeenth century, William Penn wrote sympathetically of Indian burial rites practiced in Pennsylvania.

> If they die, they bury them with their apparel, be they man or woman, and the nearest of kin fling in something precious with them, as a token of their love: their mourning is blacking of their faces, which they continue for a year. . . .

As for their graves, "lest they should be lost by time, and fall to common use, they pick off the grass that grows upon them, and heap up the fallen earth with great care and exactness." In time, this practice spread beyond the Indian community. Scraped mounds stripped of grass and other vegetation, usually located on hilltops, became characteristic of nineteenth-century folk cemeteries in Georgia, Alabama, Louisiana, and Texas, for whites as well as Indians. This is a rare instance of Native American influence on Christian burial practices. Usually the influence went the other way.

American Indians confronting European settlers struggled to maintain their age-old burial rites. Yet ultimately, as Europeans invaded and conquered what had been tribal territories, a great number of Indians came to be buried in Christian graveyards. Both Spanish missionaries in the Southwest and Protestant ministers throughout the continent took pride in the conversion of Indians and considered churchyard burial the convert's due. Christian interment was understood as the final step on the path toward God.

One of the most interesting examples of how indigenous peoples merged their burial rites with those of Christian newcomers can be seen in Eklutna, Alaska. There, in keeping with old traditions, Athabascan natives still bury the dead in small mounds surrounded by stones with spirit houses placed on top of them. These miniature houses, three to four feet long and two to three feet high, have no markings other than colorful decorations — squares, circles, and triangles painted red, yellow, and blue — that denote the deceased person's family, like a coat of arms.

Around the turn of the eighteenth century, Catherine the Great sent Russian missionaries to northern Alaska; eventually, a Russian Orthodox church was built next to the old burial ground, and Russian Orthodox crosses were placed on posts in front of the spirit houses. Today, this mix of Russian Orthodox and native funeral practices has become the norm for the population of 430 Alaskan natives living in the village.

Over the past few decades, Native Americans, Alaskan natives, and native Hawaiians have become increasingly active in their efforts to reclaim their ancient burial grounds, as well as the bones and artifacts that have sometimes been taken from them and placed in museums. Their political activism contributed to the Native American Graves Protection and Repatriation Act (NAGPRA), passed in 1990, which permits Native Americans and native Hawaiians to retrieve human remains and funerary objects. The bones of one's ancestors in a certain locale make a strong case for connection to that site, and even to ownership.

Early immigrants to America of Hispanic, English, Dutch, French, German, Swedish, and African origin, to name only the most numerous, must have felt a heightened connection to the soil once their kin were buried within it. This is the truth of all peoples who have come to the New World during the past four hundred years. Burying a family member in an adopted homeland is yet another way of claiming that country as one's own.

The connection between a newcomer's sense of identity and the burial of his fellow settlers is the subject of a cleverly humorous story written by author William Saroyan (1908–1981), himself the son of Armenian immigrants. In the late nineteenth century, the Armenians who first moved to Fresno, California, where Saroyan grew up, founded a cemetery called Ararat, in honor of the mountain that symbolized their distant homeland.

One of Saroyan's uncles, named Vorotan, obsessed to the point of madness over the need for a first burial in the Armenian cemetery. "He wanted somebody to die, and to be buried so that he, as well as the rest of us, might know that a tradition had been established . . . that we were in fact in Fresno, in California, in America, and, in all probability, would stay." When one of the immigrant group finally did die, the uncle was "overwhelmed by the good news, donated ten dollars toward the cost of the funeral, made a short talk at the graveside, and was instantly healed of his madness." Years later, Vorotan found his own final resting place in the Ararat cemetery, as did William Saroyan.

During Saroyan's lifetime, on the other side of the American continent, country folk from Mississippi still had the habit of asking a newcomer "Where do you bury?" That simple question had meanings far beyond the literal. It meant: Where do you come from? Who are your kin? What place do you call home? In short: Who are you? However mobile we Americans may be, our individual identities are often tied up with a specific piece of land — a city, a state, a region, a house, maybe just a six-foot plot of soil holding a loved one's remains.

2

MARKING
THE GRAVE

MARKING THE GRAVE of the dead reflects our need for a hallowed site of remembrance — a place to which we return, alone or in the company of others, to renew our ties with someone "gone, but not forgotten." Many of us return regularly to the grave of a loved one — a wife, husband, parent, or child — especially in the first months or years after a death. Tidying up the grave, watering plants, bringing flowers soften the pain of mourning. Sometimes we talk to the dead in the belief that the spirit still hovers near the corpse.

Far worse is the anguish experienced when a body is lost and never retrieved, such as those who disappear at sea or in natural disasters or wars. In *Moby-Dick*, Ishmael compares the fortunate widow who knows the site of her husband's grave with the less fortunate widows of husbands lost at sea "who have placelessly perished without a grave."

> Oh! Ye whose dead lie buried beneath the green grass; who standing among flowers can say — here, *here* lies my beloved; ye know not the desolation that broods in bosoms like these. What bitter blanks in those black-bordered marbles which cover no ashes! What despair in those immovable inscriptions!

Above: Skull and crossbones, Savannah, Georgia

And the saintly Melanie in *Gone With the Wind* expresses sorrow for women on both sides of the Civil War "who do not know where their sons and husbands and brothers are buried." She shocks her women's club by pulling weeds off the graves of nameless Union soldiers in Atlanta as a gesture of compassion for bereaved Yankee women.

Many countries create special monuments for the unknown soldier. Death in battle is tragic enough without the additional pathos of unidentified bodies. Some families can never rest until the body of a lost son, father, or brother; daughter, mother, or sister has been found and properly buried in a marked grave.

We in the twenty-first century have known the anguish surrounding a national tragedy in which people perished along with the skyscrapers, and body parts were carried out of the rubble for months afterward. A morgue for the human remains was erected under a huge tent, with a separate area added for the victims' families. "It was very meaningful to families who didn't have anything to bury," said a New York City representative. "This was tantamount to their mausoleum, their cemetery, their sacred space."

Eventually the remains will be transferred to the Ground Zero memorial. A spokeswoman for the World Trade Center Memorial Foundation reminded the public that this interment will make Ground Zero a sacred space not only for the nation but also for the victims' relatives, "the final resting place of their loved ones."

Early American Burials Despite the human desire to know where one's relatives are buried, many early American settlers were placed in unmarked graves. Some were buried hastily during times of famine and epidemic. The remains of others who fell victim to nature's outbursts — flash floods and sudden blizzards — were never found. Even under normal circumstances, many families could not afford a tombstone. And some radical religious groups wavered over the necessity of grave markers; for example, Quakers did not officially approve them till 1850.

Spanish missionaries in Florida and the Southwest placed wooden crosses over the graves of white settlers (plate 3), but usually buried converted Indians wrapped in shrouds without the benefit of markers or even coffins. In colonial New England, the Chesapeake (Virginia and Maryland), and the coastal South, wooden grave rails, which consisted of one or two horizontal markers held between two vertical posts, were more common than tombstones.

A typical New England headstone was made of slate with a rounded tympanum in the center and smaller, rounded shoulders on the sides. You can usually recognize a seventeenth- or eighteenth-century stone by this tripartite, or three-lobed, shape. A headstone was often accompanied by a small footstone placed at the end of the grave; these two markers indicated the length of a body, similar to the headboard and the footboard of a bed. The stones were commonly lined up on an east-west axis, a tradition assumed to derive from the belief that a body lying on its back with its feet pointing to the east would sit up and face Jerusalem on Judgment Day.

Inscriptions, Epitaphs, and Visual Motifs Although British colonies on the East Coast existed from 1607 onward in Jamestown, Virginia, and from 1620 onward in Plymouth, Massachusetts, the oldest extant gravestones date from a later period; for example, 1637 in Jamestown. In New England, the oldest surviving inscription is the one found on slate fragments from the headstone of Barnard and Joan Capen, which was removed from the North Burying Ground in Dorchester, Massachusetts, and is now preserved in the New England Historic Genealogical Society, though no one knows for sure whether the headstone was made in 1638, the year of Barnard's death; 1653, the year of Joan's death; or some time in between. Another marker from 1653, crude but still intact, can be found at the Eliot Burying Ground in Roxbury, Massachusetts. Erected for the first child of the Reverend Samuel Danforth, it bears four horizontal lines with the inscription inserted between them:

SAMUEL DANFORTH

AGED 6 MONTHS:

DYED 22 D 3 M 1653

More typically, an inscription would contain the name of the individual and the dates of birth and death. Sometimes, two numbers were given for a year; for example, 1660/61. This confusing practice originated in Europe in 1582, when Catholic countries began to use the Gregorian calendar, which fixed New Year's Day as January 1, while Protestant countries retained the Julian calendar, in which the first day of the new year was March 25. England and the colonies did not adopt the Gregorian calendar until 1752.

Occasionally an inscription also contained the Latin words "Ætatis Suae," meaning "at his/her age," followed by the age of the deceased. This venerable formula was frequently abbreviated to "Ætatis" alone or, more simply, to the letters *Æ* or *A.S.* Sometimes the place of birth was mentioned, especially if the original homeland had been England or continental Europe.

Anything added to the basic biographical data is known as an epitaph. Epitaphs are generally short and pithy, intended to make an immediate impression. This tradition goes back in the Western world as far as the ancient Greeks. At the Benaki Museum in Athens, an epitaph reaches out to grab the passerby with a freshness belying its 2,500 years:

> You, traveler, who pass by my tomb,
> Stop for a minute and think of me.

Ancient Romans, who customarily buried their dead by the roadside, used the formulaic "Sta Viator" (Pause, traveler) to draw the wayfarer in.

Similarly intended to grab attention, a common religious epitaph found in colonial America asks that the passerby reflect not only on the deceased person but also, and more important, on his or her own future demise: "As I am now so shall you be; prepare for death and follow me." Death was always on the horizon, not only because children's mortality rate was so much higher than it is today or because the dead were laid out in their homes but also because the various Christian sects focused on death with a single-mindedness that might appear macabre to many Americans today. New England Puritans, in particular, raised their children with a daily awareness of mortality, forcing them to memorize such verses as the following:

As runs the *Glass*
Man's life doth pass.

Time cuts down all
Both great and small.

Xerxes the great did die
And so must you and I.

Youth forward slips
Death soonest nips.

A striking version of this doleful mortality theme appears on the elaborate headstone made for Joseph Tapping, who died in 1678 at the age of twenty-three and was laid to rest in Boston's first Burying Ground, subsequently known as King's Chapel. The Latin mottoes "Fugit hora" (The hour flies) and "Memento mori" (Remember you must die) are there to remind us that it is never too early to think about death. For viewers unfamiliar with Latin, the ideas are spelled out graphically. In the upper half of the stone, an hourglass sits on the head of a winged skull, or death's-head, and on the lower register, Father Time appears with his scythe and hourglass while a skeletal figure of Death snuffs out the candle of life.

Such visual images complemented the text and made for a harmonious — if disconcerting — ensemble. Death's-heads, skulls, crossbones, skeletons, scythes, shovels, hourglasses, and coffins were fearful symbols of human mortality and decay. They served as cautionary illustrations for the living, who were instructed to think on their own deaths with dread and trembling. According to the Calvinist theology espoused by Puritans, only a select few would be saved; all others would be relegated to the torments of hell. Like all Protestants, Puritans rejected the Catholic belief in purgatory — a middle ground where you could work off your sins and be aided in your ascent to heaven by others who prayed for you. Instead, Puritans believed that damnation or salvation had already been decided according to a predestined plan that would be made known only on the Day of Judgment. Because God's ways were utterly inscrutable and salvation was uncertain at best, death was anticipated anxiously throughout one's lifetime.

Death's-heads, skeletons, and skull and crossbones all representing mortality were by no means limited to dour New England Puritans. In the Chesapeake region, dominated by Anglicans who adhered to the established Church of England, they were familiar motifs in every churchyard and in the private family plots set apart on farms and plantations. Skulls, in particular, became extremely popular during the last decade of the seventeenth and the first decades of the eighteenth century (plate 4). An especially grisly pair carved in profile lie side by side on two ledger stones dated 1697 and 1698 at St. Anne's Episcopal Churchyard in Annapolis, Maryland.

In Williamsburg, at the Bruton Parish Anglican Churchyard, which has the distinction of being the largest surviving colonial churchyard in Virginia, a gruesome full-face skull peeps out from under the carved draperies of an elaborate chest tomb. Imported from England and erected for the English governor Edward Nott, who died in 1706, this tomb also carries the images of two winged faces, or soul effigies, at the upper angles. A soul effigy was a representation of the soul ascending toward heaven. While the skull represented the certainty of bodily death, the soul effigy stood for the hope of "Joyfull Resurrection."

During the eighteenth century, though skulls and death's-heads dominated mortuary iconography, cherublike soul effigies became more numerous. Sometimes, as in Governor Nott's case, both skulls and cherubs appeared on the same tomb. In West Tisbury, Massachusetts, the curious marker for James Allen (died 1714) shows a curly-haired human head framed by luxurious wings; on top of this is a smaller death's-head that appears almost as if it were emerging from the man's crown.

From the 1740s onward, angelic faces with wings (plate 5) vied for popularity with the ubiquitous death's-heads. The pace of transition from the morbid death's-head to joyful resurrection was probably related to the Great Awakening of the 1730s and 1740s, a religious revival movement that pulled away from established ritual and external authority in favor of inward, more personal, sentiments. This wave of religious enthusiasm, which pitted conservatives against revivalists, would eventually reshape all the major Protestant religions save Anglican and Quaker. In time, religious orthodoxy gave way to a more optimistic theology intimating that some form of benign eternity awaits us all.

But at the end of the eighteenth century, just when winged faces on tombstones threatened to outnumber death's-heads, a new set of motifs appeared on the scene. Greek Revival symbols of mourning, namely the urn and the willow tree, were already fashionable in Europe, and in the late 1700s they were discovered and adopted by Americans. A graceful urn in the shape of a rounded body supported by a narrow foot, traditionally used to store cremated ashes, clearly represented death, while weeping willows, with their long leafy strands suggesting the hair of a woman bent over in grief, stood for the cycle of life and regeneration.

The evolution from death's-heads to soul effigies and then to urns and willows can be seen in the Old Burying Ground in Cambridge, Massachusetts, as one walks from one end to the other. In the oldest section, death's-heads dating from the 1690s are lined up shoulder to shoulder like a brigade of fierce watchdogs. Midway across the field, angels with curly hair and soaring wings, dating from the 1730s and 1740s, begin to infiltrate the death's-heads. Both death's-heads and angels stand side by side until, at the end of the field, the space is invaded by urns and willows from the final two decades of the eighteenth and the beginning of the nineteenth century.

A superb example of the urn-and-willow motif is found, appropriately, on the tombstone erected for the colonial silversmith and goldsmith Benjamin Hurd (1739–1781) in Boston's Granary Burying Ground. Silversmiths like Hurd and his brother Nathaniel and their better-known contemporary Paul Revere were forerunners of the Greek Revival movement, which extended beyond tombstones to furniture and other crafts. These examples of material culture must be understood in terms of the emerging society that created them. In contrast to death's-heads and cherubs, with their religious associations, the urn, the willow, the lyre, and other Greek Revival motifs were primarily secular icons. First popularized in Europe by Enlightenment thinkers and French revolutionaries, who looked back nostalgically to the ancient democracies of Athens and Rome, Americans too, in the enthusiasm generated by their infant democracy, adopted Greek motifs as their own.

Undoubtedly the most famous urn of this period was the miniature one made by Paul Revere to enclose a lock of hair cut from the head of George Washington by his widow. Made in gold with a crystal top, it was presented on January 27, 1800, to the Grand Masonic Lodge of Massachusetts. Both Washington and Revere are known to have been devoted Freemasons.

Post-Revolutionary America embraced Greek motifs and architecture to such an extent that they constituted a national style for most government buildings. Throughout the nineteenth century, public buildings and private mausoleums imitated ancient Greek and Roman temples, and tombstones continued to bear images of urns and willows. Often, an urn coupled with a willow would appear in bas-relief on a tombstone, or the urn alone would rise up on a pillar as a freestanding piece of sculpture. Sometimes the willow tree would take center stage and throw its branches across the headstone in an act of unbridled mourning.

Stone Messages from the Past Gravestones reflect the beliefs, values, hopes, aesthetics, and technologies of the societies in which they are embedded. When studied in the aggregate, they become indicators of mindsets, or what the French call *mentalités* — constellations of ideas and attitudes held by specific groups at a certain time and place. While generalizations on the sole basis of tombstones risk oversimplification, these monuments of individual lives suggest how whole swaths of society regarded personal identity, gender, and socioeconomic status.

Personal Identity Early markers tell us very little about the person buried beneath the stone. The most common indices of identity were, and still are, relational: Mother, Father, Wife, Husband, Daughter, Son. Lengthy, detailed inscriptions were rare, reserved for distinguished public figures or, less frequently, a beloved child, husband, or wife. Occasionally, venerable religious leaders, statesmen, or soldiers were honored with a collective monument, such as the old-style tombstone erected in the King's Chapel Burying Ground in Boston, which reads:

Here Lyes
Intombed the Bodies
Of the Famous Reverend
And Learned Pastors of the First
Church of CHRIST in BOSTON
VIZ:
Mr JOHN COTTON Aged 64 Years Decd Decembr
the 33rd 1652.
Mr JOHN DAVENPORT Aged 72 Years Decd
March the 13th 1670
Mr JOHN OXONBRIDGE Aged 66 Years Decd
December the 28th 1674
Mr THOMAS BRIDGE Aged 58 Years Deced
SEPTEMBER the 26th 1715

From the nineteenth century onward, many tombstones carried a folk epitaph, such as "He was an honest man," or "She hath done what she could," or, even more anonymously, "Gone to rest." The most ubiquitous inscription for children was "Asleep in Jesus," but children were just as likely to be buried with no stones at all, given the high infant mortality rates and the sense that an infant had not yet developed a distinctive personality. Most epitaphs are formulaic and can be found over and over again, whether one walks among stones in the rural or urban South, New England, Missouri, Illinois, Texas, or the West Coast.

Occasionally, the cause of death was included in the epitaph, as if the dead person had been marked for all eternity by the nature of his or her demise. The most commonly mentioned cause was death in childbirth, which often pertained to both mother and child, as on the Bruton Parish ledger stone for Mrs. Ann Burges that states, "She died 23 December 1771 in giving Birth to an Infant Daughter, who rests in her Arms."

Other frequently listed causes of death were smallpox, consumption, and cholera. In the South, "the fever" and "putrid fever" became catchall terms for yellow fever or any other communicable disease producing an intolerably high temperature. With epidemics breaking out regularly, it was not uncommon for several members of a family to perish at the same time.

Highly unusual deaths were also recorded on tombstones. The old cemetery in Midway, Georgia, a heavily shaded peaceful refuge, contains the tombstones of Peter Girardeau (died 1793), who was "Slain by Indians while recovering animals stolen by them," and John N. Way, who "died by Lightning Feb.y 29. 1827 Æ 32." Other calamities such as "the Fall of a Tree" (John Stockbridge, 1768, Hanover, Massachusetts) or drowning (Mr. Luther Ames, 1801, Central Burying Ground, Boston) were considered exceptional enough to be inscribed in stone.

Little John Bowers in Pepperell, Massachusetts, "was drouned in a tan pit Augst 24th 1776. Aged 3 Years 3 months & 6 days." In my mind's eye, I see this little boy flailing in a pit used to tan leather while helpless adults try to rescue him. Subsequently, his anguished parents ordered a headstone that displayed not only the peculiar cause of his death but also his portrait, which shows a boy with locks of hair lying on his forehead, a narrow collar, and three buttons on his shirt.

Scattered attempts to portray the deceased graphically can be found from the first decades of the eighteenth century onward, but most portrait stones were of a later date. While generally primitive in conception and execution, a few stand out as accomplished works of art. The fine portraits of Mrs. Mary Lamboll (died September 15, 1743) and Mr. George Heskett (died August 31, 1747) in Charleston's Circular Churchyard are exquisite pieces of sculpture worthy of museum space. The Lamson family carvers of Charlestown, Massachusetts, are known to have produced a number of fine figure stones, including the one for Anthony Gwynn (died 1776), with his three-cornered hat and stylish waistcoat. Removed from St. Paul's burying ground in Newburyport, Massachusetts, it is now in the collection of the Boston Museum of Fine Arts.

On the whole, eighteenth-century tombstone portraits were not individualized. Many carvers created identical faces and set them atop similar busts, making only small variations for gender, such as buttons for the male or a cap for the female. It is relatively easy to recognize the work of certain local carvers who used the one-face-fits-all indiscriminately for both men and women. In the Old Burying Ground in Cambridge, the low-relief faces of Mrs. Hannah Reed (died 1788), Mr. William Porter (died 1798), and Mr. Richard Hunnewell (died 1798), each surrounded by a crudely carved oval frame, look as if they are the drawings of a child. On a more sophisticated level, Asa Abbot (died 1797) and Lucy Cogswell (died 1798) have essentially the same face, one enclosed in an arch, the other in a diamond (Andover, Massachusetts). Among the most obvious and the most pathetic are the three identical heads of James, John, and Edward Brown — small boys who perished in a fire with their mother and father. Their tombstones read: "Burned in his house March 29th, 1770" (Stow, Massachusetts).

There is some question as to why nondifferentiated faces were acceptable to the populace. Some have suggested that they were never intended to be likenesses of the deceased. Like death's-heads and winged effigies, they were understood to be general representations. But given the personalized portraits commissioned for a few individuals, another possibility is that uniform faces may simply have resulted from the carvers' lack of skill. After all, most stonecutters were masons or even tanners, rope makers, smiths, or printers who worked part-time on gravestones and could not be expected to achieve sculptural likenesses. Portrait statuary would not become a full-time occupation until the second half of the nineteenth century, and then for only a small number of master carvers.

Another means of personalizing tombstones appeared with the invention of photography in the 1830s and the subsequent process discovered in 1854 by two Frenchmen that allowed photos to be bonded to ceramic, porcelain, and enamel substances. Photo-ceramic portraits were brought to America at the turn of the twentieth century by Italians and other working-class immigrants from southern and Eastern European countries. Many sent photos of the deceased back to European artisans, who would fire copies of the photos onto the desired surfaces. Soon American entrepreneurs were following their lead. In 1893, the first memorial portraits were produced by the Chicago firm of J. A. Dedouch, a family company that still produces twelve to fifteen thousand "Dedos" per year. During the first decade of the twentieth century, Sears, Roebuck began selling "Imperishable Limoges porcelain portraits" at $11.20 for the marble version and $15.75 for the granite one. These oval images became staples on the tombstones of Italian, Jewish, and other early-twentieth-century immigrants — that is, until they became unfashionable in midcentury among their descendants, who wanted gravestones that resembled the Protestant mainstream's.

Today, ceramic photos, often in color, are experiencing a revival. They can be seen on markers for blacks, whites, Asian Americans, Eastern Europeans, and Hispanics, especially for children and young adults. Even a small marker laid flush with the grass offers a final chance to immortalize the unique face of a loved one. And for those who desire more arresting monuments, laser technology now makes it possible to scan life-size photos onto highly polished headstones, which seize the eye even from a distance.

Differences in Gender For most of American cemetery history, women have been identified generically as "wife," "widow," "mother," or "daughter." A study of colonial gravestones in the Boston area revealed that more than 70 percent of kinship references were for women. As for marital references alone, the gender difference was astronomical: nine men as compared to two thousand women!

Certainly there were no collective monuments for women in early America, as in the case of the reverend pastors mentioned above. In fact, the graves of two of the pastors' wives — Sarah Story Cotton (died 1676), widow of the venerable John Cotton and mother of his children, and Elizabeth Davenport (died 1676), wife of Mr. John Davenport — fell into neglect and were described in the mid-nineteenth century as "very modest and now obscure." They had been hidden under earth and flora for almost two hundred years before they were uncovered by a determined cemetery buff.

A typical colonial woman's inscription reads:

> Here lies the Body of
> Deborah Wife of John
> Dowers who departed
> This Life Oct. 21 1761
> Aged 42 years
>
> [Trinity Churchyard, New York City]

A married woman's name was usually connected to that of her husband. If she was unmarried, her father and sometimes her mother were named. If she had been married more than once, her last husband only was listed; however, widowed men's inscriptions might mention more than one wife. Sometimes two (or more) wives were buried on each side of the husband's grave, but never were multiple husbands buried beside a wife's grave. A curious zinc monument in Chicago's Mt. Olive Cemetery, established by nineteenth-century Scandinavians, displays the names of the two wives of N. C. Brun back-to-back on opposite sides of his marker. And, of course, among nineteenth-century Mormons who practiced polygamy, a man was often buried in the company of his plural wives. A telling inscription in the historical Santa Clara Cemetery of Ivins, Utah, reads as follows:

IN LOVING
Memory of
Bishop Marius Ensign
Who departed this life Oct. 14, 1884
Aged 63 years 1 month and 26 years
Born in Limsburg, Hartford, Conn.

I shall be there and look for thee
Farewell dear Wives remember me.

Given his position as a spiritual leader in the Church of Jesus Christ of Latter-Day Saints, Bishop Ensign would have considered it his duty to set an example of polygamy, since Mormon theology professed that rewards in heaven would be granted to men with many wives and to women with many children. In that families are central to the Mormon ethos, it is still common to find on the backs of Mormon couples' tombstones lists of their numerous children and even their grandchildren.

Many nineteenth-century patriarchs of various religions were immortalized in upward-thrusting monuments — elongated rough-hewn stones or marble pedestals and obelisks — with smaller stones laid at the base to indicate the graves of their wives and children. One of the most famous patriarchal family plots is the Sedgwick Family Burying Ground, known as the "Sedgwick Pie," in Stockbridge, Massachusetts. The Hon. Theodore Sedgwick (1747–1813) — lawyer, judge, U.S. congressman, speaker of the House, and U.S. senator — lies under a marble obelisk, with his second wife, Pamela, at his side and roughly one hundred fifty descendants from six generations laid out in concentric circles around him. They are grouped in five different wedges; hence the word "pie." The present Theodore Sedgwick, who intends to be buried there as was his father, has grown up with a tremendous sense of attachment to this cemetery. When his time comes, he, too, will receive a funeral service in Stockbridge's St. Paul's Episcopal Church, before being carried in a plain, wooden box drawn by two horses along the Main Street that passes by the Sedgwick family house to the "wedge" where his branch of the family awaits him.

The Sedgwicks have honored a few of their women with substantial epitaphs — most notably, the prolific nineteenth-century author, Catherine Maria Sedgwick, and her family's surrogate mother, the remarkable freed slave, Elizabeth Freeman known as Mumbet. More commonly, the epitaphs of women in early America were cursory and extolled only their religious and domestic virtues, including childbearing. Some mothers were lauded for having been exceptionally prolific, others mourned for having died in childbirth. Consider the consequences of prolific motherhood for this woman buried in a little strip of grass adjacent to the First Presbyterian Church in Charleston, South Carolina.

> Wife of Mr JEREMIAH THEUS
> Who departed this Life in Child
> Bed of her Sixth Child Nov 8th 1754
> In the 29th Year of Her Age

Particularly in the South, we came across many heartfelt epitaphs for daughters, wives, and mothers erected by grieving parents, husbands, and children. In Williamsburg's Bruton Parish Churchyard, the women were praised for being "faithfull and Vertuous// . . . prudent and tender" (Mary Page, died 1690); "loving, frugal, and discreet" (Mary Purdie, died 1772); and "generous & endearing" (Mary E. Dixon, died 1836). The one for Mrs. Mary Arnet Galt (died 1854) stands out as unique because in addition to her virtues as "A devoted wife, a tender and faithful friend[,] A kind and compassionate neighbour[,] A loving and self sacrificing mother," she is remembered for her work outside the home: "For forty years she was matron of the Lunatic asylum."

In keeping with the social changes that occurred during the second half of the twentieth century, contemporary tombstones are beginning to reflect the new status of women. For example, the epitaph for Janet Bluestein Goldstein, who was laid to rest next to her husband in 2001, surely distinguishes her from the other Jewish matriarchs buried during the past 150 years in the Hebrew section of Wilmington, North Carolina's historic Oakdale Cemetery.

> She walked in beauty
> With grace, dignity, and charm
> An honest and forthright businesswoman.

Still, in much of America, women's achievements outside the home continue to be underplayed on their tombstones. On the grounds of the Wananalua Congregational Church in Hana, Maui, Hawaii, established by missionaries in 1838, a recent inscription shows that even a woman with unusual professional credentials is remembered with the same typically deprecating female epitaph.

> REVEREND
> EDITH H. WOLFE
> April 30, 1921
> April 8, 2005
>
> "She did what she could."

Class and Money Not surprisingly, differences in wealth and status are as striking among the dead as among the living. In fact, in early America a gravestone was often expected to indicate a person's place in society. In colonial Virginia, the stones imported from England followed the position articulated in a 1631 manual that "Sepulchres should bee made according to the qualitie and degree of the person deceased that by the Tombe everyone might bee discerned of what rank hee was living." The royalist elite who migrated to Virginia in the mid-seventeenth century fleeing the Puritan rule of Oliver Cromwell were determined to preserve the hierarchical society of their homeland. Those entitled to coats of arms had them engraved on elaborate tombstones, most of which were made in England. Colonel Richard Cole, for example, in his testament of 1674 directed that a slab of black marble bearing his coat of arms engraved in brass should be purchased in England after his death and then laid on the spot where he would be buried. Inscriptions using such titles as Honorable or Esquire indicated that the deceased was a bona fide gentleman. The term "mister" was appropriate for other respected members of the community such as clergymen, military officers, and professionals, even if they were not entitled to coats of arms. As for the "middling sort" and the servant class, they usually had either wooden markers or nothing at all.

Epitaphs for those considered "best blood," as one Virginia monument put it, could be prolix and even flowery. Markers in the Bruton Parish Churchyard laud the "Unspotted fame" of Captain Francis Page (died 1692) and the "upright conduct" of the Honorable John Blair (died 1800), who had been appointed to the Virginia Court of Appeals by General Washington. Indeed, Blair rated no fewer than twenty-six eulogistic lines, ending with the belief that "he never excited enmity nor lost a Friend."

Uncovering more subtle distinctions that favored upper-class members of society sometimes requires detective work. One historian discovered that the Massachusetts carvers Nathaniel and Caleb Lamson placed angel-faced effigies on the tombs of affluent and distinguished families during the time (1725–1769) when most gravestones, including others made by the Lamsons, were still being decorated with death's-heads. This pattern suggests that families headed by ministers, college professors, doctors, lawyers, military men, and government officials were more likely to be depicted as worthy of salvation than common folk.

Funerals, too, varied greatly according to wealth and status. In seventeenth-century Massachusetts and Virginia, volleys of gunshots were fired for leading members of the community; for example, Captain Bartholomew Gosnold in Jamestown and Governor John Winthrop in Boston. The quantity of gunpowder used for a fusillade was an indicator of rank. Presumably Thomas Wall of Surry County, Virginia, whose 1650 will specified "three volleys of shot for the entertainment of those who came to bury him," was not in the same class as Major Philip Stevens of York

County, Virginia, honored around 1660 with a fusillade of ten pounds of powder.

The Bruton Parish Church in the early colonial capital of Williamsburg was the scene of many elaborate funerals for Virginia's elite. On the occasion of state funerals, the aisle, altar, pulpit, and governor's throne were covered with black cloth. It was not uncommon for the mourners who packed the church to vent their grief with unrestrained tears.

Although Puritans in New England practiced greater restraint than Anglicans in the Chesapeake, they both indulged in lavish funeral feasts. The more money one had, the more extravagant the feast. Long before the famous Irish wake was transported to America, in the nineteenth century, colonists had come to expect huge quantities of food and drink at funeral banquets. For instance, at one Virginia funeral around 1680, the provisions for food and drink included turkeys, geese, and other poultry; a pig; several bushels of flour; twenty pounds of butter; sugar and spice; and twelve gallons of different kinds of spirits. At another funeral occurring in 1667, slaking the thirst of the mourners required twenty-two gallons of cider, twenty-four of beer, and five of brandy, as well as twelve pounds of sugar to sweeten the drinks.

People with modest resources often went beyond their means to provide lavish meals. Some seventeenth-century Virginia testators tried to limit funeral costs in their wills, one ordering that there should be "no drinking immoderately" and another expressly forbidding guns to be fired over his grave. Legal efforts, in Boston and then New York, to limit the amount of money spent on funerals proved futile. The mourners craved sustenance after a death, as if filling the internal void with food and drink would temper the vision of the open grave filling up with earth.

As mentioned earlier, in both Spanish and English settlements, burial in or beneath the church was reserved for the most eminent members of the congregation. Priests and ministers were sometimes buried right in front of the altar, and some influential churchgoers were even buried beneath the pew they had occupied in life. These practices continued into the early nineteenth century, as in the case of President John Adams and his wife, Abigail, who were buried in a vault under the boards of the Congregational Church in Quincy, Massachusetts.

Underground vaults were increasingly common during the nineteenth century. Usually made of brick, they were placed in church crypts to house the coffins of those able to afford extra protection from the elements. Some churches possessed "virtual warrens of vaults" that extended under the building, the churchyard, and even the surrounding streets. In 1823, an estimated 570 vaults existed underneath New York City churches.

At least twenty vaults for prominent members of the King's Chapel congregation in Boston were embedded in the walls of the crypt underneath the church; the practice stopped in 1890, when the vaults were closed to future interments and the entrance to each one was sealed with bricks. At present, the names on the walls are no longer visible, and the crypt resembles an abandoned storage room — a repository for the church's tools, pamphlets, clothing, and sundry odds and ends.

To this day, certain sections of graveyards are considered better than others — those to the east of the church nearest the altar better than those on the south, west, or north. In secular cemeteries, the most desirable and expensive sites are situated on central pathways or on hills with a view. In cemeteries, as in real estate, location is everything.

Though death is called "the great equalizer," cemeteries reveal age-old attempts to carry one's wealth and position beyond the grave. We do not believe, as the Egyptians did, that the dead require costly replicas of their earthly possessions in order to enjoy them in the afterlife, but many Americans in the past accepted the view that markers should be appropriate to the deceased person's status. Victorians spent as much as they could afford — and sometimes more — to ensure an ostentatious monument for the family patriarch, or a sentimental statue for a wife or child. The rows of mausoleums erected in St. Louis's Bellefontaine and Chicago's Graceland and many other cemeteries nationwide ensured that the rich and powerful would be neighbors for eternity, sharing the same exclusive community they had enjoyed when alive.

IN ONE OF HIS STORIES, the French writer Albert Camus illuminated the human condition in two words that sound almost identical: *solitaire* and *solidaire* — "apart" and "a part of." As solitary beings, each of us merits a separate grave; as members of a group, we are buried together. Cemeteries are outgrowths of the communities that create them, and they often become focal points for family, religious, ethnic, regional, or national celebrations that simultaneously honor the dead and enhance a sense of group identity among the living.

Many cemeteries, or parts of cemeteries, become venues for religious practices and folk customs brought from foreign lands. The creation and maintenance of such cemeteries are parts of a process whereby immigrant communities preserve their unique identities within mainstream America.

Attachment to one's birth country at the moment of death is beautifully expressed by a twentieth-century immigrant reflecting on burial in Chicago's St. Casimir Lithuanian Cemetery: "Even if it should not be one's lot to return to dust in one's own homeland, it is good to know that even in another land your remains will be tended by the loving hands of

Above: Wheat stalks, St. Casimir Lithuanian Cemetery, Chicago, Illinois

one's own clan. In this consecrated ground, among one's own people, among one's kinfolk."

Almost invariably, this comforting sense of belonging to a clan develops around a principle of exclusion. Those buried together because they share the same religion, language, ethnic background, and culture are distinguished from those who are refused burial rights. In the early days of Anglo-American history, Puritan burial grounds in Boston were intended for Puritans only — Anglicans, Catholics, Baptists, and Quakers had to go elsewhere. Similarly, once Virginia became a royal colony, in 1642, it banished the Puritans and later the Quakers; by the end of the seventeenth century, Anglican churches and churchyards reigned supreme in the state. Even in colonial Philadelphia, the most tolerant of American cities, Catholics, Jews, and African Americans were denied burial rights in established graveyards and were relegated to the strangers' burial ground along with yellow fever victims. Before 1840, Jews could not be buried within the Commonwealth of Massachusetts and their corpses had to be shipped out to Newport, Albany, New York City, and other locales with more generous laws. Well into the twentieth century, blacks were excluded from most white cemeteries, in the North as well as the South. Many private California cemeteries did not accept blacks and Asians until 1959, when they were required by law to do so. For hundreds of years, religious and ethnic prejudice prevailed in underground America, just as it prevailed above ground.

Catholics Though they were often discriminated against in Protestant America, Catholics have always managed to take good care of their dead. Beginning with the Last Rites offered by a priest to the dying; followed by an evening vigil service in the church, home, or funeral parlor; and culminating in the main funeral liturgy pronounced at the graveside the following day, Catholics regard death as the gateway to life everlasting. Through the death and resurrection of Jesus, they maintain hope that the faithful will eventually be raised up and reunited in heaven.

Cemeteries are seen as bridges between heaven and earth, resting places for the dead awaiting the Resurrection. They are often called Calvary "because the name of Calvary is indissolubly associated with our

Lord's death; it designated the spot where Christ died that we might live . . ." Catholic cemeteries have rich statuary aesthetics, most notably in figures of the Virgin Mary (plate 6), Jesus, heavenly angels, and, of course, the Cross, raised up over and over again as a symbol of faith in Christ's victory over death. Individual cemeteries are often indebted to specific European regions with a strong Catholic culture. There is a Spanish-missionary style in California; a French-Mediterranean style in New Orleans; Polish, Ukrainian, and Lithuanian styles in Chicago; Alsatian iron crosses in Texas and the northern Great Plains; and Italian-type carvings almost everywhere. Even from a distance, one can distinguish a Catholic cemetery from a Protestant one simply by its markers.

Consecrated ground is intended for Catholics and excludes "those who are not baptized, those who do not belong to the Church, and public sinners who have died in impenitence." But Catholic cemeteries often set apart land for the burial of certain non-Catholics, such as parties to mixed marriages. If there is doubt as to the right of burial, the bishop of the diocese must be consulted. While not condoning suicide, the Church has recently become less rigid about issues of burying or praying for Catholics who have killed themselves.

Catholic cemeteries are seen as extensions of the Church community, second only to the Church itself in its sacred nature. On the first two days of November, designated as All Saints' Day and All Souls' Day, Catholic cemeteries are often deluged with family members who come to honor their loved ones.

One of the best-known funeral rites associated with Catholicism is the wake, especially the Irish wake. Traditionally, the Irish wake took place in the house of the deceased after the body had been bathed and dressed in white garments by women and then laid out on a table or bed for viewing. As a sign of respect, all clocks in the house were stopped and all mirrors covered. The body rested amid lit candles and was not left unattended until burial.

After the somber rituals at home, in the church, and at the cemetery, the jovial wake brought feasting, drinking, even music and dancing. While the mourners experienced their grief, they were expected to be comforted by the party-like atmosphere celebrating the life that had passed. Such wakes came to the United States in the mid-nineteenth century with Irish immigrants and then became known as "American wakes," combining the same mix of mourning and gaiety found in an Irish wake.

Jews Jews too tend to look after their cemeteries. Unlike Christians, they don't place cemeteries next to their houses of worship but at significant distances from them. In particular, the *kohanim* — the category of priests descended from Aaron, the brother of Moses, who are best known today under the name Cohen — must avoid contact with the dead. In order for the *kohanim* to enter into the temple, they must undergo a series of purifications to erase any taint of traffic between the dead and the living.

Since their earliest days in America, Jews have established their own separate burial grounds, first in seventeenth-century Manhattan under the rule of the grudging Dutch governor Peter Stuyvesant; later in the liberal eighteenth-century communities of Newport, Rhode Island, and Charleston, South Carolina; and still later in such disparate locales as St. Louis, Chicago, and the California gold rush country. Well-preserved cemeteries in all of these places (and others) contain old stone markers with inscriptions in Hebrew and English, as well as German and, less frequently, Spanish, Portuguese, and Russian, depending on the European roots of the deceased.

The earliest Jewish cemeteries were established by Iberian Sephardim, who practiced a strict brand of Orthodox Judaism; they were followed by Ashkenazim — Jews of northern and central European origin — who came with their own form of Orthodox Judaism; still later, Jews from Germany introduced the liberal Reform movement to America. In time, Conservative Judaism offered a middle-of-the-road alternative to the older branches. Of course, each group had to have its own cemetery, sometimes across the road from one another or even side by side.

Jews were also allotted special portions of municipal graveyards, as in Atlanta's Oakland Cemetery, established in 1850. There, on a spacious hillside, members of the first Jewish community in Atlanta were laid to rest, most of them Reform Jews originally from Germany. Their gravestones carry both German and English inscriptions, as well as an occasional Hebrew formulaic expression. Less affluent Orthodox Ashkenazis from Russia, arriving in the late nineteenth century, were granted the remaining, narrow edge of the Jewish strip. Their upright tombstones marked in Hebrew are huddled together like bodies seeking one another's warmth.

The space apportioned to Jews in interdenominational Protestant cemeteries was usually on the margins of the land. Often, as in Chicago's Oak Woods Cemetery or Wilmington, North Carolina's Oakdale Cemetery, these sections were enclosed by wrought-iron fences (plate 7). It is hard to know today whether the barriers were intended to keep Jews at a distance from Christians, or Christians away from Jews.

Because burial space in Jewish cemeteries was limited to Jews, this exclusivity acted as a deterrent against out-marriage. In principle, you would not want to marry someone who could not be buried next to you. Yet sometimes the rules were bent to accommodate a non-Jewish spouse; one example was gunfighter Wyatt Earp, whose ashes were placed in the family plot of his Jewish wife, Josephine Marcus, at the Hills of Eternity Memorial Park in Colma, California. Today most Jewish cemeteries — Orthodox, Reform, and Conservative — take in Jews of all stripes. Some even accept non-Jewish spouses.

Traditionally, when death occurs, Jews are expected to follow certain basic rituals. Caring for the dead begins with the services of the Chevra Kaddisha, a society that prepares the body for burial, men preparing men and women preparing women. They wash the body with warm water from head to toe and dress it in a white shroud. Orthodox and Conservative Jews traditionally provide a *shomer* — a guard — to attend the corpse until burial. The *shomer* keeps the body company in the belief that its soul, or *neshama,* hovers around until the body is properly buried.

Ideally, bodies should be interred within twenty-four hours, though this period is often extended to two, three, or even more days because of practical considerations, such as the arrival of close relatives who have to come from a distance. Since nothing should impede the natural process of decomposition, traditional Jewish laws proscribe the use of embalming and of coffins made of any material other than wood, which would slow down the body's return to the earth. Washing the body, wrapping it in a shroud, providing a *shomer,* enclosing the corpse in a coffin, and burying it in the earth are the five prescribed steps for treating the dead with honor.

Before the funeral, the immediate members of an Orthodox family — siblings, parents, children, spouse — tear a piece of their clothes to symbolize their loss. Reform and other Jews usually substitute a torn black ribbon, which is pinned on his or her garment. When the mourners and their friends gather in the funeral home, the rabbi conducting the ceremony delivers a eulogy and leads the congregation in reciting psalms and prayers.

At the gravesite, the rabbi concludes the service with a recitation of the mourner's prayer, called the Kaddish, from the Aramaic word meaning "holy." Although the Kaddish is recited at the burial and afterward by members of the deceased person's family, it is less a prayer for the dead than a paean to God and an expression of hope for all humankind. At the end of the burial service, it is considered a mitzvah — both a blessing and an obligation — for family members and friends to help shovel soil upon the grave. A year after burial, family members attend an unveiling of the tombstone that has been placed over the grave. When a person visits a Jewish gravesite, he or she leaves a small stone or rock on the marker as a concrete representation of one's respectful presence at the burial site.

Jewish ideas about the soul and an afterlife are far from uniform. While Orthodox Jews believe that the righteous soul makes its way to the presence of God, many other Jews espouse the view of the medieval philosopher Maimonides, who thought that when we consider life after death, "we are like blind men trying to understand the nature of light," and that it is better to fix the center of gravity on life rather than the hereafter.

The best-known Jewish postburial rite is the practice of sitting shiva for seven days. This custom allows the family time to mourn before returning to everyday life. It is a time to talk about the deceased and share one's deepest feelings, activities that — according to grief counselors — help in the healing process. Reform Jews have reduced this period of mourning to three days. A minyan, which for most of Jewish history was defined as a group of at least ten Jewish men, is expected to gather together in the house of mourning to recite the memorial prayers. In Reform and many Conservative circles today, women also are allowed to help make up the minyan. All of these customs help shore up the Jewish sense of community.

African Americans Africans brought to America as slaves had no say in their lives but had some control over the rites of burial. For the most part, they buried their dead in forests or fields designated for them by their masters. Without the benefit of stone markers, most of these gravesites have by now disappeared, destroyed by the plow or the construction crew. Many others unrecorded on old maps have simply been reclaimed by nature.

One known slave burial ground, on Butler Island, Georgia, has been lost to posterity, but a description of an 1839 burial there has survived. It was written by Fanny Anne Kemble, a famous English actress who married the American rice and cotton plantation owner Pierce Mease Butler. Published many years after her divorce from Butler, her *Journal of a Residence on a Georgian Plantation* contains this rare account of a slave funeral.

> Yesterday evening the burial of the poor man Shadrach took place. I had been applied to for a sufficient quantity of cotton cloth to make a winding sheet for him, and just as the twilight was thickening into darkness, I went with Mr. [Butler] to the cottage of one of the slaves.

The cottage was inhabited by a man named London, who was both a cooper (barrel maker) and a Methodist preacher; he was destined to make the coffin and then perform the burial service. Kemble continues:

> The coffin was laid on trestles in front of the cooper's cottage, and a large assemblage of the people had gathered round, many of the men carrying pine-wood torches. . . . Presently the whole congregation uplifted their voices in a hymn, the first high wailing notes of which — sung all in unison, in the midst of these unwonted surroundings — sent a thrill through all my nerves. When the chant ceased, cooper London began a prayer, and all the people knelt down in the sand, as I did also.

After the prayer, the coffin was carried to the "peoples burial ground," where London read aloud portions of the funeral service from the Book of Common Prayer. He ended the service with a short address on the subject of Lazarus, using the "simple and rustic" words of his people.

This type of funeral was probably performed repeatedly all over the South. The body of a dead slave would be laid out on a cooling board while a slave carpenter made the coffin. The burial was usually held at night according to African tradition, with a procession of mourners carrying pine torches to light the way. The night funeral made it possible for other blacks from neighboring plantations to attend, since their masters were generally reluctant to give them time off during daylight working hours. Funerals were an opportunity for slaves to vent their feelings freely, even with their masters and mistresses in attendance.

On very rare occasions, slaves were buried with their owners. At the Jewell Family Cemetery in Columbia, Missouri, slaves' graves were marked by tiny uninscribed stones that peep through the grass behind the standing tombstones erected for the slaves' white masters and mistresses. In the North, before slavery was abolished there state by state, it was rare for a master or mistress to erect a stone for a slave; yet a few did, as attested to by inscribed stones bearing the words "Negro" and "servant" found in the Old Burying Ground in Cambridge, Massachusetts, and the Common Burial Ground in Newport, Rhode Island. "Servant" was a common northern euphemism for "slave."

Although most African American cemeteries now resemble white cemeteries, some, especially in rural areas, still reveal traditions brought over from Africa. In the South, one often finds conch shells and other items connected with water — cups, glasses, vases — placed on graves. These are believed to be connected to the West African Bakongo belief system, which held that spirits pass through a watery expanse on their way to the afterlife — an upside-down realm situated under the world of the living.

Another practice is to leave a personal object belonging to the deceased on the grave, often the last one he or she had touched. In our trip through the South we found teacups, mugs, and even a bikini placed on African American graves.

Blacks in the North — whether slaves or freedmen — were also buried together in sites separate from the white community. The recently discovered Negroes Burying Ground on lower Broadway in New York City, where up to twenty thousand African Americans are believed to have been buried, occasioned the ceremonial reburial of more than four hundred bodily remains — an event I discuss further in chapter 7.

The search for and restoration of old African American graveyards is now occurring in many locales. As in the case of the Negroes Burying Ground in New York, honoring one's newly discovered ancestors is a way of enhancing solidarity among their descendants.

An inspiring project has been taking place in the rural countryside of eastern Texas, at the Love Cemetery, abandoned in the early 1960s. This two-acre burial ground disappeared beneath wisteria vines and wild mustang grapes, and for almost forty years afterward, the people who had bought the land wouldn't grant access to the members of the African American community whose relatives were buried there. After prolonged legal struggles, the descendants were allowed to visit the graveyard, and working with black, white, Native American, and Latino volunteers, they were able to uncover the stones of their ancestors. Using machetes, clippers, and their hands, the volunteers removed the undergrowth and ultimately, in August 2004, reconsecrated the burial ground with an interfaith cemetery. This experience provides a model for the kind of community action that builds bridges across ethnic and religious divisions.

Protestant Sects out of the Mainstream For the past four hundred years, Protestants have dominated the American landscape, whether they be Episcopalian, Congregationalist, Presbyterian, Lutheran, Unitarian, Methodist, Baptist, or any one of the numerous denominations spawned over the centuries. Many of these sects have churchyards reserved for their parishioners, though municipal and private cemeteries now rival churchyards in the number of occupants. For the most part, it is difficult to distinguish one denomination of Protestant graveyard from another.

Some of the most distinctive burial grounds belong to marginal Protestant groups such as the Mennonites, the Amish, and the Moravians, who founded American settlements in the early eighteenth century. Their cemeteries have been preserved by descendants faithful to the ways of their forebears in spite of myriad pressures to change. Standing inside an Amish cemetery in Lancaster County, Pennsylvania, one can experience a profound sense of continuity with the past. With rows of similar tombstones facing in the same direction and family names repeated from generation to generation, the dead seem to be part of the living community. It is not hard to imagine that those buried underground can hear the *clop-clop* of a covered buggy passing by.

Asians and Other "Newcomers" Such early American religious groups, however different from the mainstream, were nonetheless white and Christian, which made it easier for them to coexist with others of European origins. But immigrants from Asia, born in countries with totally different religious traditions, were for a long time denigrated and ostracized. From the mid-nineteenth century onward, successive waves of Chinese and Japanese found their resting places in Hawaii and on the West Coast, usually in cemeteries created exclusively for each group — Chinese with Chinese, Japanese with Japanese. The Japanese who made it as far as Chicago in the late nineteenth century were greeted by open hostility; most cemeteries refused them burial, a situation that worsened during World War II, when Issei, Nisei, and Sansei were treated as national enemies.

Japanese practice cremation according to Buddhist rites, which vary from country to country. Since the Buddha himself was cremated and since funeral space is very scarce in Japan, cremation is almost universal among the Japanese in their homeland. Japanese American Buddhists continue to prefer cremation, though many who are Christian now opt for body burial.

The Chinese bury their dead underground, but in the early days of immigration, they frequently disinterred the bones of the deceased after a few years and sent them back to China to be re-interred in their native villages — a practice that died out in the early twentieth century. Today, in many interdenominational cemeteries throughout the United States, one finds clusters of markers with Chinese characters; in addition, there are cemeteries devoted exclusively to Chinese Americans (plate 8).

Both Japanese and Chinese families come to the cemetery on special occasions designated for tending the graves of their ancestors — Chinese during the Ching Ming season, in the spring, and Japanese for the Obon festival, in August. (For more on Japanese and Chinese practices, see chapters 14 and 15.)

Some more recent immigrants — Indians, Vietnamese, Russians, Armenians, Middle Easterners, and Pacific Islanders, for example — lie in the newcomers' section of nondenominational graveyards or in cemeteries designed for each ethnicity. The increasingly large number of Muslim immigrants arriving since World War II have been faced with special problems.

Muslims Muslims started arriving from the Middle East at the end of the nineteenth century. Most of the earliest immigrants came from what was then known as Greater Syria — present-day Lebanon, Syria, Jordan, Palestine, and Israel. With the collapse of the Ottoman Empire, after World War I, a second wave of immigration occurred, and many Muslims joined relatives who were already established in the United States. Following World War II, Muslims again began arriving in large numbers. Today, the estimated Muslim population in America is around six million people, many of whom have ancestors in south-central Asia and Africa as well as in the Middle East.

The first Muslim Americans settled in the Midwest — in Iowa, Indiana, and Michigan. There they established their centers for Islamic worship and buried their dead in municipal or mosque-related cemeteries. Cedar Rapids, Iowa, claims to have erected the first building in North America used exclusively as a mosque (1934), as well as the First National Muslim Cemetery in North America (1948). The first twelve acres of cemetery land were donated by Yahya William Aossey, who had come to Cedar Rapids in 1907 as an immigrant. Like many other Muslims from the Middle East, as well as Christian Arabs, Aossey earned his livelihood as a peddler. In time, with a Muslim wife at his side, he worked his way up the socioeconomic ladder and became one of the respected elders of a growing Arab American enclave.

Both Sunni and Shi'ite Muslims were drawn to the Detroit area to work at the Ford Motor Company. Until recently, despite an estimated three hundred thousand Arab Americans in metropolitan Detroit, there was no cemetery solely for Muslims, and the sections reserved for them in ecumenical cemeteries were almost exhausted. After six years of negotiations over twenty-six acres of land, in 2006 the Islamic Memorial Gardens, with space for fifteen thousand graves, opened in suburban Detroit.

This new cemetery will make it easier for Muslims to adhere to their traditional burial practices. For one thing, since Muslims, like Jews, prescribe burial within twenty-four hours, the cemetery will offer services on weekends, when most other cemeteries are closed to burials. Plots in the cemetery will be laid out to allow the Muslim deceased to face Mecca, the holiest Islamic site. In the best American spirit, non-Muslims have supported the project, with Christians among the ten major investors. According to one prominent Arab American, "If it were not for our non-Muslim partners coming in, we would not have gotten this off the ground, at this point."

Muslims share a prescribed set of funeral rituals that begin even before death. Family members of the dying person are expected to be present at his or her side to help turn thoughts to Allah. They encourage repentance and trust in Allah's mercy. When the person is confirmed dead, family members close the eyes and mouth, tilt the head to the right, supplicate Allah for forgiveness, and prepare the body for burial. Like Jews, Muslims see to it that males are washed by males, females by females, and that the body is enclosed in a white shroud. Today in America, the shroud is often made from white sheets, with cloth ties fastened above the head, under the feet, and around the body.

Then the body is transferred to the mosque, where a service is held either inside or in front of the mosque. Collective funeral prayers known as *Salat-ul-Janazah* are led by the imam, who stands by the body. Traditionally, three rows of mourners stand behind the imam: a first row of males, then children, then females. The prayers consist of ritual expressions in Arabic that praise Allah and ask Him to grant peace to the deceased and to all dead Muslims.

After the *Salat-ul-Janazah*, the body is transferred to the cemetery. Pallbearers remove the body from the hearse and carry it on their shoulders for the last portion of the journey. Traditionally, only men are allowed to attend the burial. The deceased's male relatives are expected to lower the body into the grave, without a coffin, and lay it on its right side facing Mecca. If the deceased is a woman, she is placed in the grave by her husband, her sons, her father, her brothers, or her uncles. After the body is covered with earth, three handfuls of soil are thrown upon the grave, each handful accompanied by a ritual expression in Arabic. Even after the burial, relatives are enjoined to remain in the cemetery to make *dua* (supplication) for the deceased.

Muslims believe that the person in the grave is visited by two angels, Munkar and Nikar, who raise questions about his or her faith and lifetime deeds. Martyrs for Islam go directly to heaven, but the others — both those judged worthy of heaven and those consigned to torment — will remain unconscious in the grave until the Last Judgment. On that day, the blessed will know the joys of heaven, conceptualized as a shaded garden with a fountain called Salsabil. There, wearing silk garments and reclining upon couches, they will be reunited with their loved ones and, above all, enjoy the vision of God. Evil sinners will know the torments of hell, but not eternally, for God is expected to be merciful even to them.

Devout Muslims refrain from many practices that have become common in America. They do not permit cremation or autopsies, unless one is requested by a court order. They do not put flowers, candles, or photographs on the grave. Yet like most Americans regardless of their religion or ethnicity, Muslims consider it a duty to offer sympathy and comfort to the family in mourning. In the words of a Muslim funeral guide, "This strengthens the relationships within the Muslim Community."

Long before ground breaks for the development of a cemetery, zoning issues can become a nexus of controversy. Not all religious or ethnic cemeteries come to completion as felicitously as the one in suburban Detroit. In fact, in one Georgia community, reactions to a proposed Muslim cemetery became openly contentious. In 2001, with an estimated sixty thousand Muslims in metropolitan Atlanta, the Georgia Islamic Institute of Religious and Social Studies proposed a fifteen-hundred-plot cemetery a few miles from its mosque in Lawrenceville, Georgia. Its proposal was slated for review by the planning commission on September 18, but with the intervening events of September 11, a simple procedural event escalated into a controversy over the desirability of a Muslim cemetery in a predominantly Baptist neighborhood.

Neighbors worried that the cemetery would lower their property values. They pointed to presumed health hazards created by the Islamic mandate to wrap the body in a shroud without embalming or a casket. They took pictures of a cemetery near Lovejoy, Georgia — then the only Muslim cemetery in metro Atlanta — showing open graves awaiting burials and modest wooden markers on unkempt grounds.

Eventually a compromise was fashioned for a scaled-down facility that required wooden caskets but dispensed with embalming. An eight-foot cemetery wall — two feet lower than the one originally requested by residents — would presumably keep the graveyard sufficiently out of sight from its non-Muslim neighbors.

These are the kinds of hostile feelings many newcomers to America have had to deal with throughout the centuries, even without the unfortunate circumstances affecting Muslim Americans today. Even in death, we fear the stranger. And the stranger finds comfort in bonding with those who share his or her beliefs and customs.

4

DISTANCING
THE DEAD

THE HISTORY OF AMERICAN cemeteries is the story of immigrant groups coming to the New World, claiming the land, marking the gravesite, and preserving religious and ethnic identities even beyond the grave. But there is another story interwoven with this history, one that follows the evolution of cemeteries themselves and the changes that have taken place in the way corpses are prepared for burial. These developments have had the effect of distancing the dead, geographically and sometimes even emotionally, from their families and communities.

New Haven's New Burying Ground From the early seventeenth to the late eighteenth century, Euro-American cemeteries were somber places intended not only for the disposal of bodies but also for the edification of the living. They were meant to be visual reminders that death awaited everyone. Tombstone inscriptions stated brutally: "Here lies . . ." or "Here lies the body of . . ." Later formulations, such as "In the memory of," show a collective distancing from the focus on mortality and physical decay that had previously dominated Christian, and especially Puritan, theology.

By the turn of the nineteenth century, the old colonial graveyards were often neglected and had become little more than city eyesores. Not

Above: Gravestone, Mount Auburn Cemetery, Cambridge, Massachusetts

only were they unsightly, but many people began to believe in the miasma theory — city burial grounds were contaminating agents that emitted noxious vapors. However inaccurate, this belief in the infectious properties of miasma produced by decomposing bodies would hang on for years to come.

A revolution was about to take place in the American cemetery. It began in New Haven, Connecticut, after the yellow fever epidemics of 1794 and 1795. When the old New Haven Green became too crowded to serve as the city's chief burial site, thirty citizens led by U.S. Senator James Hillhouse decided to purchase a six-acre lot at the edge of town for the establishment of the New Burying Ground, later known as the Grove Street Cemetery. As opposed to the haphazard arrangement of other burying grounds, this cemetery was divided into family lots and had special sections set aside for Yale College, Strangers, Negroes, and the Poor. All of this met the unabashed approval of Timothy Dwight, president of Yale University and a prominent Congregationalist minister, who wrote in the early 1800s: "It is believed that this cemetery is altogether a singularity in the world. I have accompanied many Americans and many foreigners into it, not one of whom had ever seen or heard of anything of a similar nature."

Dwight's praise for the New Burying Ground was linked to deep moral and religious beliefs, which he expressed by comparing the new burial location with the old.

It is always desirable that a burial ground should be a solemn object to man, because in this manner it easily becomes a source of useful instruction and desirable impressions. But, when placed in the center of a town and in the current of daily intercourse, it is rendered too familiar to the eye to have any beneficial effect on the heart. From its proper, venerable character, it is degraded into a mere common object, and speedily loses all its connection with the invisible world in a gross and vulgar union with the ordinary business of life.

Surrounded by residential and public buildings, a way station for people and cows, the old graveyards of Connecticut had, in Dwight's opinion, lost their power to evoke the spiritual world. By contrast, the New Burying

Ground on the outskirts of New Haven, a full two blocks away from Yale University, was seen as a transcendent oasis that could propel the spirit above life's quotidian cares.

Two hundred years later, with university expansion, Yale now abuts the cemetery's front gate. It is once again a familiar sight to town and gown, but with an effect Dwight could not have anticipated. By now it is a prized piece of New Haven history, the burying place of many esteemed personages and the forerunner of the American rural cemetery movement.

"The Great Tomb of Man" Dwight's concerns were part of a new philosophy of death imported from England and Europe and adapted to the New World by American clergymen and writers. Foremost among them was William Cullen Bryant, who, in his masterly 1817 poem "Thanatopsis," offered a vision of mankind more attuned to "Nature's teachings" than to otherworldly exhortations. Man was presented as a creature of the earth, "brother to the insensible rock," destined after death "To mix forever with the elements." While individuals would surely die, the cycles of Nature would assure the continuity of life. And even if one inevitably died alone, Bryant found consolation in the idea of union with all the dead from ages past, "All in one mighty sepulchre." Without excluding the possibility of a Christian afterlife (which Bryant later alluded to in the poems of his old age), the younger man romanticized death amidst Nature's bounties, in "the great tomb of man." The poem's final message is one of complete trust in God's and Nature's plan, including the promise of eternal repose: "approach thy grave / Like one who wraps the drapery of his couch / About him, and lies down to pleasant dreams."

Inspired by Bryant and his literary peers, early-nineteenth-century civic leaders set out to create idyllic settings that would indeed be conducive to untroubled rest. In fact, it was only with the rise of the rural cemetery that the word "cemetery," from the Greek equivalent of "dormitory," meaning "a place of sleep," became a popular replacement for the terms "burying ground" and "graveyard." This bucolic impetus would effect a radical transformation in cemetery design, eventually replacing the cramped urban necropolis with miniature Gardens of Eden on the city's outskirts. Instead of bleak grounds punctuated with stark slabs, the new cemeteries would have headstones and statues artfully inserted into garden settings of soothing grass, lush foliage, towering trees, and colorful flowers.

Though some old graveyards can still be found in urban centers, such as those in downtown Boston and in the historic district of Charleston, most fell victim to the general nineteenth-century exodus from urban to rural locales. This often meant that a religious congregation would sell a valuable piece of central-city real estate, disinter hundreds of bodies, and then re-inter them in less expensive acreage outside the city limits. The rationale for this move was underpinned by the belief that corpses were a source of contagion, to be placed as far as possible from human habitation. Increasingly, all across the nation, city limits were extended and cemeteries relocated farther and farther away from the city center.

The Mount Auburn Cemetery Model In 1823, when he became mayor of Boston, Josiah Quincy inherited a cemetery problem similar to New Haven's twenty-five years earlier. How was the city to deal with its overcrowded burial grounds? With a population that had reached 43,290 by 1820 and would jump to 70,000 in the next decade, Boston no longer had any space available for the dead. Moreover, it was believed that its burial grounds were contaminating the water supply. In Paris, the French were dealing with these same problems by creating the magnificent Père-Lachaise Cemetery; it originally covered forty-two suburban acres but doubled in size between 1824 and 1850. Should not Boston think big on the French scale, rather than emulate their small-town neighbors in New Haven?

The idea of a spacious burial ground found advocates within the newly formed Massachusetts Horticultural Society, which spearheaded the development of a "garden cemetery" at a site known as Sweet Auburn (eventually called Mount Auburn) in Cambridge. In 1831, the Horticultural Society agreed to purchase seventy-two acres for a sum of six thousand dollars; by August, one hundred lots had been sold at a price of sixty dollars each; and on September 24, a consecration ceremony was held before nearly two thousand people.

In his consecration address, Judge John Story reminded his audience, "It is the duty of the living thus to provide for the dead." He spoke of the universal desire "to die in the arms of our friends" and "to repose in the land of our nativity." He evoked the agony of those who "sleep their last sleep in the land of strangers," a sentiment he traced back to biblical times, when the Patriarch Jacob asked not to be buried in Egypt but in his Hebrew homeland. Judge Story's combination of personal, patriotic, religious, and moralistic exhortations sounded the right note for Mount Auburn's high-minded community.

At that time, Mount Auburn was unique among American cemeteries. With its original 72 acres expanded to 112 by midcentury, Mount Auburn offered a beautifully verdant landscape spread over seven hills, dotted with ponds, and shaded by majestic trees. Oak, pine, beech, walnut, willow, and cedar were natural features prized by the Horticultural Society. In time, numerous other species would be added, many of which are carefully labeled today with both their popular names in English and their species names in Latin.

Coming upon an exuberant pink dogwood the color of cotton candy across from the soberly understated tomb of Henry Wadsworth Longfellow, I knew the nineteenth-century Horticultural Society would be proud of its legacy. Now at 175 acres, Mount Auburn is indeed a marriage of nature and art: orderly, well maintained, tasteful. On its grounds lie such notables as the writer Justice Oliver Wendell Holmes, the painter Winslow Homer, the museum founder Isabella Stewart Gardner, poets James Russell Lowell and Amy Lowell, Justice Felix Frankfurter, the psychologist B. F. Skinner, the inventor Buckminster Fuller, and the novelist Bernard Malamud. A classic Greek temple at the edge of a bucolic pond rises in honor of Mary Baker Eddy, founder of the Christian Science religion (plate 9). Small wonder that Mount Auburn is still the burial spot of choice for many Cambridge academics and Boston's elite.

Mount Auburn would soon be followed by other rural sites near cities eager to achieve cemetery fame: Laurel Hill in Philadelphia in 1836; Greenmount in Baltimore in 1838; Green-Wood in Brooklyn in 1839; Spring Grove in Cincinnati in 1844; Allegheny in Pittsburgh in 1845; Bellefontaine in St. Louis in 1849; Oakland in Atlanta in 1850; Calvary in

Milwaukee in 1857; and Graceland in Chicago in 1860. By 1861, there were some sixty-six garden cemeteries in the United States. One of my favorites is the Sleepy Hollow Cemetery in Concord, Massachusetts, where authors Henry David Thoreau (1817–1862), Nathaniel Hawthorne (1804–1864), Ralph Waldo Emerson (1803–1882), and Louisa May Alcott (1832–1888) are all buried within visual distance of one another. Designed in 1855 by the noted landscape firm of Cleveland and Copeland, Sleepy Hollow offered an earthly paradise of trees, flowers, and undulating greenery. If, as historian Simon Schama has brilliantly argued in *Landscape and Memory*, individuals cast in the same mold as Thoreau preferred their nature wild, others were content to see it tamed. The rural cemetery model offered a meeting place between civilization and the wilderness. No longer the unruly land feared by their colonial ancestors, nature had become for many nineteenth-century Americans a gentle homeland ready to embrace them.

The Memorial Park The rural or garden cemetery was to the nineteenth century what the memorial park was to the twentieth. Although both emphasized landscape, they had different aims. The garden cemetery privileged nature as a sweet setting for the dead and a consolation for the living; the memorial park practically hides death altogether. Memorial parks are characterized by markers set flush with the ground, barely visible among the acres of lawn that encompass them (plate 10). Without tombstones to interfere with maintenance, power mowers and water systems keep the grounds blanketed with manicured grass. In many memorial parks, green carpet stretches out like a golf course as far as the eye can see.

The memorial lawn-park runs counter to the desire for individualization apparent in certain recent tombstones bearing porcelain and laser portraits and other engraved images connected to the deceased, such as a musical instrument. Instead, flat granite and bronze markers are incorporated into the ground covering, producing an overall effect of anonymity. What gets lost, of course, are the numerous possibilities offered by old-fashioned tombstones. A twelve-by-twenty-four-inch marker simply does not offer a surface large enough for elaborate carvings or lengthy epitaphs. There is barely space for a full name accompanied by the dates of birth and death. Ironically, the use of efficient maintenance technology has led us back to the spare markers of the earliest Anglo-American burying grounds.

Many memorial parks do, however, provide additional features designed to vary the landscape: shrubs and trees, ponds and streams, fountains and statues, group mausoleums and even mourners' chapels that double as sites for wedding ceremonies. The larger-than-life statuary erected in Southern California's Forest Lawn cemeteries amaze millions of visitors each year.

The memorial park is just one more step in the direction of taming death, a process that began in the eighteenth century when angelic faces with wings started replacing death's-heads. At that time, optimistic Enlightenment ideas of human progress, followed by romantic visions of harmony between man and Nature, and increased confidence in the scientific ability to control illness all contributed to the sense that death was no longer the central concern of life. Death was further distanced by another major development — the funeral parlor.

The Rise of the Funeral Industry Until the late nineteenth century, most Americans died in their homes and were prepared for burial by their kin. The body was washed, wrapped in a shroud, and laid out in a wooden coffin by family and friends. Deathbed scenes were a staple of American lives and literature, as sensitive young men and women recalled the painful, permanent departure of grandparents, parents, and siblings from their homes.

While most individuals still died at home well into the twentieth century, the appearance of the professional undertaker in the aftermath of the Civil War would — quite literally — change the face of death. The first national meeting of undertakers, in 1882, established a set of standards that called for the presence of the funeral director in the home and later in the funeral parlor, where he would clean the corpse, embalm it for a final viewing, and ultimately usher it to the cemetery.

In his semiautobiographical novel *Look Homeward, Angel,* Thomas Wolfe recreated the last days of Ben, a fictional brother whose imminent death brought together — at least briefly — a dysfunctional family. Eliza, the mother from whom Ben had been estranged, was allowed to come to him only after he had died:

> It was almost four o'clock in the morning. Eliza straightened out Ben's limbs, and folded his hands across his body. She smoothed out the rumpled covers of the bed, and patted out the pillows, making a smooth hollow for his head to rest in. His flashing hair, cropped close to his well-shaped head, was crisp and crinkly as a boy's, and shone with bright points of light. With a pair of scissors, she snipped off a little lock where it would not show.

In a subsequent scene, two of Ben's brothers, Eugene and Luke, go to the funeral parlor to consult the undertaker. It is apparent that even in 1929, when this book was published, the undertaker's profession was suspect. The selling of the coffin in the novel is a gem of understated satire, and the sight of Ben later in the day after he had been embalmed left the brothers in a state of astonished despair. "Eugene thought, it is not Ben. . . . In this poor stuffed crow, with its pathetic barbering, and its neat buttons, nothing of the owner had been left. All that was there was the tailoring of Horse Hines [the undertaker], who now stood by watchfully, hungry for their praise."

For Ben's middle-class family in North Carolina, the funeral parlor was already a necessary way station between the home and the graveyard. But among poorer folk in isolated regions, burial by family and friends was still common even as recently as fifty years ago. Sarah Middleton, a one-hundred-year-old black woman living in rural South Carolina, recalled in 1996 that during much of her life the body was laid out in the home for bathing and dressing. Coffins were built at or near the home of the deceased, then loaded onto horse-drawn wagons. "We dressed and sang hymns . . . some of us carried torches. It was a long time ago, but I still remember it."

With the growth of the funeral industry, undertakers — also known as morticians and funeral directors — assumed control of all stages of death, from the moment the body breathed its last breath until it was buried. Though the word "undertaker" has been around since Middle English, the word "mortician," generally used more in the United States than in England, did not appear until the nineteenth century, and "funeral director" did not become common until the twentieth. But whatever they were called, undertakers became particularly adept at staging the funeral ceremony in a formal manner commensurate with the deceased person's income and status. Because the funeral industry was largely unregulated in its early days, it frequently fattened itself through questionable practices, many of which were exposed by Jessica Mitford in her 1963 bestselling book *The American Way of Death.*

Mitford had many quarrels with America's funeral directors. She portrayed them as a deceitful lot dedicated to the commercial exploitation of the bereaved. She depicted their venal efforts to sell the most expensive metal caskets (rather than simple wood coffins) and other costly accoutrements deemed essential for a viewing of the body. Most of all, she criticized the routine practice of embalming that had been sold to the American public as a necessary step in the burial process, though few states absolutely required it, and some religions — Orthodox Judaism and Islam — specifically prohibited it.

Embalming is the process whereby preservatives and disinfectants are injected into the arteries as a substitute for blood. This ancient procedure practiced by the Egyptians went out of use during the Christian era but was revived in America for "sanitary purposes," especially when the body was not to be buried until several days after death.

Embalming was first used on a grand scale in America during the Civil War to permit slain soldiers to be shipped back to their homes. Thomas Holmes, a physician, is credited with having made embalming popular. When called upon to embalm Colonel Elmer Ellsworth, President Lincoln's former clerk from his Springfield, Illinois, law office days, Holmes did such an excellent job that his services were subsequently much in demand. At this point, opportunistic undertakers charging as much as eighty dollars for an officer and thirty dollars for an enlisted man "competed for corpses" on the battlefield, and the industry took off.

Most states passed laws requiring the procedure in three instances: (1) when the person dies of a communicable disease, (2) when the body is to be moved across a state line, or (3) when the body is to be held more than twenty-four (or thirty or forty-eight) hours before burial. Yet some states held that embalming was not mandatory under any circumstance.

Recently, the popular TV program *Six Feet Under* brought the mortician's practice to the attention of numerous bemused viewers, as Thomas Lynch's *The Undertaking* did for thousands of readers. Instead of lugubrious professionals, we see the human side of the trade: the tensions among family members engaged in running a mortuary; the concealed anxieties of those trained to clean, dress, and embalm corpses; the sense of pride in their craft, as well as the slights and humiliations they experience from the community at large.

A Cemetery Itinerary We turn now to a cemetery itinerary through time and space. Each of the following eleven chapters is linked to a specific city or region. Collectively they tell the story of our nation, from seventeenth-century New England Pilgrims to twenty-first-century Hawaiians. The distinctive atmosphere of these burial sites — affluent and poor, large and small, city and rural, sectarian and nonsectarian, private and municipal — has been captured in Reid Yalom's photos, which evoke, with the immediate claim of the visual, the treasures you will find if you follow in our footsteps.

5

DEATH'S-HEADS AND FUNERAL GLOVES

BOSTON, MASSACHUSETTS

IN THE HEART OF Boston, with cars emitting noise and pollution from busy Tremont Street, Boston's original Burying Place transports us back to the seventeenth century. Rough-hewn greenstone with no decoration and slate slabs featuring ghoulish death's-heads mark the graves of New England's first families: Winthrops and Cottons, ubiquitous Johns and Marys, and quaint given names like Obadiah, Hepzibah, and Mehitable. Their tenacious hold on valuable property belies the modern metropolis that has grown up around them.

King's Chapel Burying Ground The Burying Place — later known as King's Chapel — was founded almost immediately after the arrival of the *Arbella,* the flagship of the seventeen vessels that sailed to Massachusetts in 1630 bearing English Puritans. On board was Lady Arbella Fiennes, for whom the ship had been named; her friend, the future poet Anne Dudley Bradstreet; Anne Dudley's parents and her husband, Simon Bradstreet; the future governor of Massachusetts John Winthrop; and a sturdy contingent of other Puritans who had chosen exile in order to escape harassment in their home country. Unlike the Pilgrims who had settled Plymouth ten years earlier, the Puritans wanted to "purify" the Church of

Above: Skull and crossbones, Granary Burying Ground, Boston

England, not separate from it. Far from the Anglican Church, with the rituals it had carried over from Catholicism, Puritans would practice a simple yet uncompromising form of worship.

They observed the Sabbath rigorously starting at sundown on Saturday; work and play were forbidden under penalty of fines. Sexual intercourse was also taboo on the Sabbath. Laws drawn from the Pentateuch ordained that crimes such as blasphemy and bestiality were punishable by death. Hanging for capital crimes, maiming and whipping for other serious offenses, stocks and pillories for lesser infractions — all were legitimate means of enforcing the law. Puritans set out to create a meticulously regulated theocratic society. In 1633, there was even a law enacted prohibiting idleness. Having risked everything to found settlements in the wilderness, they felt the need to protect themselves by strictly defining acceptable behavior and by excluding any who might threaten their new community.

Despite the mind-boggling changes that have taken place since 1630, the King's Chapel Burying Ground (plate 11) still bears the hallmarks of its Puritan origins: simplicity, sobriety, order. Its plain stones are packed together in an egalitarian enclave; the only exceptions are a few larger collective tombs, which were erected at a later date. Although the graves were originally laid out randomly, with no pathways, over time the markers have been rearranged in a more linear fashion, so now the bones below do not necessarily correspond to the names inscribed above. The 611 remaining gravestones and 29 tabletop tomb markers probably represent but a fraction of the actual burials in these grounds.

Puritans had very clear ideas about how they should be buried. In an effort to dissociate themselves from Anglicans and Catholics, they established their burying grounds under municipal rather than church control, and at a distance from the meetinghouses, which served as churches. Instead of "churchyard," they used the term "burying ground" or "graveyard" for the secular sites that became the norm throughout the Massachusetts Bay Colony.

In a further effort to avoid popish symbols, they did not place crosses or any other images of divinity on the grave. In fact, prior to the mid-seventeenth century, they took little care to mark graves at all. There were probably wooden markers, which have since disappeared, before the carefully carved stones that began to proliferate in the 1650s.

The earliest surviving tombstone in King's Chapel is that of William Paddy, a Boston merchant. Its typical inscription reads in uppercase letters:

HERE LYETH

THE BODY OF MR. WM. PADDY,

AE. 58 YEARS

DEPARTED

THIS LIFE AUGUST THE —— 1658

Paddy is buried next to his second wife, Mary (1615–1675) and his son Thomas (1647–1690). Between his two wives, he is known to have had eleven children.

Many of the tombstones from the seventeenth and eighteenth centuries carry the death's-head image of a skull with wings. The stark skull was a vivid reminder of mortality and the certainty of physical death. But the wings spoke for the spirit and the possibility of resurrection. Puritans understood death as punishment for Adam's original sin in the Garden of Eden, a sin that had been transmitted to all mankind. Depravity, the natural state of all mankind, was succinctly summed up in a popular couplet: "In Adam's fall, we sinned all." Nonetheless, some would be saved, according to the Calvinist doctrine of predestination, which attributed salvation solely to the grace of God. Contrary to Catholic doctrine, election could not be earned by good works or acts of repentance and was not influenced by indulgences or prayers sent upward to help the deceased. Every Puritan was taught from early childhood to fear God, to accept His will, and to prepare for the Day of Judgment. Puritan graveyards were thus somber places intended to convey the twin truths of inevitable human decay and ultimate confrontation with one's Maker.

Initially, New England Puritans, following their reformed brethren in the home country, were firmly opposed to elaborate ceremony in the graveyard. Ostentatious processions, pompous eulogies, and other marks of worldly distinction were discarded as High-Church travesties of true Christian comportment. An English traveler to New England in the late 1630s and early 1640s reported, "At burials, nothing is read, nor any Funeral sermon made, but all the neighborhood, or a good company of them, come together by tolling of the bell, and carry the dead solemnly to his grave, and there stand by him while he is buried."

While such simplicity prevailed for the first generation of Puritans, by the middle of the century more grandiose ritual had crept back into the burial procedure. In 1649, when Governor John Winthrop died, his funeral was carried out with conspicuous ceremony. A barrel and a half of gunpowder was discharged by Bostonians eager to show their "love and respects to the late honored Gounor which they manifested in solemnizing his funeral."

Until his death in 1649, at the age of sixty-one, Winthrop had been the dominant force in the Massachusetts Bay Colony, serving as its governor twelve times. His journal chronicling early Puritan society in America leaves behind the picture of a disciplined, energetic leader, committed to the idea of a Christian community that would shine as a beacon to the world. "We shall be as a City upon a Hill, the eyes of all people are upon us" encapsulated his utopian hopes for the fledgling colony.

Envisioning Massachusetts as a theocracy, Winthrop took the side of the clergy in their confrontation with the outspoken religious dissident Anne Hutchinson during the upheaval known as the antinomian heresy. As a voice who proclaimed the priority of individual conscience over church dictates and the doctrine of God's grace over good works, Hutchinson was eventually tried as a heretic by the general court, sentenced to banishment, and excommunicated. She moved to Rhode Island, which welcomed religious dissidents, and after the death of her husband, she migrated farther south to New York, where she and five of her children were killed by Mahican Indians in 1643. A plaque marking the presumed site of her murder was erected in 1911 on the Split Rock in present-day Pelham Bay.

In contrast to Hutchinson's gory demise and uncertain resting place, Winthrop's raised ledger tomb — a 1920 replacement for an earlier marker — is now the most sought-out shrine at King's Chapel. He is buried with his son and grandson, each a governor of Connecticut.

Throughout much of the seventeenth century, ongoing religious strife in England would directly influence the Boston colonists and, specifically, their first burying place. In 1685, the restored king James II resolved to reestablish the Anglican Church in England and the colonies. To that end, he sent Sir Edmund Andros to Boston in December 1686 as New England's first royal governor-general. Andros planned to build an Anglican chapel on property purchased from the town. When the Puritan town councilors rejected his request, he approached Judge Samuel Sewall (see below), who also refused to sell some of his private property for the purpose of Anglican worship. Finally, Andros simply appropriated a portion of the burying ground that was public property, and by June 1689, a tiny wooden church named King's Chapel was dedicated. To this day, King's Chapel — now a Unitarian congregation — stands on the front corner of the original Puritan burying ground, while the graveyard itself remains the property of the City of Boston.

In the early years, cattle were allowed to graze in the Burying Ground, until the Boston selectmen decided on March 15, 1679/80 that "noe Cattle be suffered to feed" there. Infractions of the grazing prohibition would continue despite fines for the owners of the offending cattle. On May 26, 1718, it was "Agreed that William Young is to pay fifteen shillings for his Cows grazeing in the Old burying place this Last Summer." Another hundred years would pass before it became customary to build fences around cemeteries to keep the cattle out.

In the mid-nineteenth century, author Lydia Sigourney (1791–1865) was asked to contribute a poem to a book on the King's Chapel tombstones. Known as a successful poet of death literature (like her contemporary William Cullen Bryant), she would do honor to the list of names carefully compiled by Thomas Bridgman in his *Memorials of the Dead in Boston* (1853). In the course of his visits to King's Chapel, Bridgman managed to discover the graves of Sarah Story Cotton and Elizabeth Davenport and called attention to their neglected condition. He also lamented the fact that many of the early gravestones had been lined up in straight rows, noting with dismay: "By a singular caprice of a former superintendent of burials, many of the grave-stones in this burial-place have been removed from their original locations and placed in rows; an act which it is very desirable should never be repeated." This separation of gravestones from the remains they marked had already been the fate of most early burying grounds in the Boston area.

Phipp's Street Burying Ground Across the river from Boston, in the suburb of Charlestown, another burying ground was also established in 1630. Now known as the Phipp's Street Burying Ground, it has remained close to its original design, without the realignment of stones that altered King's Chapel and other colonial graveyards. If you want to see what an early New England burying ground looked like before the stones were lined up in rows, Phipp's Street is the best example in metropolitan Boston. All the extant gravestones — 1,558 in toto — have remained in their original clusters, going every which way. They adorn a small hill on the edge of a neighborhood that, despite creeping gentrification, still carries traces of its working-class origins.

One of the graveyard's earliest inhabitants was a modest minister named John Harvard. Before coming to America, Harvard received his bachelor's and master's degrees from Emmanuel College in Cambridge, England. An immigrant to Charlestown in 1637, he served as assistant to the pastor and as a teaching elder in the local church. When he died in 1638, at the age of thirty-one, he bequeathed £780 (half his estate) and his library of 320 volumes to the newly founded college in Cambridge, Massachusetts, which was subsequently named in his honor. Today an obelisk at the top of the hill marks his grave. Surprisingly, few Boston or Cambridge residents seem to know where John Harvard is buried, as opposed to the large number of inhabitants familiar with John Winthrop's permanent resting place — perhaps because the Phipp's Street Burying Ground is located in unfashionable Charlestown rather than Boston or Cambridge.

Harvard's neighbors in the cemetery represent a wide range of Charlestown residents, from Nathaniel Gorham, a signer of the Constitution, to Prince Bradstreet, an "honest man of color." One of the wonders of this graveyard are the tombstones carved in a recognizable, dramatic style by a man known only as the Charlestown Stonecutter, who worked from the mid-1670s onward and was followed by four generations of Lamson family members. The Lamson stones appear thicker, sturdier, and more ornate than many others from the same period. The ubiquitous death's-heads have a family resemblance, like cousins leering at one another. Lamson stones can be found throughout New England and as far away as Charleston, South Carolina. Unlike many anonymous carvers who plied their trade in colonial America, the Lamson family carvers were well known for their craft and were widely imitated.

Joseph Lamson (1658–1722), the first of the line who can be identified by name, probably came to work under the Charlestown Stonecutter about 1678. He supplemented his income by moonlighting as a seaman, a shoemaker, and a surveyor. Headstones that are attributed to him in the Phipp's Street Burying Ground include the ones for Zechariah Long (died 1688) and Ensign Timothy Cutler (died 1694). Each shows a winged death's-head under a central arch with leaf and fruit borders on the sides. On the Long stone, two imps separated by an hourglass shoot mortal darts into the death's-head skull. On the Cutler marker, two imps carry a coffin right under the death's-head chin.

Joseph Lamson's own tombstone was carved by one of his two sons, either Nathaniel (1692–1755) or Caleb (1697–1760), and follows the pattern established by the father: a death's-head in the tympanum under an edge of pleated drapery with foliate swirls on the sides. The death's-head has the by-now-familiar wings, round eyes, triangular nose, square jaw with two straight rows of clenched teeth, and eyebrows that were found on nearly all of Joseph Lamson's stones. But there is a noticeable difference in quality between the masterly work of the father and that of his somewhat more pedestrian sons.

A Lamson double tomb devoted to two children who perished at the same time raises unanswerable questions (plate 12). Why did "Jonathan Bunker Aged 5 years, 6 Mo & II Ds" and "George Bunker Aged 4 Years & 7 Monts" both die in November 1721? Were they victims of an epidemic or a fire? What was their place within the Bunker family, a name famous for the nearby Battle of Bunker Hill?

Jonathan and George were the descendants of George Bunker and Judith Major Bunker, who came to Charlestown sometime before January 1633. These early English immigrants, founders of the Charlestown branch of the prolific Bunkers, acquired hundreds of acres in the area, including a pasture that reached over the summit of the hill that was subsequently given their name.

There they lie, Jonathan and George, plucked from life in early childhood. The winged death's-heads on their twin headstones may appear to modern observers grotesquely comical, but they were dead serious images for the boys' contemporaries. Death's-heads would continue to be the most popular gravestone motif in America until the late 1700s.

Copp's Hill Burying Ground Less than three decades after the establishment of the first two burying grounds in Boston and Charlestown, the city needed new land for the dead. The North Burying Ground, later known as Copp's Hill, was laid out in 1659, and the Granary in 1660. From the vantage point of Copp's Hill in the North End of Boston, one could look down on the Charles River and Charlestown on the other side. It was, and still is, a choice site, the only one of Boston's original three hills that has not been whittled away or completely flattened over time (plate 13).

Apparently, the North Burying Ground began to be called Copp's because of a shoemaker named William Copp living on the hill. The oldest gravestone, uncovered in the late twentieth century, belonged to a member of his family: "David, son to David Copp and Obedience his wife, aged 2 weeks Dyed Dec, 22 1661."

It is estimated that Copp's Hill contains approximately ten thousand graves, though there are now only 2,300 markers. One hundred and twenty years ago, some three thousand markers still remained, but many were carried away and used for a variety of purposes — for example, the foundations of nearby buildings, closures to entrances for belowground tombs, and even a baker's hearth!

The cemetery has the distinction of containing the Mather family tomb, including Congregational ministers Increase Mather (1639–1723), Cotton Mather (1663–1728), and Samuel Mather (?1706–1785). The Mathers were major re-interpreters of Puritanism and dominant figures in both church and state. Increase was, among other things, president of Harvard College, pastor of North Church, and the author of forty religious books.

When he died in Boston in 1723, an immense funeral procession including virtually every important public figure in Boston made its way to the burial ground.

Increase's son Cotton Mather, his partner and successor as pastor of North Church and an author even more prolific than his father, died in 1728. He too was the recipient of a very large funeral gathering, "almost as if it were the funeral of the Country," according to one contemporary report. Because both men believed in witches and defended the witch trials, the honor afforded them today would probably be less generous. Yet it should be said in defense of Cotton that he eventually played a significant role in bringing the trials to an end. And one should also remember that witchcraft in the colonies resulted in only about fifty deaths, as opposed to the tens of thousands in Europe.

Samuel Mather, heir to the family vocation, requested in his will that his body "be deposited in the same Tomb with the remains of my honoured Father and Grandfather, and of many other esteemed Relatives, besides my most respected and beloved Wife." But in contrast to the fanfare surrounding his father's and grandfather's funerals in the early eighteenth century, Samuel wanted something less ostentatious. He specified "no Funeral Encomiums" and "only one Bell tolled just before Sun down, and that but for Five Minutes." Perhaps this scion of celebrated leaders did not feel he merited the same attention as his prominent forebears, or perhaps he truly wanted a return to the simplicity of the first New England Puritans.

The Mathers share Copp's Hill with many other colonial worthies, among them Captain Thomas Lake, commander of the Ancient and Honorable Artillery, "perfidiously slain" by Indians in August 1676; Recompense Wadsworth, "First Master of yᵉ Grammar School of yᵉ North End of Boston," who died at the age of 25 in 1713; and Revolutionary War hero Robert Newman, remembered for hanging out the signal lanterns in the Old North Church steeple on April 18, 1775, to inform the patriots of British movement — "one if by land, two if by sea," in the words of Longfellow's poem "Paul Revere's Ride."

By the time of the Revolutionary War, more than a thousand African Americans were also buried at Copp's Hill, though in a separate section.

African Americans had been brought to Boston as slaves from the West Indies as early as 1638, but slavery never grew to the large proportions found on plantations in the South, and New England households usually had no more than one or two slaves, euphemistically called servants. Some few African Americans were even buried with elaborate funerals, as indicated by the following account in the *New England Courant*, July 22, 1723:

> On Wed. morning last dyed here Mrs. Carlington, consort of Mr. James Carlington, an African belonging to Robert Achmuty, Esq. Her corpse was carried in a coach to her mother's house at the North End on Wed. night and on Thur. night she was magnificently interred in the North Burying Place [Copp's Hill], the velvet pall being supported by 6 blacks of the first rank and her funeral attended by 270 more of the same color.

By 1765 there were about 950 slaves and a large number of free blacks within the city. During the Revolution, many on either side fought in exchange for their freedom. After the war, they petitioned in court for an end to slavery. Finally, in 1783, it was officially abolished in Massachusetts, but not until 1810 did it completely disappear in Boston.

The most famous antislavery black activist to be buried in Copp's Hill is Prince Hall (died 1807). Born a slave in 1735, Hall was freed by his master on April 7, 1775, as a reward for twenty-one years of faithful service. He became a significant leader in the movement to secure rights for black people, including the right to public education. He is perhaps best known as the founder of the first African American lodge of Freemasons, organized in 1787. Freemasons of color claim him as their spiritual ancestor and remember that when he died of old age, in December 1807, his funeral was celebrated in accordance with Masonic rites.

Granary Burying Ground The largest of the central Boston burying grounds is the Granary, established in 1660 on what was then part of the Boston Common. Popularly called the Granary because of the barn that once stood on the property, it was intended to help alleviate the overcrowding at King's Chapel, barely a block away.

The Granary contains approximately 2,350 gravestones, although it is estimated that 5,000 people are buried here. Unlike King's Chapel and Copp's Hill, the predominantly slate grave markers were arranged in an orderly fashion from the start according to instructions from the 1660 Boston selectmen, but as the gravestones have been rearranged several times, many of the stones no longer stand over the remains of the people named on them.

Originally, cows were allowed to graze freely among the stones, but later grazing and breakage fees were instituted to provide a source of revenue for the city, as noted in the Boston selectmen's report of 1713, when a certain James Williams was held responsible for damages to the graves "by reason of his cows going there."

The twenty-five-foot obelisk in the center marks the tomb of the parents of Benjamin Franklin, whose own grave is in Philadelphia. Three signers of the Declaration are buried here — Samuel Adams (1722–1803), John Hancock (1737–1793), and Robert Treat Paine (1731–1814) — as is that other Revolutionary patriot Paul Revere (1734–1818), still resting from his arduous midnight ride.

One of the oldest and most impressive stones is the 1671 marker for the four children of Andrew and Millicent Neal, which is attributed to the Charlestown Stonecutter. Andrew Neal, the innkeeper of the Starr Inn, apparently had the wherewithal to commemorate the lives of his four dead children with one large eye-catching stone carrying their names: Andrew, Hannah, and two Elizabeths. (In colonial times, it was not unusual for parents to name a new child after one who had died.) Andrew died at eighteen months, Elizabeth I at three days, Elizabeth II at two weeks, and Hannah at an unknown age. Their unusual stone has a triangular pediment enclosing a classic death's-head. Underneath, there are outlines of three headstones commemorating three of the four children; perhaps Hannah was born and died after the stone had been commissioned. Elizabeth I has crossbones above her name; Elizabeth II has an hourglass; and Andrew has spades for digging a grave.

In America today, the loss of four children would be a dire tragedy, but in the seventeenth century it was a common occurrence: approximately one fourth of all children died before the age of one, and one half before the age of five. This doesn't mean that parents failed to grieve. We know from many documents that families throughout the colonies felt deeply bereft at the deaths of their children, though they tried to accept such losses as part of the inscrutable workings of Providence.

Judge Samuel Sewall's family, buried in the Hull-Sewall tomb in the Granary, bears poignant testimony to the rampant loss of children. Of Samuel and Hannah Sewall's fourteen children, one was stillborn and seven died in infancy. We know about these deaths from Sewall's remarkable diary, a precious record of social life among the third generation of Puritans.

In one arresting entry from December 1696, Sewall described his visit to the Hull-Sewall family tomb following the burial of his two-year-old daughter, Sarah. Seven other children had preceded her to the grave, so Sewall took the opportunity to visit them as well as his in-laws, John and Judith Hull. He noted: "I order'd little Sarah to be set on her Grandmother's feet." Then he mused: "'Twas an awfull yet pleasing Treat; Having said, The Lord knows who shall be brought hether next, I came away." Obviously, Sewall took comfort in seeing the coffins of his beloved dead housed together in an orderly fashion.

Sewall's friend Cotton Mather tried to comfort him for the loss of so many children in such rapid succession. When Mather's own first child, Abigail, died at four months old, on December 25, 1687, he preached a sermon that very afternoon in Charlestown. When the sermon was published two years later, it was titled *Right Thoughts in Sad Hours, Representing the Comforts and the Duties of Good Men under all their Afflictions, And Particularly, That one, the Untimely Death of Children,* and was dedicated to his "very Worthy Friend, Mr. S.S." A deep, abiding faith in God, divine justice, and eternal life allowed Mather to write:

> It was from God that we received those dear pledges, our children, and it is to God that we return them. We cannot quarrel with our God, if about these loans he says unto us, give them up; you have had them long enough! We know what they were when first we took them into our arms; we know that they were potsherds, that they were mortals,

that the worms which sometime kill them, or at least will eat them, are but their name-sakes; and that a dead child is a sight no more surprising than a broken pitcher, or a blasted flower.

Mather's faith would be sorely tested during his lifetime, since he would lose all but two of his fourteen children before he died. Samuel Sewall shared his friend's resignation to God's will in all things, even the deaths of his children. If he had any quarrel, it was with himself for his "Omission of Duty towards them." As a Puritan, he was obliged to accept death as God-given and to help others in their waning days. It was his habit to pray with his dying friends, to read aloud passages from the Bible at their bedside, and to encourage them to surrender to the grace of God.

When Sewall died, on January 1, 1729, at the age of seventy-seven, he joined his first wife, Hannah, and eleven of their children in the Hull-Sewall tomb. He had survived Hannah's death in 1717 and the 1719 death of his second wife, Abigail, who was dead within six months of their marriage. Only his third wife, Mary, survived him, as did three of the fourteen children he had had with Hannah.

Sewall was eulogized as an upstanding citizen and exemplary Christian. A sermon given in his honor at Old South Church, based on First Samuel, praised his learning, piety, humility, justice, and compassion. He is remembered today not only for his diaries but also for publishing in 1700 *The Selling of Joseph,* considered the first American antislavery tract.

While orthodox Puritans still dominated New England in the late seventeenth century and the death's-head continued to reflect their gloomy cosmology, funerals did not remain as simple and inexpensive as they had once been. The practice of giving gloves to invited mourners is a case in point. In 1633, the will of Samuel Fuller of Plymouth designated the sums of money to be distributed at his death for the specific purpose of buying the mourners gloves: "I give to my sister Alice Bradford twelve shillings to buy her a pair of gloves," two shillings six pence for a pair for Rebecca Prence, and five shillings for a pair to "be bestowed on" Governor John

Winthrop. The quality of the gloves varied according to the status of the recipient or that person's relationship to the deceased. Fuller's sister got the most expensive pair, Governor Winthrop a pair costing considerably less, and Rebecca Prence — possibly a servant — a cheap pair. As a principal mourner, Fuller's sister would have had gloves that were black or purple. If there were attendees at Fuller's funeral other than these three, they did not necessarily receive money for gloves or the gloves themselves.

But by the last decades of the century, sending funeral gloves as a form of invitation to all mourners had become de rigueur. Judge Sewall reported in a diary entry of 1700 that he "went to the Funeral of Mrs. Sprague, being invited by a good pair of Gloves." Since the amount of mourning gloves needed could number several hundred pairs for a single funeral, their cost was not incidental to the total expenses. The Reverend Andrew Eliot was so frequently invited to funerals that he acquired almost three thousand pairs of gloves in thirty-two years of service at Boston's North Church!

Once the pair of gloves had been received, the recipient was obliged to attend the funeral, almost as if he had been served a court summons. He or she would put on the gloves and other symbols of mourning — a black ribbon, a black armband, a black cloak — and join the funeral cortege that began at the home or the church where the dead person had been laid out. Members of the family preceded the coffin, while the other mourners walked behind. The coffin, made of wood and lined with cloth, might be carried by designated mourners or by a horse-drawn hearse. The horse too might wear signs of mourning, such as black ribbons and death's-heads.

After the coffin had been placed in its grave, the mourners returned to the deceased's home, where they were offered a feast. Here at last, Puritan restraint was loosened and New Englanders found comfort in eating and drinking, often to excess. Even little children sometimes became intoxicated. Before the feast was over, funeral tokens were offered: scarves, rings, and even silver spoons. The costly rings, usually made of gold or silver, were often engraved with a death's-head, a skeleton, or a coffin. The spoons given to the principal mourners followed a custom that had been imported into New England from the Dutch in New Amsterdam. With all these expenses, wealthy people could expect to spend as much as 20 percent of the deceased person's estate on a suitable funeral.

Things got so out of hand in Massachusetts that laws were passed three times during the first half of the eighteenth century to restrict lavish gifts at funerals, under penalty of fines. Men were prohibited from purchasing new mourning clothes and permitted to wear black armbands only. Women were allowed new bonnets, gloves, fans, and black ribbons only. Nevertheless, when the wife of Governor Belcher died in 1736, the mourning family gave away more than a thousand pairs of gloves. And when the Reverend Samuel Buxton of Salem, Massachusetts, died in 1758, he left a quart tankard filled with funeral rings.

By this time, orthodox Puritanism was being challenged by a different, more emotional approach to religion, which produced the Great Awakening of the 1730s and 1740s. Revivalist ministers such as Jonathan Edwards in Northampton, Massachusetts, preached a more personal love of God and encouraged public confessions of faith. The revivalists' rousing sermons fueled an evangelical movement based on the heart that was to have long-lasting influence on American Christianity.

Simultaneously, the ubiquitous death's-head began to be replaced by the benign image of the soul effigy or cherub. The transition from the death's-head to the soul effigy represented a softening of the earlier grim symbolism and a greater emphasis on the joys of Resurrection. Epitaphs too shifted their focus from human frailty and mortality to the anticipation of heavenly rewards. Increasingly, New Englanders at the turn of the nineteenth century would think of death as a release from earthly sorrow and a flight into "realms of bliss where joys eternal reign / Devoid of care, and uncontrol'd by pain" (inscription for Mrs. Mary Loring, 1804, Central Burying Ground, Boston).

This religious softening would have been anathema to the early Puritans. They would not have recognized their eighteenth-century descendants, with their revival religion and cosmic optimism. They would have been appalled by their showy funerals, frivolous attire, and tolerance toward other sects. By the time of the Revolution, "so many religious denominations existed in the colonies that the Founders brilliantly decided that they could not have a state religion." Religious liberty and the separation of church and state ultimately took precedence over the ideal of Puritan hegemony, and the country went on to follow a model established not in Massachusetts but in Rhode Island by breakaway Christians.

6

"GONE ARE THE LIVING,
BUT THE DEAD REMAIN"

———

NEWPORT, RHODE ISLAND

NEWPORT RATES STAR BILLING among cities judged for their worth in cemeteries. Tombstones greet you as you enter the city and bid you good-bye as you leave along the aptly named Farewell Street. The presence of the dead is palpable here, stone sentinels of the past stretching back four centuries. Unlike their Boston neighbors, the Newport settlers were determined to build a community that allowed for religious liberty, and remarkably, they did just that. Cemeteries of diverse religious persuasions — Baptist, Quaker, Jewish, Anglican, Catholic — sprang up close together, reflecting the living conditions of inhabitants who managed to coexist peaceably despite their different faiths.

While most of the early settlers were of English extraction, there were also non-Anglo enclaves, such as Sephardic Jews of Spanish and Portuguese origin and Africans brought over as slaves. The Common Burial Ground, situated on a land grant dated 1640, had to make room for all comers. Other residents were interred in their own private family plots or in graveyards belonging to their churches. Three of Newport's founders, William Coddington, John Clarke, and John Coggeshall, are buried in cemeteries that bear their respective names.

■

Above: Death's-head, Common Burial Ground, Newport, Rhode Island

Coddington and the Quakers William Coddington came from England to the colonies in 1630 with his first wife, Mary Mosely. He served as treasurer of the original Massachusetts Bay Company and became a leading merchant in Boston. In 1637, owing to religious differences with the Puritan establishment, Coddington left Boston for Rhode Island, where the Puritan clergyman Roger Williams, who had been banished from Boston for his own unorthodox views, was establishing a new colony open to religious diversity.

Coddington joined a group of settlers, including the exiled Anne Hutchinson and the physician John Clarke, who purchased the island of Aquidneck (later part of the state called Rhode Island) from the Narragansett Indians for forty fathoms of white beads. After a break with Hutchinson, Coddington and the others founded the town of Newport. They agreed to share equally in the governance of the town, with the judge having "a double voice." Coddington served as Newport's first judge, from 1639 to 1640.

At different times over the course of the next decade he served as judge, governor, or president of the various towns that sprang up in Rhode Island. Then, in January 1649, he sailed to England and managed to procure a commission as governor of the entire area, which went counter to the compacts he had originally signed. Alarmed at this move, the colonists dispatched John Clarke as their agent to secure a new charter. Though Coddington acknowledged he had no more right to govern Rhode Island than his associates, he still refused to lay down his commission, and he remained in ruling positions until his death, in 1678.

Sometime in the early 1660s Coddington became a member of the Religious Society of Friends (Quakers), founded in England by George Fox (1624–1691). Quakers believed that Christians should be guided by an inward light supplied by the Holy Spirit. They were called Quakers because they trembled with emotion at their religious meetings. They had refused to worship in Anglican churches, to pay church taxes, to take oaths, and to bear arms in war, and were thus persecuted in England. The earliest Quakers who appeared in America in the 1650s were treated as rudely in Massachusetts, New York, and Virginia as they had been in their homeland. A decade later, they were able to form stable communities in Rhode Island, with mixed-gender worship services in their meeting-houses and single-sex business meetings in their homes.

Coddington attended Newport's first Friends Meeting House, as well as the monthly meetings of the Men Friends of Rhode Island, often held at his house or at the home of Joshua Coggeshall. According to the records of these meetings, the men's concerns revolved around financial matters and "differences" between Friends, while the women's meetings focused on other interpersonal issues, such as the marriage intentions of prospective spouses — a subject rigorously scrutinized and ultimately approved or rejected by the men's group. Both the women's and men's records are typically terse, leaving today's reader with many unanswered questions. One obvious difference between the men's and women's records lies in the handwriting: the women's are consistently more legible and prettier.

By the time of his death, Coddington had had three wives and ten children, four of whom died in infancy. His widow, Ann Brinley, left a will dated June 7, 1708, that made various bequests, including a silver saltcellar, a rug, two Dutch blankets, and a silver tankard. Tankards, sometimes filled with jewelry and other valuables, were among the most treasured items mentioned in colonial wills.

Coddington is buried on land from his own large property, which he had given to the Friends' community. Known today as the Coddington Burial Ground, it is a rectangular strip in the historic center of Newport. Cars drive by on each side, unaware of the long-dead Quakers lying peacefully beneath the neat tombstones. Coddington's oversized monument, erected in 1839 on the second centennial anniversary of the founding of Newport, enumerates his many accomplishments. In death, as in life, he presides over the community he dominated so long ago.

Clarke and the Baptists John Clarke arrived in the Massachusetts Bay Colony in November 1637 at the age of twenty-eight, having studied law, medicine, and theology at the University of Leyden in Holland. Thrown immediately into the stormy religious controversy surrounding Anne Hutchinson, he joined those who left Boston and made his way to Rhode

Island. Although he had come to Massachusetts as a Puritan, he took up residence in Newport as a Baptist. In 1638, Clarke became the first pastor of the United Baptist Church in Newport and held that office for the rest of his life, in addition to continuing his work as a physician.

Baptists had two major quarrels with Puritans. First, they renounced infant baptism and substituted in its place baptism for people old enough to choose it as an expression of faith. Also, unlike Catholics, Anglicans, and Puritans, Baptists subscribed to full bodily immersion for the baptism.

Second, parting company with the theocratic society established in Massachusetts, Baptists believed in a total separation of church and state; they felt government should have no say in matters of faith. Left in the hands of Baptists, dissenters could be excommunicated from the church but never subjected to banishment, as they were in Massachusetts. The new ideal was one in which individuals of different religious beliefs could live peaceably together.

Because of Coddington's attempt to usurp power, Clarke was compelled to travel to England with Roger Williams in 1651. He stayed a full twelve years before returning in 1663 with a remarkable charter signed by King Charles II that granted the citizens of Rhode Island toleration in matters of faith. That royal charter authored by Clarke has been hailed as a milestone in the history of religious freedom in America.

On April 20, 1676, the day of his death, Clarke made out his will. Like many individuals in the past, he had not bothered to write his testament until he felt death was near. The original document, carefully preserved by the Newport Historical Society, has many provisions, including a trust "for the reliefe of the poor or bringing up of children unto learning from time to time forever." It was the first charitable trust set up in America.

Dr. Clarke was buried in a family graveyard adjacent to the lot where it is believed his house had been situated. His remains lie between two of his three wives, Elisabeth and Jane. The sparse tombstones of Clarke family members and a few later Baptist pastors are grouped together at one lonely edge of the largely unoccupied cemetery.

The Coggeshall Family Cemetery The Coggeshall burial ground deserves special mention because it contains the earliest locally carved gravestones — those of John Coggeshall (1647), his wife, Mary (1684), and Patience Throckmorton (167–), the second wife of Coggeshall's son, another John. These three stones are similar in style and were probably all carved by the same person not too long after Mary's death. A crude death's-head with wings appears at the top of each of them, and foliate borders run down the sides. Mary Coggeshall's inscription reads:

> HERE LYETH Yᴱ BODY OF
> MARY COGGESHALL WIDO
> WHO DECEACED Yᴱ 19TH OF
> DECEMBᴿ 1684 AGED
> ABOUT 89 YEARS

The inscription, with its haphazard spelling, contractions, and insertions, has survived for more than three hundred years in remarkably good condition.

The Coggeshall burial ground also contains the remains of the Abraham Redwood family. Redwood is justly remembered for having founded, around 1747, the Redwood Library, which is America's oldest library in continuous use.

Family burial grounds were common throughout America's early history; the small state of Rhode Island still contains at least 3,300, some with only five or ten headstones. Local historians say that this large number of private graveyards reflects Rhode Island's origins as a place of religious tolerance, with few centralized churches and considerable freedom for individuals to choose family property, municipal property, or churchyards for their final resting places.

Church-Affiliated Burial Grounds Some burial grounds in Newport, even those that started out as family graveyards, were eventually taken over by religious institutions. The Golden Hill Friends Cemetery was originally called the Clifton Graveyard, after the first owner of the land, Thomas Clifton, who willed it to the Society of Friends in 1675. Its two hundred burials with a hundred and fifty inscriptions dating from 1670 include such notable citizens as Freeborn Clarke, a daughter of Roger Williams, and her second husband, Governor Walter Clarke. By the mid-eighteenth century, Quakers had become the largest denomination in Rhode Island, thus necessitating numerous other Friends burial sites throughout the colony.

The lovely small Episcopal Trinity Churchyard, a standard on Newport tours, contains approximately two hundred inscriptions dating from 1704 to 1900. Several of the early pastors of the church lie here, as well as members of Newport's wealthy merchant class. One of Trinity's notable parishioners was Clement Moore, remembered for his poem "A Visit from St. Nicholas," more familiarly known as "'Twas the Night before Christmas." He died in Newport in November 1863, and his funeral was held at Trinity Church, but there is neither gravestone nor written record indicating the whereabouts of his remains.

St. Mary's Old Catholic Cemetery was originally laid out for St. Joseph's, the first Catholic church in Rhode Island, established in 1828. It contains the graves of twenty-four early Catholic immigrants, whose birthplaces in Ireland are inscribed upon their stones along with their names and their years of death, which range from 1828 to 1853.

It is believed that both the Sabbatarian Church, founded in the United States in 1672 and committed to strict observance of the seventh day (Saturday rather than Sunday), and the Moravian Church, established in Newport in 1749, had sites of burial. But once these churches died out in Newport in the mid-nineteenth century, the remains in their cemeteries were removed to the Common Burial Ground.

The Touro Jewish Cemetery Perhaps the most famous of Newport's religious burial grounds is the Touro Jewish Cemetery, established in 1677, two decades after the Sephardic Hebrew congregation was formed. The nearby synagogue, designed by the noted colonial architect Peter Harrison (who also designed King's Chapel in Boston), was erected in 1763, and now stands as the oldest Jewish place of worship in North America. Up the hill from the synagogue, its cemetery is entered through gates that were designed by Isaiah Rogers (also credited with the gates of the Granary Cemetery in Boston). The Touro cemetery holds about one hundred known burials, though no markers have survived from the earliest period.

Those that are visible today, forty stones in all, span the years 1761 to 1866. The inscriptions are in Portuguese, Spanish, Hebrew, Latin, and English, indicating the Sephardic origins of the congregation. Many begin or end with the formulaic Hebrew words: "May his or her soul be bound up in the bonds of eternal life" — a quotation from 1 Samuel 25:29 that can mean one of two things in Jewish theology. The older interpretation limits itself to the idea that life continues after death, biologically through one's offspring and spiritually through the influence one has on others. As long as one is remembered, one is symbolically still alive. A second interpretation, which dates back to the first century BCE, posits belief in an afterlife — an Edenic eternity for the righteous linked to the coming of the Messiah. Generally speaking, Orthodox Jews espouse the second view, while many other Jews are concerned less with the hereafter than with life on earth.

The date of death written on Jewish tombstones is of primary importance because pious Jews, especially children of the deceased, are expected to observe its anniversary by visiting the grave and lighting a *Jahrzeit* candle at home. In the Touro cemetery, the death date is commonly inscribed according to both the Gregorian and Hebrew calendars. For example:

JACOB LOPEZ.
died 18. March 1822.
or 25 of the Hebrew month
Adar 5582.
Aged 70.

(plate 14)

In the center of this quiet burial ground, sacred to the memory of Newport's pioneer Jewish community, is a plot with four obelisks of ascending size. They are dedicated to members of the once-prominent

Touro family, for whom the synagogue is named. Although the *hazan* Isaac Touro (1738–1783) was buried in Kingston, Jamaica, he is commemorated here, alongside his wife, whose epitaph reads:

> Beneath are deposited
> the remains of
> Mrs. REYNA
> the worthy relict of
> Revd ISAAC TOURO.
> who died in Boston on the
> 11th of Tisri A. M. 5518.
> and the 28th of September 1787.

Note the archaic word "relict" for "widow," a usage frequently found on both Christian and Jewish tombstones from this period. The memorial was erected by Isaac and Reyna's son, Abraham, as a "tribute of filial piety." Abraham is also buried there under an obelisk with an inscription in Hebrew that says: "Monument of the Burial place of the worthy and esteemed Abraham, son of the Sweet Singer of Israel, Isaac Touro, of blessed memory." Nearby lies Abraham's sister, Rebecca, also remembered for her kinship to her father, as well as her husband, who was a member of the prominent Lopez family. Following the patriarchal Jewish mode, neither Rebecca's nor Abraham's tombstones mention their mother, as if both children had sprung full grown from the head of their esteemed father, the Reverend Isaac Touro.

The tallest obelisk marks the grave of another son, Judah Touro, who amassed a great fortune in New Orleans and was known for his various philanthropies, including gifts to restore the Touro cemetery. By the early nineteenth century, when many members of the congregation had moved to other cities, the burial ground had fallen into neglect and would have suffered the fate of other abandoned cemeteries were it not for the largesse of the Touro brothers, each of whom was unmarried. In 1843, Judah is known to have replaced the cemetery's fence and gate, costing the substantial sum of $12,000. Following his death in 1854, his body was taken back to Newport and interred in the family plot. On his tombstone are inscribed these words: "The last of his name, he inscribed it in the Book of Philanthropy to be remembered forever." Then as now, philanthropy was a much-touted Jewish virtue.

In the year of Judah Touro's death, the Cambridge poet Henry Wadsworth Longfellow was inspired to write "The Jewish Cemetery at Newport," a moving tribute to Americans with a religion different from his own.

> How strange it seems! These Hebrews in their graves,
> Close by the street of this fair seaport town,
> Silent beside the never-silent waves,
> At rest in all this moving up and down!
>
> The trees are white with dust, that o'er their sleep
> Wave their broad curtains in the south-wind's breath,
> While underneath these leafy tents they keep
> The long, mysterious Exodus of Death.
>
> And these sepulchral stones, so old and brown,
> That pave with level flags their burial-place,
> Seem like the tables of the Law, thrown down
> And broken by Moses at the mountain's base.
>
> The very names recorded here are strange,
> Of foreign accent, and of different climes;
> Alvares and Rivera interchange
> With Abraham and Jacob of old times.
>
> Gone are the living, but the dead remain,
> And not neglected; for a hand unseen.
> Scattering its bounty, like a summer rain,
> Still keeps their graves and their remembrance green.
> . . .

Common Burial Ground In contrast to the small urban cemeteries restricted to a specific family or religion, the Common Burial Ground is a sprawling nondenominational tract on the outskirts of Newport. Laid out after 1640 and situated on one side of Farewell Street, it is the oldest and largest public cemetery in the city, containing some 7,500 to 8,000 graves. In the earliest sections, the stones are set in small, seemingly haphazard groups with family members clustering together as in life, but in the newer sections, the stones are more orderly and usually arranged in rows. The first quaint slate headstones with their simple inscriptions and death's-heads gave way in the mid-eighteenth century to many finely carved stones, some with angels and cherubs, and in the nineteenth and twentieth centuries to more elaborate markers with all manner of religious and secular symbols.

One section of special interest, known as God's Little Acre, contains the graves of African slaves and their descendants. Although the first record of slaves in Rhode Island goes back to 1652, these 282 gravestones date mainly from the eighteenth century. They have been identified as belonging to African Americans owing to the fact that they are marked with the word "servant" — a common euphemism for "slave" — or have some other sign of African origin. For instance, boys were often given Anglicized versions of African names: Cuffe instead of Kofi, the name given to boys born on Friday; Quamino (Kwame) for boys born on Saturday; Quash (Kwasi) for boys born on Sunday; Cudjo (Kojo) for boys born on Monday; Quarco (Kwaku) for boys born on Wednesday. Tombstones bearing the names of Quarco Honeyman, Cuffe Gibbs, John Quamino, Quarker Rivera, Cudjo Lopez, Quamino Brown, and Quash Dunbar attest to idiosyncratic naming patterns derived from African, English, and Portuguese or Spanish sources.

The names of classical heroes and gods, such as Caesar, Cato, Pompey, Hector, Hannibal, Hercules, and Neptune, are also very common in God's Little Acre. These names were given by white masters familiar with Greek and Roman history and mythology to their African "servants," along with the master's own surname. Thus we find Caesar Lyndon, Hannibal Collins, Hector Butcher, Cato Clarke, Hercules Brown, Neptune Sisson, and Pompey Brenton.

Geographical given names were also popular; for example, Cambridge Bull, Newport Redwood, Portsmouth Cheeseborough, Boston Vose, Bristol Marsh, and Africa Burk.

One woman with the exalted name of Duchess Quamino, identified as a "free black" on her gravestone, was known as the Pastry Queen of

Rhode Island. But typically, black women had (in contrast to the men) very common English names, such as Mary, Ann, Margaret, Jenny, Millie, Katherine, Nancy, Violet, Dinah, Lucy, Diana, Judith, Phyllis, Phoebe, Betsy, and Elizabeth.

Many Newport "servants" were children when they were brought from Africa to work and live in their owners' homes. The evidence of children's tombstones erected by their masters and mistresses suggests that some of them were treated decently and even affectionately. The one for Ann, "A Negro Child Belonging to Mr. Robert Oliver & Daugr to his Negro Mimbo aged 2 Yr Died June 1743" has a death's-head shaped like a light bulb, with lifeless eyes, a triangular nose, and five upper and five lower teeth (plate 15).

The one for Peg is more benign-looking, if not yet angelic. It reads:

In Memory of
Peg a Negro Serv
To Henry Bull
Esqʳ died July
Yᵉ 25 1740.
Age 6 Years.

By the 1770s, the death's-head and other sinister-looking images were a dying breed in God's Little Acre, as elsewhere in New England. In their place one finds cherubs with conventional wings and naturalistic human eyes, noses, and mouths. The fine tombstone made for Pompey Brenton in 1772 shows a man with widespread nostrils and tight curly hair, probably suggestive of the deceased's own features. In life, Pompey Brenton was a cook for the notable Brenton family and later a freed slave, a self-employed caterer, and a public leader.

One of the most touching portraits is that of Mercy Buliod and her baby, the infant's head resting against the mother's cheek and a pair of wings in the background framing them both (1771). Photos of these and other tombstones were made in the 1970s, fortunately before some of them were stolen or vandalized.

All these stones recall the African slave trade and Newport's colonial prosperity, to which slaves contributed substantially. Though they had been abducted from West Africa in the same inhumane manner as their brethren who were sent to plantations in the South and the West Indies, these Newport slaves probably led lives that were somewhat less horrendous. For one thing, it was customary in colonial Newport for slaves to have Sunday off for religious worship and family relaxation. Another difference from most slaves in the South concerned working for wages outside the master's home. Skilled and unskilled Africans in Newport were often allowed to work for their own profit, which made it possible for some of them to buy their freedom and that of their family members.

A few developed skills in the making of tombstones. We know from the account books of the Stevens stone-carving establishment (see below) that "Negroes" were paid to work in the family shop. One, named Sypeo, came for a month in July 1727 and spent at least "one day rubing [sic] stones." Another, named Prince, was presumably the same man whose own tombstone bears the inscription "Prince Servant of Jn Stevens died 1748/49 about 32 years."

A slave called Zingo is reputed to have practiced the art of stone carving, yet all we know for certain from the will of John Stevens the younger (eldest son of the shop founder), dated May 8, 1774, is that Zingo was left to John's wife, Elizabeth, for seven years after John Stevens's death, at which time Zingo was to be set "free and at Liberty." There is no known gravestone for Zingo, though his three successive wives lie side by side in the Common Burial Ground.

John Stevens's brother, William, ran another stone-carving shop. Among William's "servants" was one Pompe Stevens, whose signature "cut by P. S." is inscribed on the tombstone of a two-year-old named Pompey Lyndon (1765). Unusually, we know something about the circumstances of this death, from the diary of the baby's father, Caesar Lyndon. He wrote: "Our Darling Pompey was born ye 2nd Day of May 1763 taken ill on the night Thursday with the Bloody Flux September 5 1765 and died Wednesday Morning ¼ after 9 o'clock being the 11th of said Sept. 1765."

The stone carver, who identified himself only as P. S. on the baby's marker, gave his full name three years later on the tombstone of Cuffe Gibbs:

> This Stone was
> cut by Pompe
> Stevens in Memo
> ry of his Brother
> Cuffe Gibbs who
> died D 27th 1768

Pompe Stevens and Cuffe Gibbs, though brothers, carried different family names — those of their respective masters.

In addition to the slave population, there was a significant group of free blacks in Newport; as many as 145 individuals were listed in the Newport census of 1774. In 1780, they established a benevolent society entrusted with the responsibility of burying its members.

Caesar Lyndon, the father of baby Pompey Lyndon mentioned above, was one of the founders of Newport's Free African Union Society — a self-help group that, among other things, regulated conduct at black funerals. Blacks were often under pressure to relinquish certain African funeral practices, especially dancing and singing, that were deemed pagan by white Christians. Eventually, many blacks internalized the dominant culture's etiquette for proper funeral decorum and behaved themselves accordingly, though not without some notable exceptions; one need think only of New Orleans funeral processions with jazz bands rendering "When the Saints Go Marching In."

The "last colored undertaker" of Newport is known to have presided over early-nineteenth-century burials in the Common Burial Ground. Unfortunately, the only description of his activities comes from a somewhat mocking white source. George Champlin Mason, in his 1884 *Reminiscences of Newport,* described a certain Mintus in a blue swallow-tailed coat and bell-crowned hat as "walking ahead of the hearse in the middle of the street, one hand under his coat-tail and taking long strides which carried him some distance ahead of his charge; then he turned his head, and jerking his thumb over his shoulder, exclaimed in a hoarse whisper,

'Come along with that corpse.' . . . Mintus sought to do everything 'decently and in order' which meant with him as much pomp and ceremony as he could muster."

Keith Stokes, the executive director of the Newport County Chamber of Commerce, is dedicated to restoring the history of Newport's black communities through their tombstones. He goes regularly to visit his own maternal grandparents, uncles, and father, all buried in God's Little Acre.

The John Stevens Shop As one drives back into town from the Common Burial Ground along Thames Street, one finds the John Stevens Shop on the right. Established in 1705, this stonecutting establishment has been providing gravestones for three centuries, not only in Newport but throughout New England, and even nationally. The fine 1736 tombstone of the first John Stevens, its founder, is in the Newport Common Burying Ground. Probably carved by one of his sons, the stone bears a striking image of a curly-headed, heavy-jowled angel at the top and is encased by side panels with fruit and leaves.

For more than two hundred years, the shop remained in the hands of the Stevens family, but since 1927, the Bensons have been in charge. The present owners, John Benson and his son Nicholas, have held on to the ledger dated 1727 that lists orders and expenses going back to 1705. Initially the shop was not confined to gravestones; it also did masonry work, built chimneys and foundations, and repaired stone walls. But it is the legacy of magnificent stone carving for the dead that has made this shop rightly famous.

Carvers there often reproduce eighteenth-century tombstones and inscribe new ones with ancient lettering. Whether they use power tools or the brute force of their hands, these craftsmen work the stone with the same patience and care as their forebears.

7

CEMETERIES AS
REAL ESTATE

NEW YORK CITY

SKYSCRAPERS, NOT CEMETERIES, are the hallmarks of New York City. The visitor's eyes are drawn up to the top of awesome buildings, icons of the present rather than the past. One does not usually associate dynamic New Yorkers with dead bodies crumbling under the earth.

And yet, the five boroughs that make up New York City are rich in graveyards, some of which go back almost four hundred years. In the 1620s, when the Dutch began to settle New Amsterdam, the dead were buried close to their homes at the southern end of Manhattan Island. Then, as the colonists spread out over the growing city, new burial grounds were established in mid-Manhattan and the outlying boroughs. An estimated one hundred graveyards once existed in Manhattan alone.

But as time went by, especially during the nineteenth century, most human remains were exhumed from their original Manhattan graves and re-interred elsewhere. It's as if long-dead bodies immigrated to the suburbs, a pattern familiar in many American cities. By 1853, following prohibitory legislation, city interments had "nearly ceased," and cemeteries ringed Manhattan, with Brooklyn as the main suburban site. Today, Queens claims the distinction of providing more space for the dead than any other borough, with 3 million graves in Calvary Cemetery alone (plate 16).

Above: Flowers, African Burial Ground, Manhattan

Of all the burial grounds that once were part of the Manhattan landscape, less than a dozen remain, and these are mere fragments of their former dimensions. Finding their remnants requires dogged detective work, as evidenced by Carolee Inskeep's book *The Graveyard Shift*, which locates the original sites of Manhattan cemeteries and traces their moves from one locale to the next. Such information is extremely useful for people tracking down the bones of their ancestors. A few colonial graveyards, or bits of graveyards, can still be found right in the heart of commercial Manhattan between high-rises and storefronts and under buildings and sidewalks. These range in size and grandeur from the splendid Trinity Churchyard on Wall Street, where a sizable portion of the original space still survives; to the tiny pocket at Chatham Square, reduced to a handful of Jewish tombstones; to the African Burial Ground, completely obliterated by urbanization before it was rediscovered in the 1990s (see below).

Colonial New Amsterdam It should not surprise us to think of New York graveyards as real estate. After all, commerce has been at the heart of New York since its inception. Unlike the Puritans who came to Massachusetts or the dissenters who moved to Rhode Island for religious reasons, the Dutch came to New Amsterdam for the explicit purpose of trade. In 1623, the Dutch West India Company, formed by a group of businessmen, sent thirty families and a few fur traders to the region that had been explored in 1609 by the English navigator Henry Hudson. In 1626, they appointed Peter Minuit to govern the territory, and within months of his arrival, another ship sailed from Amsterdam to New Amsterdam and returned with a valuable cargo of furs and wood. The official report of this voyage includes a description of Minuit's purchase of Manhattan Island from the Indians — variously referred to as Manhattes, Manatthans, or Manates — for the by-now-legendary sum of sixty guilders, or twenty-four dollars.

By 1628, 270 Dutch men, women, and children were living in Manhattan. A fort was built on the southern point of the island, a countinghouse erected in stone, and a meeting place constructed for Sunday worship. Although there were as yet no regular clergymen, two Consolers for the sick and dying (*Kranck-besoeckers*) led religious services according to the liturgy of the Dutch Reformed Church.

The *Kranck-besoeckers* were a singularly Dutch institution. They were sent over by the practical-minded West India Company directors even before clergymen because of the immediate need to care for the seriously ill. If a member of the household was in danger, the Consoler was brought in, along with the nearest relations; the relatives did not leave the house until the patient had either died or recovered. The Consoler was expected to visit frequently to talk with the invalid or read aloud and pray.

When the patient's end approached, the family called in the neighbors. All knelt down in the sickroom while the Consoler read the prayers for the dying. It was customary to record the last words of the person about to die. When he or she breathed no more, the nearest blood relation approached the corpse, closed its eyes, and gave a parting kiss. A mirror was held before the mouth of the deceased or smoke blown into the nostrils to make sure that he or she was truly dead. If the person was married, as was almost always the case for adults, the wedding ring was taken off and given to the widow or widower. A sheet was spread over the body, and the curtains of the bedstead were drawn.

The neighbors returned to lay out the body. They undressed and washed it and combed its hair. Both men and women were dressed in the death "wade" — a long shirt with wide pleats and black trimmings. The head was covered by a linen nightcap with a black plume. A man was laid out with his arms straight down along the sides of his body, a woman with her arms crossed or with folded hands. When a woman and her baby both died in childbirth, the babe was placed in her arms.

Following the model brought over from Holland, the coffin was set up in the front room on two black trestles, with the corpse's feet pointed toward the door and the head facing eastward, as it was believed that Christ would come to judgment from the east. Mirrors and pictures were turned to the wall, and the room was draped with black.

Another tradition brought over from Holland was that of the *aanspreecker* appointed to invite the friends and relatives of the deceased to the funeral. The *aanspreecker* might also be the gravedigger, church-bell ringer, or the schoolmaster. He performed the function of a newspaper's obituary notice, going from home to home dressed in black to deliver his solemn message and give funeral information. No one would think of going to a funeral without a specific invitation. The *aanspreecker* was paid by the bereaved family in part according to the distance traveled. In 1682 in Flatbush, Brooklyn, the *aanspreecker* received twelve guilders per funeral, with four additional guilders if he had to go into New York City. The funeral procession of family members, neighbors, the Consoler, and the minister would proceed to the burial ground, where interment took place as expeditiously as possible. Early Dutch settlers paid their respects to the dead but without any of the expensive pomp displayed by later generations in their New Amsterdam and New York funerals.

In 1647, Governor Peter Stuyvesant arrived in New Amsterdam. He had previously directed the Dutch colonies of Curaçao, Aruba, and Bonaire and had lost his leg while attacking the Portuguese island of St. Martin. Thereafter he wore a wooden leg, and behind his back he was called Pegleg Pete.

From the moment of his arrival, Stuyvesant set about putting his forceful mark on the colony. A stern taskmaster, he often came into conflict with the local inhabitants, who chafed at his despotism and even plotted his recall. But Stuyvesant, with the resolve of an experienced military man and the shrewdness of a born politician, managed to squelch his Dutch enemies in New Amsterdam, maintain stability and order, and coexist peaceably with his Anglo-American neighbors in New England until he was ousted by the English takeover of Manhattan in 1664.

Like Governor Winthrop in Massachusetts, Stuyvesant did not believe in religious freedom. The only religion tolerated in his colony was that of the Dutch Reformed Church, and he saw to it that it was practiced rigorously. The notorious Sunday laws forbade various activities on the Sabbath, such as working, drinking excessively, taking jaunts in boats or carriages, and playing cards or ninepins — all under penalty of stiff fines.

Dutch Reformed Churchyards
Manhattan's St. Mark's Church in the Bowery and the Flatlands Church in Brooklyn The first churchyards in New Amsterdam were established under the auspices of the Dutch Reformed Church and laid out adjacent to the church buildings. In Manhattan, the only remaining seventeenth-cen-

tury Dutch Reformed churchyard is St. Mark's Church in the Bowery at the corner of Second Avenue and Tenth Street. The original property belonged to Governor Stuyvesant, who set aside part of his "Bouwerie" (the Dutch word for farm, from which New York's Bowery takes its name) for a chapel, built in 1660. In those days, this section of Manhattan was mostly meadows and marshes, small patches of forest, and Stuyvesant's farm, which covered three hundred acres. With his family, neighbors, and slaves, he worshipped every Sunday in the original chapel, and when he died, in 1678, he was buried under it in a vault that eventually housed his widow and six generations of descendants.

The churchyard was used until 1851, when New York City passed laws prohibiting burials below Eighty-sixth Street. At that time, many city cemeteries were considered unhealthy eyesores and encouraged to relocate elsewhere. But given its long history of continuous worship and the vaults containing so many Stuyvesants, St. Mark's held on to its church-cum-churchyard, even though the churchyard was increasingly neglected. By 1969, it was little more than a garbage dump. That year, under the influence of its determined pastor, the burial ground was transformed into a playground. Cobblestones were laid out in circular patterns around the few surviving tombstones, and several trees were planted. Today, children run, jump, skip, and hop over the cobblestones, happily unaware of the bones under their feet.

Unlike the paved-over churchyard in the Bowery, a sister church founded under Peter Stuyvesant in Brooklyn has retained its burial ground almost intact. The Flatlands Reformed Dutch Churchyard is a bucolic island in a poor neighborhood at the end of the subway line. Dating from around 1663, it stands as a testimonial to a time when Dutch was the lingua franca of Manhattan, Brooklyn, the Bronx, Queens, and Staten Island. "Hier ligt" or "Hier leit" (Here lies) are the first words on many seventeenth-century Dutch tombstones, and this formula continued well into the eighteenth century, long after the British had taken over New Amsterdam and renamed it New York.

Other Dutch inscriptions included "Hier rust het lighaam" (Here rests the body), "Hier leydt het stoffelyk deel" (Here lie the earthly remains), or simply "Hier leyt begraven" (Here lies buried). To counter the stark evidence of mortality and to emphasize belief in an afterlife, many gravestones also carry the soothing words "In den Heere Ontslapen" (Sleeping in the Lord).

The founders of the Flatlands Dutch Reformed Church had come from a Dutch outpost in Brazil that had been captured by the Portuguese. Ordered to convert to Catholicism or leave the country, the Dutch set sail for New Amsterdam and established their Flatbush congregation in February 1654 under the leadership of the Reverend Johannes Theodorus Polhemus. It would be another nine years before a consecrated church was erected in which he could preach.

Many early interments were made under that church and sometimes even under the seat that a church member occupied when alive. The cost for interment inside the Flatbush church was proportionate to age; for example, two pounds for a child, three pounds for a person from six to sixteen years of age, and four pounds for an adult. But most interments took place outdoors, on the land edging the church that is still used for burials to this day.

For 350 years, the church and churchyard (plate 17) have served the needs of a changing Flatbush community. Yesterday's Dutch have been replaced by today's Afro-Caribbeans, and one now hears the strains of gospel and island music alongside traditional hymns and prayers. The beautiful white wooden structure with a steeple, built in 1794 on the site of the first church, has the simplicity and elegance of bygone days. Because the church is well endowed and owns rent-producing property, it has perks that might not otherwise be available to a congregation in this part of Brooklyn: a full-time minister conducting regular services; a parsonage housing various activities, including a nursery school; and — for those members of the congregation who request it — a free cemetery plot! I know of no other seventeenth-century graveyard that still has plots to spare and makes them available for free.

The history of cemeteries in New York, like the history of the city itself, must be understood in terms of real estate. Most colonial burying grounds disappeared because the land was eventually considered too valuable for the dead. Over and over again, a congregation (Protestant,

Catholic, or Jewish) would decide to sell its property and re-inter its dead in a cheaper location. Contrary to this general pattern, the Flatlands Reformed Church has refused to budge, even though it has been offered $40 million for its city block. For the present, at least, the bones resting in this peaceful corner of Brooklyn have nothing to worry about. They remain undisturbed under a grassy lawn, with trees shading many of the tombstones, indeed pushing them apart in some places. New interments must be in the form of ashes and are marked only by newly planted trees.

Stuyvesant would be proud to know that the two churches founded during his governorship are still functioning, even if one of them — St. Mark's — is no longer Dutch Reformed. (It became Episcopal more than two hundred years ago.) He would probably be apoplectic to see the changes within his once rigorous religion and, worse yet, the proliferation of other sects. In his day, his determined persecution of Lutherans, Quakers, and Jews put him at odds with the directors of the West India Company, who reprimanded him on more than one occasion. Religious tolerance might have already taken root in Holland, but it was virtually unknown in Stuyvesant's New Amsterdam. He issued a proclamation declaring that the exercise of any religion but the Dutch Reformed would be punished by a fine of fifty guilders. He was particularly harsh with the English Quakers, whom he saw as frenzied proselytizers and generally troublemakers. They were subject to fines, arrests, and imprisonments, as was anyone who abetted them.

Similarly, when a group of twenty-three Sephardic Jewish refugees from Brazil landed in New Amsterdam in 1654, Stuyvesant's first reaction was to expel them. But influential members of the Amsterdam Jewish community put pressure on the directors of the West India Corporation and, through them, on Stuyvesant. Stuyvesant did not yield easily. He tried to restrict Jewish trade, to make Jews pay for the town watch, and to prohibit them from owning property. When they applied for a plot of land for a graveyard in 1655, the governor denied the request on the grounds that no Jew had as yet died. But a year later, when one of them did die, the governor was compelled to designate "a little hook of land" beyond the town wall for the first Jewish burying ground — a site that has since disappeared.

The Jewish Cemetery at Chatham Square That same year, Sephardic Jews founded the congregation Shearith Israel, which is active to this day. Miraculously, a tiny piece of their early graveyard, in use from 1682 to 1831, has managed to survive. Located at St. James Place just below Chatham Square on the edge of present-day Chinatown, it is squeezed between stores with Chinese characters and low-rise tenements. Were the Portuguese- and Spanish-speaking Jews able to listen from their graves, they would hear the voices of New York's polyglot Lower East Side.

The markers for Sephardic Jews were predominantly flat tablet stones set over the graves, in contrast to the upright headstones for those with Ashkenazi backgrounds. Both types exist in the little Chatham Square Cemetery, with inscriptions in Portuguese, Spanish, English, and Hebrew. The writing on the stone of Benjamin Bueno de Mesquita (died in 1683) consists of eight lines in Portuguese. Since there were no Jewish stone carvers in New York before the nineteenth century, all the early stones were carved by Christian masons unfamiliar with Hebrew characters. A Hebrew inscription appeared on the marker for Rachel Pinto (died 1815) consisting of sixty words, with fourteen additional lines of English, and was signed by the stonecutters W. and J. Frazer.

During the eighteenth century, the Shearith Israel Cemetery was much larger than today's small remnant. Expanded in 1729, it eventually covered all of Chatham Square. But real estate rarely leaves things as they are. In the early 1800s, the city pushed through streets that destroyed major parts of the cemetery. The cruelest blow of all occurred in 1855 and 1856, when the extension of the Bowery caused more than 250 graves to be moved elsewhere in Manhattan and Queens.

In 1851, when further burials were forbidden by law in Lower Manhattan, the Shearith Israel congregation acquired a large section of the newly established Cypress Hills Cemetery in rural Brooklyn. Since its opening in 1849, Cypress Hills, a nonsectarian for-profit cemetery, has offered special group rates to various religious congregations and secular associations, such as local chapters of the Masons, Odd Fellows, and Sons of Temperance. Today it continues to receive the remains of New York's amazingly diverse population. Its most famous resident is undoubtedly the great Dodger second baseman Jackie Robinson, the first African American to play Major League Baseball.

African Americans in New Amsterdam and New York The history of blacks in New York goes back to the city's earliest days under the Dutch. In 1626, the same year that Peter Minuit was sent to govern the colony, eleven African men were brought to New York on one of the Dutch West India Company's ships. It is not certain how they were acquired, but four of their names are still known: Paolo d'Angola, Simon Congo, Anthony Portuguese, and John Francisco. Although their surnames suggest that Paolo had come from Angola and Simon from the Congo, both geographical names were used indiscriminately in the early slave trade for any person brought from the west coast of central Africa to America. It was from this region that an estimated ten million people were abducted during the seventeenth, eighteenth, and nineteenth centuries, stowed like cargo in ships' holds, and carted across the turbulent Atlantic in such unsanitary conditions that many, perhaps two and a half million, died aboard ship and were buried at sea. The men who survived and landed in New Amsterdam were set to work as laborers in construction and farming, and the luckier ones as house servants. Women and children too were torn from their homelands and sent to a strange land where they became the slaves of white masters and mistresses.

A 1628 letter from a peevish Dutch settler named Jonas Michaelius reveals the prevalent state of mind that existed in New Amsterdam toward Africans: "the Angola slaves are thievish, lazy and useless trash." The directors of the West India Company may have shown a tolerant spirit toward Jews, but they were typical of their time in their inhumane attitude toward Africans.

Yet in some instances, slaves were freed by Dutch colonists in return for long service. Some former slaves were even given land or acquired the means to purchase property and enjoyed limited legal rights, such as recording their marriages. By the time of the English takeover of New York in 1664, there were about three hundred slaves and a small community of freed blacks.

Where were black slaves and freedmen buried under the Dutch regime? Initially, when there was no separate burial ground for people of African descent, they were buried along with other settlers in the graveyard situated near the Hudson River on property owned by the West India Company. Some domestic servants may also have been buried in family plots. Soon, however, African Americans were excluded from burial within New Amsterdam's city walls; at that point the area of steep hills known as the Kalch-hook became the major burial ground for the black community.

After the English acquired Manhattan, segregation between blacks and whites, in death as in life, became even more rigid. Trinity Church, the Anglican stronghold founded in 1696, decreed in writing: "No Negro shall be buried in Trinity Churchyard." But by then Africans, numbering about a fourth of a population of some three thousand families, had their own large burial ground not very far away.

The African Burial Ground The rediscovery of the African Burial Ground in Manhattan is worth a book unto itself. Indeed, one for young adults has already been published, and an electronic archaeological report fills four volumes. These texts record the unearthing of a site known in the eighteenth century as the Negroes Burying Ground, consisting of nearly seven acres outside the city limits on the northern side of the protecting wall that gave Wall Street its name. The Dutch had used slave labor to build this wall in 1653, in an attempt to ward off Indian attacks. Until 1796 when the African Burial Ground was officially closed, an estimated twenty thousand people were buried there, stacked layer upon layer.

Subsequently neglected and abandoned, the burying ground was eventually forgotten and paved over, preparing the way for the office buildings, stores, and restaurants that now line lower Broadway. However, in the early 1990s, when a new federal building was about to be constructed on that site, the archaeological excavation mandated by law revealed the skeletal remains of more than four hundred bodies. Most of the men, women, and children had been buried in plain coffins made from inexpensive woods such as cedar, pine, and spruce. The bodies had been wrapped in cloth coverings — shrouds and winding sheets fastened either with hand-tied knots or small straight pins that had wire-wound heads. Hundreds of other artifacts found at the site included buttons, beads, cuff links, tobacco pipes, nails, coffin handles, and a single silver child's earbob. A seashell found with one of the skeletons suggested a direct link to the Congo, where shells placed on tombs were believed to enclose the dead person's soul and carry it to the afterworld.

Five coins were found at various graves, three of which had been placed on eye sockets. This practice, found in several cultures, including that of the ancient Greeks, was used to close the eyes of the dead and provide a propitiatory offering to the spirits believed to mediate the passage from the land of the living to the land of the dead.

What was New York City to do with all those bones and artifacts? Since there were no laws protecting the burial grounds of Africans as there were for Native Americans, nothing could stop the government from constructing the intended building. The construction plans were not halted, but they were altered so as to include a space outside the building for a commemorative burial site that would be designated as a national historic landmark. And in this space, on October 4, 2003, the remains of 419 Africans and all the artifacts that had been dug up with them were reburied and laid to rest.

The re-interment was unlike anything else in the annals of American cemetery history. Four hundred and fifty hand-carved coffins were commissioned from Ghana in West Africa, the homeland of many of the long-dead bodies. The carvings on the coffins depicted scenes of village life and symbols reflecting a sense of homecoming. Each coffin was lined with kente cloth of Ghanaian origin.

A ceremony called the Rites of Ancestral Return had begun five days earlier at Howard University in Washington, D.C., and it proceeded north to several cities where memorial events took place, finally arriving by flotilla at the foot of Wall Street. The next day, the coffins were placed in seven large mahogany crypts, sealed, and lowered into the ground amid prayers, singing, drumming, and dancing. Thousands of people took part in this tribute to their unknown New York predecessors. Five thousand "ancestor cards" containing wishes for the dead were also buried with the coffins.

Reflecting on these events, Dr. Sherill D. Wilson, director of the Office of Public Education and Interpretation of the African Burial Ground, would not recommend that such burial sites be excavated in the future. She maintains that one should memorialize and educate, but not excavate.

On October 5, 2007, after the site had been declared a national monument, a stone memorial designed by architect Rodney Leon was unveiled. New York Mayor Michael Bloomberg and poet Maya Angelou invoked the presence of those men, women, and children whose forced labor helped make New York City the thriving metropolis it ultimately became.

In the eighteenth century, slavery was just as pervasive in New York as it was in the South. In fact, it is believed that about four in ten New York households had slaves. Contrary to its liberal image, New York was among the last of the northern states to abolish slavery, an event that didn't occur until 1827. As the oldest and largest graveyard for persons of African descent, the African Burial Ground confirms their historical claim to America's most populous city.

Trinity Churchyard Nothing could be further from the history of the African Burial Ground than that of Trinity Churchyard, located on the other side of Wall Street (plate 18). Established in 1696, it soon became the final resting place for a large portion of New York's English Protestant population, including its most prominent members.

By the mid-eighteenth century, New York funerals had become very costly. Not only did the family of the deceased distribute gloves, rings, and spoons to the invited mourners, as in New England, but the Dutch also added linen scarves and bottles of wine. These gifts and the mandatory funeral banquet were not just signs of respect for the dead; they were a way of keeping up with one's peers or betters, even if the expense meant financial hardships for the survivors. Stories of excessive eating, drinking, and pipe smoking, both in city residences and upstate manors, are now part of American lore. If they could not afford such a feast, people of lesser means would limit themselves to cake and wine.

A distinctive kind of Dutch funeral cake called a "doed-koeck" (dead cake) was given to the mourners. It was made from flour, sugar, butter, water, salt, and caraway seed, cut four inches in diameter, and marked with the initials of the deceased. The cakes were often carried home and kept as mementos of the dead.

The extravagance of New York funerals prompted one resident to write a protesting letter to the *Independent Reflector* on March 17, 1753. He bemoaned the burdensome expense to the survivors, many of whom spent "at least a fourth Part of their whole Fortune" on scarves, rings, liquor, and the entire panoply of funeral rituals. "One would think that the Sorrow we feel at the Death of a Relation, was a sufficient Calamity, without the Aggravation of making ourselves anxious about the Preparation of a pompous Interment." The letter writer suggested that New York should follow the model of Boston and set a legal limit on the sum that could be expended for a funeral. While such legislation in New York was not forthcoming, attempts to change costly funeral habits continued into the nineteenth century, as in the case of John Pintard, founder of the New-York Historical Society, who wrote to his daughter in 1817 that he was no longer planning to give scarves to his eventual pallbearers and would set aside the scarf money for the support of poor widows instead.

The most famous funeral in Trinity Churchyard was that of Alexander Hamilton — lawyer, general, Founding Father, protégé of George Washington, and the first secretary of the treasury. After he had been killed in a duel with Aaron Burr, he was buried on July 14, 1804, with ceremony fitting his renown. The Common Council determined that "there shall be a solemn procession at his funeral" and that "the bells should be tolled." One observer noted:

> On the day appointed, the procession composed of the Militia, the Cincinnati, the Reverend, the Clergy of all denominations, the Common Council, foreigners of distinction, the gentlemen of the bar, students of law and of the college, incorporated bodies, societies, & followed by a great number of citizens, moved from Park place, at 11 o'clock, and after proceeding in a slow manner through the principal streets, arrived at Trinity Church about 2 o'clock. The Hon. GOUVERNEUR MORRIS, with the general's four sons, mounted a stage, which had been erected in the portico of the church, and after

being seated for a short time, he arose and delivered a short, eloquent and truly pathetic eulogium on his deceased friend. . . . few of those who heard him remained unmoved. Most of them shed tears. The body was interred with military honours.

New Yorkers were in a state of shock and grief. Never before, even when George Washington died, had they expressed such collective sympathy. For thirty days, many wore black bands on their arms.

Hamilton's tomb bears a squat obelisk at its center and an urn at each of its four corners. At the turn of the century, urns became fashionable as part of the trans-Atlantic Greek Revival movement, and obelisks followed suit after the French invasion of Egypt under Napoleon. The monument's long inscription praises Hamilton as a "patriot, soldier and states man." No mention is made of the duel that carried him away. Since then, millions of words have poured forth in an effort to explain why Aaron Burr, then the vice president of the United States, challenged Hamilton to a duel; why Hamilton "wasted" his first shot; and how Burr inflicted the mortal wound. As a means of restoring one's honor, the dueling culture imported from Europe still existed in post-colonial America, especially among politicians and the military, despite state laws that tried to outlaw it.

At Hamilton's side lies his wife, Elizabeth Schuyler, left a widow with seven children by her husband's senseless act. She survived him by fifty years. It is appropriate that Alexander Hamilton, the first secretary of the treasury, is buried on Wall Street, at the heart of New York's financial district.

Today more than a thousand gravestones carved from marble, slate, or red sandstone remain in the churchyard. These represent a fraction of the burials, since it was estimated in 1800, after only a century's use, that the churchyard already contained more than a hundred thousand New Yorkers. How was this possible on so few acres? It appears that the same burial space was reused many times, with bodies placed one on top of the other so often that the level of the churchyard was raised by several yards.

Edged on one side by the American Stock Exchange and shaded by steel and concrete skyscrapers, Trinity Churchyard gives the impression of an unexpected time warp. New Yorkers walking through the graveyard on their way to and from work or stopping to rest on its benches treat it as a cozy neighborhood park. Indeed, with its trees, hedges, paths, and flowers, Trinity Churchyard offers a quiet retreat in urban Manhattan, for the living as well as the dead.

St. Paul's Chapel and Churchyard Five blocks to the north of Trinity Church, St. Paul's Chapel takes pride in being the oldest church building in Manhattan continuously open since it was erected, in 1766. It was in this Episcopal church that George Washington prayed during the year when New York was the capital of the United States. In the late twentieth century, tourists would often photograph its spire in the opening formed between the two colossal towers of the World Trade Center.

After the September 11, 2001, terrorist attacks, St. Paul's became the center of relief for the firefighters, police officers, and workers who painfully carried away dead bodies and laboriously cleared the site. For a full eight months, people there served meals, made beds, and offered support to the needy. Hundreds of volunteers — medically trained personnel, massage therapists, musicians, and ordinary citizens — came from all over the United States to help in this effort.

Outside on the churchyard fence, desperate messages were posted in search of loved ones. Messages of hope and inspirational pictures came from schoolchildren. Foreigners sent compassionate letters in a spirit of solidarity. Today, many of these messages are on display inside the church.

There was so much debris and damage from the destruction of the two towers that it took two years for the churchyard to be cleaned up and reopened. Though the events of September 11 are still very much on our minds, it is soothing to sit awhile in the shady yard among picturesque eighteenth- and nineteenth-century tombstones reminiscent of an age when destruction did not descend from the skies.

Washington Square Not far away in Lower Manhattan is the public park known as Washington Square, laid out with playgrounds, swatches of green, dog runs, busts of once-famous people, game tables, benches, and fountains. Chess players congregate in one corner, and couples, gay and straight, push their baby strollers along the well-kept paths. It is a popular meeting place for local residents, tourists, students, and artists.

But before Washington Square became an official park in 1827, before the Greek Revival mansions were built on its edge in the 1880s, this city block was a burial ground. In 1797, when this space was little more than a marsh, the Common Council acquired it for use as a potter's field — a burial ground for the poor — and for public executions. For thirty years it served those functions, receiving the remains of society's unknown and unwanted.

Whether one stops to rest here in trendy Greenwich Village, or at the churchyards of Trinity or St. Paul's, these are good places to remember all the unknown millions whose bones are hidden beneath New York's towering cityscape.

8

PLAIN AND FANCY

PHILADELPHIA
AND
LANCASTER COUNTY

IN 1681, KING CHARLES II granted his close friend William Penn proprietorship of Pennsylvania, a colony of 40,000 square miles, bounded on the north by New York and on the south by Maryland. As a convert to the Quaker faith, Penn saw his province in the New World as a refuge for civil and religious liberty. Before long, not only Quakers but numerous other faiths — Anglicans, Mennonites, Amish, Moravians, Catholics, Methodists, Presbyterians, and Jews — gravitated to Pennsylvania.

Following the teachings of the Society of Friends founded by George Fox, Quakers believed that an emanation of the divine passed into every human being, making it possible for anyone to be saved. Differing from Puritans with their inexorable doctrine of predestination, Quakers allowed for individual effort in the process of salvation once a person had recognized the inner light. Theirs was a God of love more than a God of fear. Quakers saw no need for a specially trained clergy and permitted anyone, male or female, to speak at their meetings and spread the word of God. Emphasizing the spiritual over the material, they dressed plainly, avoided outward show, and minimized ceremony of any sort.

When they buried their dead, they did so austerely: no large processions, no gifts of rings or gloves, no expenses beyond those required for a

---

Above: Benjamin Franklin's tombstone, Christ Church Burial Ground, Philadelphia, Pennsylvania

linen shroud and a wooden coffin. However, funeral feasts were never totally suppressed, although the Quaker leadership discouraged them. Cakes and wine were served before a Quaker burial and a full meal afterward, but never with the excess seen among Catholics and Protestants in New England, New York, and the South. The Quakers even eschewed gravestones — a contested subject among them throughout the eighteenth century, and one not fully resolved until an 1850 approval by their London yearly meeting.

The Arch Street Meeting House Burial Ground In the early years, from 1701 onward, Philadelphia Quakers were laid to rest in the burying grounds around the Arch Street Meeting House. It appears that those eighteenth-century Quakers did not place markers on the plots. During the great epidemic of 1793, the grounds filled up quickly with yellow fever victims. To this day, the long wooden sleigh used to transport the dead to their graves has been preserved within the meetinghouse.

Fair Hill Burial Ground A second Quaker burial ground in Philadelphia was established in 1703; it was on four acres of land that had been given by Penn to Fox and willed by Fox to the Friends "for a meeting house and school house and a burying place; and for a playground for the children in the town to play on, and for a garden." Eventually the graveyard expanded to its present five acres, and a beautiful wrought-iron fence was placed around its perimeter.

Unfortunately, in the late twentieth century the neighborhood departed from the peaceful ways dear to the Quakers. The area around the cemetery in what is now North Philadelphia became a dangerous, drug-infested part of town, with rampant theft and vandalism spilling into the hallowed grounds. It took the strenuous efforts of a group of concerned Friends to restore the cemetery to its original tranquillity. Today it is an idyllic oasis in the heart of a rough section, protected by a locked fence and the respect of nearby residents.

On the days when the gates are unlocked and entry is allowed, it is possible to imbibe the sense of repose generated by the soft green grass, arching trees, and rows of unassuming headstones, all equally small and dated in the distinctive Quaker manner: "Born 12ᵀᴴ mo. 16ᵀᴴ 1827 / Died 2ᴺᴰ MO. 28ᵀᴴ 1901." Slightly longer inscriptions add only the age at death, for example: "Lillian Claire Smith / died 12. month 29. 1873 / aged 15 years 4 months / & 12 days."

One finds among the dead the graves of Robert Purvis, an African American businessman and prominent abolitionist (1810–1898), and Lucretia Mott, also an eloquent abolitionist and a fervent advocate of women's rights (1793–1880). Like the others buried here, Mott and Purvis have simple stones faithful to the principle that Quakers should avoid ostentation in death as in life.

Christ Church Burial Ground Although Quakers are popularly identified with early Pennsylvania, Anglicans became increasingly prominent during the eighteenth century, and their Philadelphia burial ground, established in 1719, contains an impressive community of distinguished citizens. Statesmen, physicians, lawyers, and military men are represented here in disproportionate numbers to the greater population, buried alongside their wives and sometimes their children. Foremost among them is Benjamin Franklin (1706–1790), who lies under a flat stone with his wife, Deborah (died 1708–1774), beside him.

Printer, inventor, statesman, diplomat, signer of the Declaration of Independence and the Constitution, Franklin is too well known to require an introduction, yet the facts of his funeral are worth noting. When he died, at the age of eighty-four, twenty thousand mourners joined his funeral procession. The cortege from his house was led by clergy from various religious institutions and dignitaries from the political, educational, and cultural realms he had served. Along with friends and private citizens, they all walked through a saddened city where the flags were flying at half-mast and the church bells tolled their loss.

At the time of Franklin's death, the population of Philadelphia was around fifty thousand. It was a city often racked with epidemics that periodically decimated the population. (Almost five thousand perished from yellow fever in 1793.) Franklin's own son, Francis, died of smallpox on November 21, 1736, at the age of four, and Franklin never forgave himself for not having had him vaccinated against the disease; at that time, vaccination was still a new, controversial procedure. Today the Franklin grave is a pilgrimage site for many who honor the memory of America's most original forebear; they leave their shiny pennies on the simple ledger stone he specified in his will.

Flat slabs, known as ledger stones, are numerous in the Christ Church Burial Ground, but there are also headstones, box tombs, obelisks, columns, pyramids, pedestals, and pedestal tables, and even one unusual oval-shaped tomb for two spinster cousins, Katharine Inglis (1750–1821) and Margaret McCall (1754–1824), who lived together in their later years. It is an orderly assembly of markers laid out in well-tended rows on a two-acre field surrounded by a brick wall. Some of the plots are marked with brass plaques indicating personages of historical interest.

Among them, one finds the grave of Benjamin Rush (1745?–1813), considered the father of American psychiatry, with his wife, Julia Rush (1759–1848). Rush was a physician, professor of chemistry, member of the Second Continental Congress, signer of the Declaration of Independence, treasurer of the U.S. Mint, faculty member at the University of Pennsylvania, and surgeon at the Pennsylvania Hospital. In that last capacity, he authored his *Medical Inquiries and Observations upon the Diseases of the Mind* (1812), which advocated more humane psychiatric treatment than was practiced at that time. Rush also crusaded for the abolition of slavery and of the death sentence, as well as for the promotion of a property tax to support free public education. Though his place in the American historical consciousness is smaller than Benjamin Franklin's, Rush certainly deserves the title of Renaissance man as much as his older Philadelphia compatriot.

Laurel Hill Cemetery By the early 1830s a new cemetery concept had reached America. The rural or garden cemetery concept, imported from France, made its appearance in Cambridge, Massachusetts, in 1831 and in Philadelphia in 1837. When John Jay Smith, a Quaker librarian and entrepreneur, buried his daughter in Philadelphia's Arch Street Meeting House burial ground, it turned into a dismal affair because the ground was so damp and muddy. He resolved that "Philadelphia should have a rural cemetery on dry ground, where feelings should not be harrowed by viewing the bodies of beloved relatives plunged into mud and water." With the example of Cambridge's Mount Auburn Cemetery in mind, Philadelphians set out to create a rural cemetery that would be second to that of Bostonians only in chronology.

Laurel Hill was originally a splendid country estate set on a promontory above the Schuylkill River almost four miles from the city. An early observer of the cemetery site noted that it was "shaded with pines and other ornamental trees of great age and beauty. The views down upon the river ... are unsurpassed for sweetness and repose." The speaker went on to assert with civic pride:

> The elegance, which marks everything Philadelphian, is shown already in the few monuments erected. . . . The whole was laid out in gravel-walks, and there was no grave without its flowers. I look upon this and Mount Auburn at Cambridge, as delightful indications of a purer growth in our national character than politics and money-getting.

Yet despite the "money-getting" comment, Laurel Hill's founders went about promoting the new cemetery with aggressive marketing skills. To attract potential customers, they oversaw the re-interment in Laurel Hill of several Revolutionary War heroes who had previously been buried elsewhere. The most famous was:

GEN. HUGH MERCER
Who fell in the battle
of Princeton
January 3rd 1777
And Died January 12th 1777.

His monument states explicitly that he was "Removed from Christ Church yard on the 26th of November 1840." Charles Thomson, a signer of the Declaration of Independence and secretary of the Continental Congress from 1774 to 1789, and his wife were removed from their estate without permission, triggering a quarrel with family members that went on for decades.

The Laurel Hill managers succeeded so well that they began to have a visitor problem — an estimated 140,000 people in 1860. Imagine a cemetery with so many visitors that it had to issue admission tickets! On Sundays, only bona fide plot holders and their families were allowed to pass through the cemetery portal. In the mid-nineteenth century, before Philadelphia had a public park or art museum, the grounds and monuments at Laurel Hill provided a favorite destination for outings, picnics, and aesthetic contemplation.

In time, the original twenty acres were expanded to ninety-five, and Philadelphia's elite filled the grounds with grand monuments reflecting affluence and status. During the burgeoning economy of the post–Civil War years, industrialists, manufacturers, and financiers constructed elaborate tombs that stood out from conventional headstones and even from the obelisks that had proliferated during the protracted building of the Washington Monument in the nation's capital. (After an initial construction period from 1848 to 1854, work was suspended on the Washington Monument for two decades, and it wasn't until 1885 that the 555-foot-high obelisk was completed.) Laurel Hill's "Millionaires' Row" was lined with mausoleums constructed in the Greek, Roman, Italian, and Egyptian styles that were popular during America's Gilded Age.

Foremost among the monuments are the spectacular tombs that make up the Warner family plot. The one on the right end, created by sculptor Alexander Milne Calder (father of the maker of mobiles), is a highly original work of art. It depicts a life-size female figure opening the lid of a sarcophagus just wide enough for a young man's winged head to appear (plate 19). As a modern representation of the spirit escaping from the bonds of death, the noble visage is a far cry from early American death's-heads; and while it bears a distant resemblance to the winged cherubs that proliferated during the nineteenth century, his is no baby face. Rather, one beholds the sleeping head of a dreamy adult male:

WILLIAM, SON OF
WM & ANNA CATHARINE WARNER
DIED JAN. 20, 1889.

William Warner's brother and sister also rate monumental tombs, all lined up in the front row. Behind them lie the headstones of their father,

William Warner (1780–1855); their mother, Anna Catharine, remembered as "wife of William Warner" (1783–1830); and an earlier wife who had died in 1809. The three older headstones in a clearly different style — Gothic revival as opposed to the modern tombs — were probably removed from an earlier burial ground so they could be placed with those of their children.

A very different set of markers lies embedded in the ground not far from the spectacular Warner tombs. These are flat marble stones for members of the Pennsylvania Institution for the Blind, established in the early nineteenth century by Julius R. Friedlander. Friedlander brought humane methods of teaching the blind to Philadelphia from his native Upper Silesia. There is something immensely moving about these stones, stones that members of the blind community could not have seen. If any of the blind were brought to the cemetery, perhaps they bent down to feel the markers of their former friends and teachers.

Set apart from the others is the obelisk erected for Friedlander by the institution he served for eight years before his death, in 1839:

> To pure Philanthropy
> Disinterested devotion, and for
> Unwearied & Successful labors,
> To Ameliorate
> The condition of the BLIND.

At his funeral oration, Friedlander was eulogized as "our friend and tutor" by the Reverend Henry Jewett Gray, himself a member of the blind community.

Once Laurel Hill had filled up, at the turn of the twentieth century, it went into a gradual decline, accelerated by the Depression and post–World War II financial woes. Like other parts of the city, it became the victim of neglect and vandalism. Then, in 1976, the Friends of Laurel Hill organized to restore the cemetery and develop programs that would once again bring admiring visitors to its grounds.

Today, in comparison with Mount Auburn, which launched the American rural cemetery movement, Laurel Hill has a more helter-skelter look.

The roads are not so immaculate and the foliage is less abundant. Yet however much Laurel Hill suffers by comparison with Mount Auburn, it definitely has its own emphatic style: dramatic monuments still vie with one another to catch the visitor's eye, all set against the distant backdrop of the Schuylkill River with its busy bridges and huge trees on both banks.

The Pennsylvania Dutch of Lancaster County Seventy miles west of Philadelphia, one enters into what is known as Pennsylvania Dutch country, though the Pennsylvania Dutch are not of Dutch extraction. Their ancestors were Swiss and German, brought to Pennsylvania through the express efforts of William Penn, and they are called Dutch probably because the word "deutsch," meaning "German," was unpronounceable to English-speaking Americans. Today, the Pennsylvania Dutch include seventy thousand "Plain People" clustered in Lancaster County — Old Order Amish, mennonites, Brethren, and several other conservative religious groups. Old Order Amish dress in old-fashioned clothing — white caps called prayer caps and solid-colored dresses with long sleeves and full skirts for girls and women; dark-colored suits, wide trousers with suspenders, and black or straw broad-brimmed hats for boys and men. The men wear beards, and the women never cut their hair. Old Order Amish ride in horse-drawn buggies; refrain from using electricity, the telephone, or other technological inventions like the Internet; and remain largely separated from the surrounding world.

The Amish have their roots in the Mennonite community, which goes back to the Reformation, when Anabaptist groups were persecuted by both Catholics and Protestants. Anabaptists believe that baptism should be given only to adults capable of making a free religious choice. Though Amish, Mennonites, Brethren, and the other Anabaptist sects still share the same beliefs concerning baptism and basic Bible doctrines, they disagree in matters of dress, approach to technology, and adaptation to modernity. Differences between and among the Amish and the more liberal Mennonites and Brethren are apparent even in their cemeteries.

The Amish Cemetery at Bird-in-Hand The Amish cemetery outside the town of Bird-in-Hand may very well be the most peaceful we have seen in all our travels (plate 20). Surrounded by farmlands as far as the eye can see, it is enclosed within a rectangular, whitewashed wooden fence divided into two parts. The first half of the rectangle forms a vestibule where one can hitch up the horses. The second half is occupied by graves.

Why did we find this small cemetery so moving? This question touches our deepest reasons for undertaking this book, reasons we did not understand until we stood in the middle of those upright tombstones — curved slabs of equal size no larger than two feet high ranging in color from dark to light gray, all facing in the same direction, toward the entry gate. The stones were hewn with a sense of craft that is rare in our era. A few of the stones that were beginning to show their age had been propped up with carefully constructed iron or steel braces. Even the temporary wood markers for recent graves were hand cut and beautifully crafted, unlike the throwaway pieces of junk we have sometimes seen in other cemeteries. Such workmanship inspires respect.

But there was more to it than the quality of the stones. There was the sense of continuity issuing from the repetition of names — Fisher, King, Stoltzfus, Smucker, Esh, Beiler, Zook, Riehl, Glick — family names appearing in every generation from the mid-nineteenth century until the present. There are few places in America where the same families have stayed together in the same community for so long.

And above all, there was the harmony between the tranquil burial ground and its pastoral surroundings. I thought of those five acres of Quaker graves in North Philadelphia encircled by a nightmare of urban poverty. Here, a two-acre rectangle reserved for the dead was part and parcel of the countryside, a familiar setting for those who had spent their lives laboring in the fields and preparing the fruits of the earth. The only buildings we could see were silos in the distance. The only sounds we could hear were the *clop-clop*s of an occasional horse and buggy. Such was the stillness of the scene that I imagined skeletons underground stirring to the vibrations of the passing carriages.

This cemetery belongs to Old Order House Amish, who still worship in their homes and follow the tradition of placing graveyards in the open countryside. Church Amish, who worship in churches, establish their burying grounds next to their churches.

When a member of the Amish community dies, friends of the family come to the home and lay out the body in a separate room. In the past this space, called the *doed-kammer,* or dead room, was mandatory for any newly built Pennsylvania-German house. Its doors had to be wide enough to allow the pallbearers to bring in and carry out the coffin. To this day, the Amish place the corpse in a coffin provided by a local carpenter and transport it to the cemetery in a horse-drawn conveyance. It is the men's duty to dig the graves. One custom still practiced by the Amish is that the women are buried in their wedding dresses. The dress, usually blue and always unadorned, would have been made by the bride and served as her Sunday best throughout her lifetime.

Mennonite Cemeteries The first group of Mennonites came to Pennsylvania in 1710 at the invitation of William Penn. This radical religious group advocated nonviolence, separation of church and state, adult baptism, and free religious choice. Though they have by now spread to other states, their greatest concentration is still in Pennsylvania.

Mennonite cemeteries are typically found next to sturdy Mennonite churches. The tombstones, too, are sturdy and carefully maintained. The whole ensemble stands for a community that respects order, conformity, and prosperity.

Across the parking lot from the Stumptown Mennonite Church — a huge red-brick building topped with a steeple — one finds a rustic churchyard with many old and new tombstones. A special marker has been erected for Christian Wenger (1688–1749). It reads, "With many Swiss pioneers he helped convert a wilderness into a garden." The Wenger name appears in several nearby cemeteries and is the object of a major genealogical search among Christian Wenger's numerous nationwide descendants.

Some old-style tombstones bear German inscriptions, such as:

> Ruhe sei mit ihre ashe
> Und fried mit ihren geist.

> (Rest be with your ashes
> And peace with your spirit.)

The newer stones demonstrate an openness to modernization not found among many of the Amish. Some are large and polished with laser-inscribed portraits of the deceased, such as one sees more commonly outside Plain People communities.

At the small Kinzer Mennonite church, the churchyard reveals a congregation that has moved with the times. While its late-nineteenth-century stones bear the sober earmarks of an earlier age, more recent markers carry images of crosses, hands in prayer, flowers, birds, and hearts. Marriage is privileged in the headstone adorned with a heart representing the 1955 union of C. Victor and Florence Groff, as in the double headstone with a colored porcelain photo of the Rubicam couple, married in 1947.

No wall or fence surrounds the cemetery, which opens out to a landscape dotted only by barns and silos, and one senses here the same harmony that exists in more traditional Amish burying grounds. Whatever advantages modernization brings to life, in death there is much to be said for old-fashioned rustic settings.

Lititz Moravian Church Cemetery The Moravians trace their roots to the Catholic reformer John Hus, who was burned at the stake in 1415. In 1457, his followers, known as Hussites, gathered on the estate of Lititz, located about a hundred miles east of Prague. They next migrated into neighboring Silesia and Moravia. In 1722, some Moravian Brethren settled in Saxony on property owned by the reformer Count Nicholas von Zinzendorf, and they formed a community named Herrnhut, which became a haven for many other Brethren. Invited to the American colony of Georgia by Governor James Oglethorpe, a Moravian group moved there in 1735, but after many hardships, they relocated to Pennsylvania. They now number eight hundred thousand members worldwide, fifty thousand in the United States and Canada alone.

Moravians settled the town of Lititz, Pennsylvania, in 1756, named in honor of their first European community. They still worship at the white-steepled church built in 1787, and they still bury their dead in the eighteenth-century graveyard.

In the Lititz cemetery, the burial markers are all flat and uniform in size to show that all men and women are equal in the eyes of God. Referred to as breast stones, in contrast to the headstones and footstones of more conventional American cemeteries, these markers are laid out chronologically and divided by sex. Men are buried on one side of a central path, women on the other. Girl children and boy children are buried in separate patches.

Many of the early stones bear German inscriptions, indicating birth in Heidelberg or Dresden or Elsheim bei Mainz. Others state proudly in German or English that a person was born in Philadelphia in 1721, or in Lancaster County in 1737, or "near Lititz, Pa. March 10th 1809." Surprisingly, John A. Sutter (1803–1880) is buried here. Sutter, a German-born immigrant, was the owner of Sutter's Mill in California, the place where gold was discovered in 1849. After a period of great wealth, he became impoverished and chose to spend his last years in Lititz among other German Americans.

The German terms for death tend to have a euphemistic touch; instead of the word "gestorben" (died), these markers bear the words "entschlafen," "entschlief" (fell asleep), and "entschied" (disappeared). Even the English markers avoid the word "died," using instead the verbal locution "departed this life." Similarly, the epitaphs "Schlaf in Frieden" (Sleep in peace) and "Ruhe Sanft in den Armen deines Erlosers" (Rest sweetly in the arms of your Redeemer) suggest that for Moravians, death is only the passage into eternal life.

It is interesting to compare Lititz with a similar cemetery in Winston-Salem, North Carolina, the home of another early Moravian community. The Winston-Salem Moravian cemetery also dates back to the eighteenth century and has flat white marble stones. These are ceremoniously cleaned and decorated with flowers every year on the Saturday before Easter, making the cemetery look from a distance like a giant sheet of graph paper with squares of various colors.

Middle Creek Church of the Brethren Cemetery The Church of the Brethren is one of the largest in this region, with a huge parking lot and spacious cemetery surrounded by hilly countryside. Entering the churchyard by a small iron gate, one is transported into an earlier era. Old stones from 1801 and 1806 are carefully lined up by the gate, as if to establish the community's pedigree. Many have German inscriptions and some — unlike Amish and Moravian stones — bear carved images, such as flowers, lambs, an open Bible, or a hand pointing upward. It is clear that the Church of the Brethren was at an early date influenced by visual motifs from the greater Protestant community.

The very latest headstones from the twenty-first century look similar to stones found in most other American cemeteries. Under the name Ober, two hearts and entwined wedding rings celebrate the 1976 marriage of Karen and Brian.

Recent stones with Russian inscriptions remind us that even in the deep heartlands, America is still a nation of immigrants. Yevgeniy "John" Belyy, dead at the tender age of twenty-two in 2001, was surely mourned by the parents who placed the word "Son" on his headstone right above his name and an epitaph in the Cyrillic alphabet beneath it.

Yet despite these accommodations to the contemporary moment, there is a strong sense of continuity over the centuries. This came home to us with special force as we stood before the large polished tombstone inscribed: "Kenneth K. Wenger / 1918–2003 and Emma Carvell / his wife / 1920–1948." Wenger must have been one of the descendants of Christian Wenger, who had died 250 years earlier and whose marker we had seen in the Stumptown Mennonite Church.

The relationship between the Brethren and the Mennonites, not to mention the Moravians and other Anabaptist sects, is extremely complex. Suffice it to say that Brethren is a term that encompasses several denominations, all springing from reform Protestant groups from Czechoslovakia, Germany, and Switzerland. Although Count Zinzendorf transported many Brethren to America with the desire of uniting all German-speaking groups under one religious roof, this dream did not materialize. Instead, sects continued to split off from one another. By the end of the nineteenth century, a three-way division had been effected among the Brethren: Old German Baptist Brethren represented the conservative wing in dress and worship, progressive Brethren stressed evangelical missions, and moderate Brethren formed their own subculture.

While German is no longer used today on Pennsylvania Dutch tombstones, German words inscribed on old stones, sung in ancient hymns, and recited from Scripture still bear authoritative weight, like Latin for Catholics, Hebrew for Jews, and Arabic for Muslims. However different the Pennsylvania Dutch sects have become from one another, they continue to agree that the graveyard is only a temporary respite before the faithful will be gathered up by the Lord.

9

THE SOUTHERN
WAY OF DEATH

SOUTH CAROLINA

AND GEORGIA

AT FIRST GLANCE, historic cemeteries in the South seem similar to those in the North, most notably in their tombstones. Colonial settlers along the coasts of Virginia, the Carolinas, and Georgia — areas that have virtually no rock — looked to New England and even England for the slate and marble markers that would honor their dead. Local stone carvers tended to follow the trends set by the master carvers in the North, even when they developed a style of their own using red sandstone or other indigenous field rock.

Epitaphs were, on the whole, similar to epitaphs found elsewhere in early America, if occasionally marked by the florid rhetoric for which the South was famous. Those in churchyards often brimmed with religious sentiment, while those in municipal graveyards were predictably more secular. Mainstream southerners were every bit as Christian as mainstream northerners, every bit as devoted to their families, and every bit as patriotic during the Revolutionary War years, if we are to judge by their epitaphs. Certainly, that is how they wanted to be remembered.

And yet, for all the similarities with the North, there is something de-

Above: "Be of Good Courage," Bonaventure Cemetery, Savannah, Georgia

cidedly "southern" in southern cemeteries. Unyielding stone is softened by the presence of moss-draped trees, wandering vines, abundant shrubs, and brilliant flowers. This is true not only of the garden cemeteries established in the nineteenth century but also of central city spaces reserved for the dead one and two centuries earlier. The Unitarian churchyard in Charleston, used as a burial ground since the late 1700s, is a riot of flora with an artfully untamed appearance. The old Colonial Cemetery in Savannah served the city for a hundred years until it was closed in 1853; in 1896 it was landscaped with a variety of trees and aptly renamed Colonial Park Cemetery. And it is impossible not to mention Savannah's Bonaventure — one of the most spectacular garden cemeteries in the South and now one of its most famous due to John Berendt's book *Midnight in the Garden of Good and Evil*. But even small, obscure southern cemeteries are usually blessed with towering trees and dazzling azaleas that turn burial grounds into springtime Gardens of Eden. The smells in the South are also distinctive, sweet and spicy in the spring, cloying in the summer.

In the past, residents of the South paid a high price for their lush gardens. Death from tropical diseases such as malaria, yellow fever, typhoid, and dysentery contributed to a high mortality rate. By comparison, during the colonial period, the death rate in New England, with its colder climate, was considerably lower. On old southern tombstones, it is not uncommon to find the mention of fever as the cause of death. An example from St. Michael's Episcopal churchyard, Charleston:

> GEORGE AUGUSTUS CLOUGH
> a native of Liverpool
> Died Suddenly of Stranger's Fever
> Nov 5th 1843

Stranger's fever was the popular term for yellow fever, owing to the fact that so many visitors from more temperate climes would catch swamp-related sicknesses upon their arrival in the South. But even natives were vulnerable to the disease, as exemplified by the following inscription from Circular churchyard in Charleston:

Only and
Greatly Beloved Child of
Thomas and Rebekah
Napier
Born in Charleston, S.C.
March 16th 1824
Died of Yellow Fever
On Sullivan's Island
Novr 6th 1858

The warm climate of the South was a boon to agriculture, but as the temperature rose each year, so did the death rate. Periodically, individual deaths would coalesce into epidemics that carried away southerners in great numbers. Savannah's Colonial Park contains nearly seven hundred people felled by the great yellow fever epidemic of 1820. In 1854, several more outbreaks led to the creation of the Savannah Benevolent Association, which was expressly organized to aid families who had suffered fever-related deaths.

Another difference between southern and northern cemeteries is the lingering presence of the Civil War. It is a sobering experience to come upon row after row of markers bearing the names of men who fell in battle fighting for the CSA — the Confederate States Army. As Union general William Sherman swept through Georgia from north to south, southerners were faced with the immediate necessity of carting their dead to already existing cemeteries or to newly created spaces, like the Marietta Confederate Cemetery in northern Georgia, which received soldiers from the horrendous Atlanta campaign. Subsequently, no respectable southern burial ground lacked a memorial to the Confederate dead. Many of these are still tended by women's associations organized during and after the Civil War.

A Confederate cemetery in Franklin, Tennessee, maintained by the United Daughters of the Confederacy, inspired author Robert Hicks to write his best-selling novel *The Widow of the South*. It starts with the historic battle of Franklin on November 30, 1864, in which 9,200 men lost their lives. Since the battle took place very close to the home of Carrie McGavock and her husband, John, their house served as a field hospital for wounded Rebels. In 1866, following the war, when the field where the soldiers had been hastily buried was in danger of being plowed up by its owner, Carrie McGavock stepped in and offered two acres of land abutting her own family cemetery for reburial of the Confederate dead. She oversaw the transfer of almost fifteen hundred bodies and looked after their graves for the next half century. Hicks's fine novel is a fictional tribute to Carrie McGavock, who became a legend during her lifetime as the caretaker of hallowed ground. She saw to it that the original wooden markers were periodically whitewashed; she preserved their inscriptions in her cemetery record book; and she corresponded with bereaved families inquiring after their lost men. When she died, in 1905, she was eulogized by newspapers throughout the South, and as far north as Chicago and New York. Unfortunately, the cemetery then fell into a long period of decline and remained untended until the 1980s, when a nonprofit organization began the work of restoration.

What you won't see in antebellum white cemeteries are any black people's graves. Blacks and whites were segregated even more after death than in life, a situation that continued well into the twentieth century. Although venerable white cemeteries are everywhere in evidence, cemeteries for slaves and free blacks are very, very difficult to find. Slaves were usually buried in forests or fields without benefit of tombstones. At best, their graves were indicated by rocks, wooden markers, or seashells. Most slave burying grounds have by now disappeared, covered over by weeds and vines, plowed up by farmers, or destroyed by builders. Our success in finding a few out-of-the-way Negro burying grounds provided high points for us in our travels through South Carolina and Georgia.

Charleston's Old Burying Grounds Eighteenth-century Charleston was the colonial equivalent of Newport, Rhode Island, insofar as religious freedom was concerned. Named after the permissive King Charles II, who had gifted the land of Carolina to certain members of his court, the fledgling city attracted a variety of nonconformists from England and New England, assured by Carolina's Fundamental Constitutions of 1669 that all would be welcome — "Jews, Heathens, and other dissenters." Although the Church of England was the only religion maintained at public expense, it was agreed that "any seven or more persons agreeing in any religion, shall constitute a church or profession, to which they shall give some name, to distinguish it from others."

By 1681, settlers had formed a Dissenters' meetinghouse that included Puritans, Baptists, Congregationalists, Presbyterians, and Quakers. A century later, there were a dozen separate churches in the city, each with its own burying ground. Today, in the heart of Charleston's historical district, one still finds ten colonial graveyards, most clustered within a few blocks of one another.

Circular Congregational Churchyard Foremost among these is the burying ground established next to the original Dissenters' meetinghouse, later called the Circular Church for the unique building erected there in 1801. Though that building was later destroyed by fire, the name stuck. The Circular congregational was a fiercely independent lot — it even accepted African Americans. Yet it was not so unconventional as to grant them burial rights in the adjoining churchyard.

It was at the Circular churchyard that we recognized Lamson tombstones made in Charlestown, Massachusetts. Owing to Charleston's milder winters, some early markers look almost as fresh as they must have when they were carved in the eighteenth century. The stones for Martha Peronneau (died 1730), Desire Peronneau (died 1740), and Mary Peronneau (died 1741), attributed to the brothers Nathanial and Caleb Lamson, are still in excellent condition.

Many colonial tombstones carry the traditional death's-head, such as the one on the stone for "Mr John Young Marriner / Born in . . . Old England / . . . and Died / in Charlestown South Carolina / March 8th 1768." His light-bulb-style skull with its two rows of locked teeth contrast with the cheerful cherubs, secular urns, and drooping willows that appear just a few feet away on tombstones of a later date.

Equally remarkable are the outstanding sculptural portraits on other colonial headstones. Elegant ladies and gentlemen in their sartorial splendor remind us that Charleston was once a wealthy, fashion-conscious port. The portrait of "Mrs. Mary Lamboll / The wife of Mr. Thomas / Lamboll Died September 15th 1743 / Aged 33 years" shows a décolletage that would do a French woman at the court of Louis XV proud. A man with long curly hair, a fine jacket, and a flowing jabot is identified as "Mr. / George Heskett / Who was Born in Boston / N. E. 1690 and Departed / This Life August the 31st / 1747 Aged 57 Years." Yet despite their outer resemblance to European aristocrats — Catholic in France, Anglican in England — these southerners were distinctly American in their Protestant diversity, ranging from High-Church Episcopalians to austere Presbyterians, expressive Baptists, and liberal Unitarians.

St. Michael's Episcopal Churchyard Vying with the Circular congregational for preeminence among the city's historic cemeteries, St. Michael's Episcopal churchyard boasts a fine assemblage of Charleston notables: John Rutledge (1739–1800), the first governor of South Carolina; Edward B. White (1806–1882), a prominent architect; and scions of the illustrious Pickney family, one of whom is buried beneath the vestry room. But what makes this churchyard special is the harmony between gravestones and greenery. Plants at the bases of tombstones soften their harsh edges, and trees arching over pathways offer protection from the strong southern sun. It is easy to imagine a bonneted lady leaning over the Young family plot to admire a finely carved tomb bearing a prominent six-pointed star. Here, on the tomb of an Episcopal priest who died in 1852, it is not the Jewish star of David that became popular in the twentieth century but an icon representing the Old Testament.

A unique feature is the columbarium laid out as a pathway. With no space left for burials, the church devised this ingenious method to bring more souls into the fold, even if it means walking on their ashes.

First (Scots) Presbyterian Churchyard In close proximity to Circular and St. Michael's, the First Presbyterian churchyard has lost some of its acreage yet has managed to preserve many of its tombstones in a novel way. A short walk from the old churchyard, one finds two smaller areas with ledger stones inserted into concrete walls. These stones had been disinterred from the original churchyard in order to make room for a parking lot.

One of the smaller areas is still a graveyard, the other a children's playground. Jungle gyms and marble headstones form a dramatic juxtaposition. What do the children think as they swing above the wall and cast their lithe shadows over the static stones? Does it give them a spooky feeling? Or perhaps, to paraphrase what novelist Diane Johnson once said in remembrance of her own childhood, when you regularly ride your bicycle through a graveyard, the dead simply become part of the landscape.

Unitarian Churchyard The Charleston Unitarian Church grew out of the Independent Society of Dissenters, becoming "avowed Unitarian" with the arrival of the celebrated Reverend Dr. Samuel Gilman and his wife, Caroline, from New England in 1819. The burial ground, in use since the late 1700s, is a marvel of plants, flowers, shrubs, and trees tended today by the Eden Keepers, a volunteer society whose name was taken from Bronson Alcott's aphorism "Who loves a garden, still his Eden keeps." Charlestonians love this natural-looking island of repose, tucked away in the middle of an urban area and accessible on one side by a long shaded pathway.

Over the years, Caroline Gilman and her husband enlarged the grounds by acquiring adjoining parcels of land, where she oversaw the planting of numerous flowers. Today there are azaleas, irises, gladioli, narcissus, snowdrops, spiderworts, roses, lilies, and many pass-along plants of earlier centuries. It was Caroline Gilman's hope that "our cemetery may hence forth, as now be consecrated to sacred thoughts . . . if the mourner goes unto the grave to weep there, perchance, a vision of angels may be seen, and a voice heard saying 'Not here but risen.'"

The epitaph on the neo-Gothic monument erected to the Gilmans is a beautiful tribute to their harmonious union and one that would do honor to any married couple.

> THEY WERE LOVELY AND PLEASANT
> IN THEIR LIVES TOGETHER.

Huguenot Churchyard Following the English dissidents, French Protestants came to South Carolina in the late seventeenth century fleeing the persecutions of King Louis XIV. In 1685, he revoked the Edict of Nantes, which had granted Protestants some measure of religious freedom; an estimated four hundred thousand refugees fled to Holland, Germany, the British Islands, and ultimately the New World. The old Huguenot Church with its small well-kept cemetery is a concrete reminder of the influential French presence in Charleston, which went far beyond prominent names such as Manigault or Gibert.

The large plain vault on the south side of the church has been the burial place of the Manigault family for more than two hundred years. Although the original Manigaults arrived in Charleston with scanty funds, they acquired one of the largest fortunes in eighteenth-century America, enabling their son Gabriel to loan the State of South Carolina $200,000 at the outbreak of the American Revolution. Gabriel Manigault also gave the Huguenot church its Communion silver, which unfortunately disappeared during the Civil War. Still hoping it will turn up, the church lists the missing silver as (1) a tankard marked "donné pour l'usage de l'Eglise Francois de Charlestown, 1745" and (2) two chalices marked "Coupe de l'Eglise Francois de Charlestown."

Congregation Beth Elohim Burial Ground Charleston was also a haven for Jewish refugees. Jews first came to Charleston in 1695, but it was not until 1749 that they were numerous enough to organize a congregation, and not until 1764 that they acquired a communal burial ground. They bought it for the sum of seventy pounds from Isaac Da Costa, a founder of the congregation and its first *hazan* — cantor. It was to be "for the use of Jews . . . who do and shall conform to the Jewish rites and ceremonies in general and the regulation of the Jews' congregation in Charles Town named Beth Elohim." These rituals were drawn from a very strict Orthodox Sephardic tradition, which did not prevent Charleston's Jews from becoming, by 1800, the most numerous and prosperous Jewish community in North America.

The cemetery still holds several hundred tombstones from the eight hundred burials that took place there. The oldest identifiable stone is that of Moses Cohen, the first religious leader of the congregation. He died in 1762 at the age of fifty-three and was buried when the property was still the private burial ground of his friend Isaac Da Costa. The heavy slab over Cohen's tomb is remarkable for the image of two hands in the gesture of

priestly benediction placed under a crown. The epitaph, given first in Hebrew and then in stilted English, reads in part:

> Thou wentest up to God with righteousness
> To shine and glorify in Heaven
> Whilst upon Earth thou wast a guide to thy people

It is not surprising to find a rabbi in a Jewish cemetery, but one may
not expect to find ten Revolutionary soldiers, seven veterans of the War of
1812, and twenty-one Confederate soldiers. The obelisk erected to Confederate hero Marx E. Cohen Jr. bears the crossed flags of the State of
South Carolina and the Confederacy, as well as a cannon pointing down-
ward in the position symbolizing death.

Quite a few inscriptions honor the memory of successful men of
business, always a respectable Jewish occupation. The one to Mordecai
Cohen (who died July 1848 at the age of eighty-five) is exemplary.

> He was a good citizen, an enterprising
> Merchant and one of the largest
> Contributors to the improvement
> And revenue of the City.
> By his strict integrity, his just
> And charitable disposition
> He won the confidence and esteem of the community.

Tribute is paid to several women for their domestic virtues. Sarah
Cardozo (1766–1853), wife of Revolutionary War soldier David N. Cardozo,
is honored as: "An affectionate parent and a fond wife / Of unbounding
charity and social disposition / . . . a model of the household virtues." Another Revolutionary War veteran's wife, Rachel Lazarus (who died in 1847
at the age of eighty-five), left behind a record of extraordinary fertility:

> Fifty-two of her descendants preceded her to the grave
> And one hundred and twenty-one survived her!
> Our mother! She taught us how to live and how to die.

Catherine Lopez, the woman with the most distinctive tomb, figures
in a story so bizarre that it is emblematic of religious divisiveness found

everywhere. As mentioned earlier, Beth Elohim was originally an Ortho-dox Sephardic congregation, and so it remained until around 1824, when it became the first Reform Jewish temple in America. Seventeen years later, its increasingly assimilated members voted to install an organ in their brand-new synagogue. Since organs were anathema to traditional Judaism, the more conservative members decided to secede and form their own Orthodox congregation, which they named Shearit Israel. How-ever, the problem of burial remained. Should members of these two now-antagonistic groups be buried in the same ground? Shearit Israel solved the problem by buying land next to the old cemetery, elevating the soil by a few feet, and demarcating this elevated section with a low wall. Now the Orthodox would not be contaminated by their more liberal Reform neighbors. Incidentally, the philanthropist Judah Touro, mentioned in the chapter on Newport, contributed $5,000 to the construction of the new Orthodox cemetery.

The story becomes more convoluted as one walks toward the back of the Orthodox cemetery and sees a small addition jutting from it. This is the private burial ground of David Lopez (1809–1884), builder of the 1840 Beth Elohim synagogue and afterward a member of the split-off Shearit Israel congregation. Entering his family resting place through a waist-high wrought-iron gate bearing his name, one immediately notices an unlikely structure. Against the back wall there is a neo-Gothic alcove, the kind constructed in medieval churches as a repository for saintly indi-viduals or wealthy nobles. How does such a *porche* come to serve as a backdrop for the conventional Jewish tombstones in front of it?

It appears that David Lopez, however Orthodox, married a Christian. When his wife, Catherine, died in 1843 and was denied burial privileges in Shearit Israel, David Lopez simply bought the adjoining land, which was big enough to hold his wife and other members of his family.

Although neither of the first two Jewish cemeteries has anything so undeniably Christian as Mrs. Lopez's burial niche, some of the Beth Elohim tombstones carry distinctly non-Jewish funerary motifs. Images of willow trees, urns, and the palmetto tree, which is the state tree of South Carolina, appear among more traditional tombstones lacking graph-ics and inscribed with Hebrew and English words only (plate 21).

Where Are the Old Black Cemeteries? It is easy to find old all-white Christian cemeteries in Charleston, even Jewish cemeteries, but old black cemeteries are another matter. It took determination and the help of knowledgeable locals to track down the burial sites listed below.

Bethel United Methodist Churchyard In contrast to almost all southern churches, the Bethel United Methodist Church on Calhoun Street, founded in 1797, not only accepted slaves and free blacks as full members but even designated a portion of the church property as a burial ground for them. However, in the late nineteenth and early twentieth century, many Bethel tombstones were moved — the markers for both blacks and whites — to make way for Sunday school buildings and a parking lot. Some of these stones remain today, lined up against the parking lot wall. The ones for the black members look no different from those of the whites, except for three that are in the shape of coffins (plate 22).

Ann Andrus, the official church historian, is able to say with certainty that on the basis of her research into court documents indicating race, some of the tombstones definitely marked the graves of slaves and free blacks. She remembers one inscribed with the words "Dorinda — Our faithful servant and Humble friend. Died 1860."

Brown Fellowship Graveyard for Light-Skinned Blacks and Thomas Smalls Graveyard for the Society of Blacks of Dark Complexion The historic cemetery that once belonged to the Brown Fellowship Society for Light-Skinned Blacks also fell victim to a parking lot. Formed in 1790 by free mulattos who worshipped at St. Philip's Episcopal — one of Charleston's most prestigious white congregations — the Brown Fellowship had extremely rigid admission criteria: one had to be the male offspring of a white father (presumably a slave owner) and a black mother (his slave or black mistress) and possess light skin and straight hair. The initial members bought property for a meetinghouse and a cemetery, the latter consecrated by Thomas Frost, the rector of St. Philip's, in 1794. Until the Civil War, the Brown Fellowship functioned as an exclusive society, refusing membership and burial rights to anyone of a dark complexion who did not have "blowing in the wind hair."

In 1843 a free black named Thomas Smalls, a member of the Circular Congregational Church, applied for admittance to the Brown Fellowship, but was turned down because his skin was considered too dark. Smalls then formed his own organization, the Society for Free Blacks of Dark Complexion, which required its members to be of "pure" African blood. It purchased property for a cemetery directly adjacent to the Brown Fellowship graveyard, forcing the light-skinned "browns" to become neighbors of the dark-skinned blacks, whom they regarded as inferiors. A second cemetery, named Ephrath, opened by the Free Blacks of Dark Complexion who were members of the Circular Congregational Church, is still largely intact, with the exception of several large headstones that are now lined up as a walkway.

As for the Brown Fellowship Society, renamed the Century Fellowship Society in 1892, it held on to its cemetery until the mid-twentieth century. Then in 1945, it sold its property to the Catholic diocese. Subsequently, many of the tombstones were removed, and the cemetery was turned into a parking lot for the Bishop England High School. It seems that other small stones, as well as the remains of numerous bodies, were simply paved over. As late as January 2001, bodily remains and headstones were still being discovered on the former Bishop England property, now the College of Charleston.

Magnolia Cemetery Some of the Brown Fellowship Society artifacts ended up in the huge Magnolia municipal complex, established in 1849 on a former rice plantation outside the city. Magnolia is still a working cemetery, with approximately 35,000 people already interred and fifty acres available for future plots. It is the only graveyard we have seen that explicitly prohibits the feeding of alligators. Magnolia boasts a community of "planters, politicians, military leaders, bootleggers, whorehouse madams — you name it, anybody from the last 150 years of Charleston's history," says Ted Phillips, who is working on a book about Magnolia. It is perhaps best known for its Confederate dead laid out in 1,700 graves. Since the end of the Civil War, this section has been the focal point of Charleston's Confederate Memorial Day (plate 23).

Separated from the white graves, African Americans are grouped according to associations, such as the Humane Friendly Society and the Brown Fellowship. It was here in 1990 that members of the Brown Fellowship celebrated their bicentennial by re-interring the remains of ancestors who had been removed from the society's first cemetery. Markers on the African American graves range from marble stones with finely carved crosses and celestial crowns to rough cinder blocks in the form of rectangles. The plots are sparsely decorated with flowers and the occasional conch shell. We would find more examples of white conch shells placed conspicuously on individual graves as we drove to the coastal islands off South Carolina and Georgia, then to Savannah, and finally to Atlanta.

St. Helena Island's Churchyards It took a trip to St. Helena Island across the bridge from Beaufort, South Carolina, to find an intact antebellum African American churchyard. Established in 1855 by freedmen, the First African Baptist Church has served members of the Gullah community for more than 150 years. Known for their distinctive dialect, called Geechee — a mix of English and African vocabulary and syntax — as well as for their crafts and food, Gullah people are descendants of the slaves who were brought to work the island's indigo, rice, and cotton plantations. Living in relative isolation after the Civil War, they managed to preserve their folk culture.

The old burial ground of the First African Baptist Church, popularly known as the Brick Church, contains several nineteenth-century headstones, ledger stones, and obelisks. Many of the oldest tombs are enclosed in rectangles made from a cementlike mixture of oyster shell, sand, and lime — a composite known as tabby that is found throughout Gullah country and other parts of the South.

Several miles away, the Chapel of Ease built by Gullah slaves for their Episcopal plantation owners is a scenic site redolent of the island's colonial past. Erected around 1740, the chapel was burned by forest fire on February 22, 1886. What remains are charred brick ruins and early grave markers, some of these surrounded by wrought-iron fences or tabby enclosures. Many of the stones are broken, defaced, or hidden under ground cover. Yet amid all this neglect, one finds ledger and upright stones in various stages of legibility, some partially covered over and effaced by beds of oak leaves and acorns, others remarkably preserved.

One dual tombstone, inscribed, "Daughters of J. A. P. and Sarah A. Scott," was in exceptionally fine condition. Side by side as they had been for their short lives, Caroline Mary Scott (October 7, 1829, to August 31, 1833) and Adaline Matilda Scott (October 5, 1827, to September 3, 1833) were presented as "Blessed Little Lambs" who would be "Gathered to the Fold of the Only True Shepherd."

A few yards away from these sentimental markers stands an ostentatious vault bearing the name Fripp and the year 1852. Even in a state of decay, this red sandstone structure with its Egyptian columns has an imposing aura, as if its owner were still saying, Look at me!

Nassau Island's Black Cemetery A short distance from St. Helena Island, Nassau Island is the site of a still-active black cemetery, located down a dirt road at the water's edge under a thick clump of palmettos. With its unkempt aura, burned-out areas, and wind whistling through the palm fronds, it has an unsettling, desolate feeling, at least at sunset. On one of the mounds a skimpy bikini had been laid out, probably in keeping with the tradition of leaving at the grave the object last used by the dead. This custom, which was carried to the South from western Africa, was once seen as a way of propitiating the dead spirit and preventing it from harming the living.

In the late 1930s, a group of investigators, the Georgia Writers' Project, toured the Georgia coastal area abutting South Carolina, and they recorded the responses of rural blacks who had held on to many folk beliefs of African origin. Despite the fact that these responses were recorded in a quasi-phonetic manner that is difficult to read, they do give us firsthand information rarely found elsewhere. Concerning the practice of placing possessions on a new grave, one woman said (according to the report): "Dis wuz a common ting wen I wuz young. Dey use tuh put duh tings a pussen use las on duh grabe. Dis wuz suppose tuh satisfy duh spirit an keep it frum followin yuh back tuh duh house." The conviction that "the spirit don't stay in the grave," as one man put it, and is capable of working evil was one of the most persistent beliefs found among coastal blacks (plate 24).

Midway Cemetery, Midway, Georgia Continuing south across the state border, we came upon several historic white cemeteries, including the peaceful site in Midway, Georgia. In 1754, two shady acres were set aside by Puritan immigrants from South Carolina and lovingly preserved by members of the Midway Church erected on the other side of the road.

"Mrs. Margaret Osgood . . . born Jan. the 19ᵗʰ 1748 & maried Aug. the 2ⁿᵈ 1768 and died Janʸ the 24ᵗʰ 1800" represents a generation that had moved away from unforgiving Puritanism toward a more joyful Christianity. Her epitaph reads:

> My flesh shall slumber in the ground
> Till the last trumpets Joyfull sound
> Then burst the chains with sweet surprise
> & in my saviours immage rise.

The epitaph on the tomb of "Mr. Thomas Baker / Who died / On the 5th of June 1837 / In the 32nd Year of his age" also expresses an acceptance of Christian eschatology, though in his case it was hard-won through illness and the foreboding of an early death.

> After protracted illness of nearly two years, leaving a wife and two children with numerous friends and relatives to mourn his irreparable loss. For more than a year before his death, the concerns of eternity seemed to engross his thoughts and when Death, the King of Terrors came his visit was not unexpected, but met with calmness and serenity. His friends entertain the consoling hope that his peace was made With God.

The reference to death as "the King of Terrors," in use since the early eighteenth century, became something of a cliché in the nineteenth. It certainly suggests the mental torments Mr. Baker had endured before he was laid to rest.

Two other epitaphs are unusual in that they may contain references to slavery. The one for Mr. Robert Quarterman (1742–1786) states, "He was a sincere Christian, affectionate / Husband, a tender Father & a kind Master." Reverend Quarterman was the pastor of his community and the father of four sons who became ministers and two daughters who married ministers.

The other epitaph is on a red sandstone marker erected for Josiah Osgood Jr. (died February 8, 1801); it calls him "an affectionate Husband, a / tender Parent and kind Master." It is rare to find tombstones that honor a man for being good to his servants and slaves.

Midway is proud of its Revolutionary War heroes — patriots, soldiers, statesmen. It also has a section for its Confederate dead and a posted reminder that the cemetery was desecrated by General Sherman's soldiers, who corralled their horses in it while they used the Midway Church as a foraging post.

Sunbury Missionary Baptist Churchyard Deep in rural Georgia lies Sunbury, once a busy colonial seaport, now a sleepy town. Today one of Sunbury's few attractions for outsiders is the African American cemetery adjoining the Sunbury Missionary Baptist Church. There we were stunned to find highly original grave markers, the likes of which we had not seen anywhere else. These had glass inserts and unusual carvings based on both Christian and African iconography.

A five-petaled flower on the strings of a necklace and a hand with a pointed index finger adorn the headstone of Joe and Martha Baker. This same five-petaled flower sits in the center of a handsome necklace incised into a tombstone inscribed, "Ceaser Hamilton / born Sept 1867 died Jan 1938."

On the headstone for George Bowens (died Aug 7, 1931), the graphics included a cross, a three-fingered hand with the index pointing upward, and two portions of a circle resembling parentheses. Clearly the markings had religious significance: the first two are Christian signposts for eternal life, the last an African symbol for the unending nature of the cosmos. Africans from the Congo-Angolan region believed that the land of the living is separated from the land of the dead by a watery barrier. Each day the sun rises over the earth and moves in a counterclockwise direction across the sky to set in the water. Then during the nighttime, the sun illuminates the abode of the dead on the underside until it rises again. The cycle continues incessantly from birth to death to rebirth. Like the cross, the parentheses represent a rich religious cosmology that had been transported across the ocean far from its original setting.

Space considerations seemed foremost on the small headstone carrying a single inscribed word, "Boston," with an aqua-colored glass insert above it. The glass inserts set into the Sunbury stones may be unique in the United States. However, there are glass pieces inserted into nineteenth-century African funerary statuettes known as *nkisi*. These protective fetishes made by the Kongo people each feature a miniature man with a projection in the middle of his body that is capped with a piece of mirror. Any connection between the Sunbury stones and the Kongo *nkisi* has to be speculative, but after one sees both of them (examples of *nkisi* are in the new museum for African art on the Quai Branly in Paris), it is hard not to infer a direct influence from the Kongo.

Another tombstone with a glass insert looked like this:

LUC

LBO

WEN

SATO

It is easy to make out the name Luc L. Bowens, but what does "ATO" stand for?

Even more unorthodox is the writing on the tomb of:

RACHA

˥ BOW

EN ƨ — PA

P И ARC

H 1937 A

GE 51

By turning the *L* upside down and reversing the *S* and *N*, one can read the name Rachal Bowens Papnarch. Despite all the dyslexic printing on the stone, the glass insert and carved hand were clearly the work of a master craftsman.

That master craftsman was, we discovered, Siras Bowens (1900–1961), descendant and namesake of an earlier Cyrus Bowens buried in this churchyard in 1866, the year the church was founded. On the first Cyrus Bowens's slab, someone had placed a bone-white conch shell, providing the loved one a symbolic portal to the next life.

Siras Bowens the tombstone maker was a well-known local figure. Described by the eminent art historian Robert Farris Thompson as "an intense black man with burning eyes," he reportedly announced one day that he heard voices telling him to make images in honor of the family dead. Bowens set about roaming the pine forests surrounding Sunbury in search of unusual pieces of wood — twisted twigs and roots with crooks in them, which were believed to communicate mysterious powers. These became the material for the wooden tombstones, standing sculptures, and columns he fashioned for the Bowens family burial ground adjoining the Sunbury church. They could be seen in the late 1930s, when the aforementioned team from the Georgia Writers' Project wrote this account of Bowens's work:

> These were wooden images set on graves that were close together. One resembled a large bird; another represented a snake writhing upon a stand; and the third was the figure of a man, round and pole-like of body, with a head that resembled a ball and rudely sculptured features. Another Bowen marker was of clay painted yellow; in its surface was roughly cut the outline of an open hand with a small mirror glittering in the palm.

Unfortunately, all the wooden markers have since been carried away by collectors or thieves. The remaining stone markers with their glass inserts, scratchy inscriptions, and linear images are all that's left of a unique Afro-American craftsman who, according to Robert Farris Thompson, was almost certainly influenced by religious forms coming from Congo and Angola, and who produced "a monument in the transatlantic tradition of black art history." Thompson's conclusions, based on his considerable knowledge of Kongo culture, seem to confirm my impression that the Sunbury glass inserts had direct African antecedents.

When the members of the Georgia Writers' Project visited the Sunbury Baptist churchyard in 1938, and when Robert Farris Thompson saw it thirty years later, they both were impressed by the decorations that visitors had placed on the graves — bottles, glasses, pitchers, and vases, as well as certain possessions that had belonged to the deceased. One that we saw was clearly of this ilk: a two-handled heavy glass cup set at the foot of the stone for Frank Jackson (1908–1952). Other objects left at the graveside were turned upside down, symbolizing death.

In the past, crockery was often broken before being placed on the grave. The tradition of breaking dishes and bottles before laying them on the grave was explained by one black woman in the 1930s: "Yuh break duh dishes so dat duh chain will be broke. You see, duh one pusson is dead, an ef yuh dohn break duh tings, den duh udduhs in duh fambly will die too."

As we were leaving the Sunbury Baptist cemetery, an elderly man arrived to check on his forebears. He pointed out the boundaries of his family plot, delineated by bricks at the four corners. There was his grandfather Andrew W. Hague (1854–1924), who had made a good living harvesting oysters three miles away and selling them in Sunbury. His descendants still own property in the area.

Savannah: Colonial Park Cemetery Fifty miles north of tidewater Georgia, with its sleepy towns and quiet graveyards, lies the lively city of Savannah. Colonial Park served as Savannah's flagship cemetery from around 1750 to 1853. Today it contains approximately 9,000 graves, 557 of which are still marked. Everyone who had been anyone was buried there during Savannah's antebellum period.

Caroline Couper Lovell, born in Georgia in 1862, remembered playing in Colonial Park when she was a girl at a time when the cemetery had fallen into a state of benign neglect. "Sometimes we played in the old cemetery, where General Nathanael Greene and Malbone the painter were buried. . . . Many of the doors of the old vaults had fallen in, and I always glanced a little fearfully at the cavernous dark inside, but the spookiness did not prevent us from cracking coconuts on the tombstones and eating them with relish." The tomb of Edward Malbone (1777–1807), America's celebrated miniaturist, is still there, as are the brick vaults, all in a better state of repair than they were when Caroline Couper feared their crumbling insides.

Today it is a calm, orderly public space with a parklike feeling. Dogwood, azaleas, conifers, live oak, and other moss-covered trees have been strategically planted, and paths made of oyster shells embedded in cement wind around the tombstones. Savannah residents and tourists cross through the cemetery on their way to somewhere else, stopping occasionally to read the signs posted before major notables.

Among them one finds both Button Gwinnett (1735–1777), a signer of the Declaration of Independence, and General Lachlan McIntosh, the Revolutionary War hero who killed Gwinnett in a duel. Their bitter rivalry was one of the less noble moments in the American Revolution.

A half century later, James Wilde, Esquire, was also killed in a duel with a fellow officer.

> He fell in a Duel
> On the 16th of January 1815
> By the hand of a man
> Who a short time before would have been
> Friendless but for him
> And expired instantly in his 22nd year
> . . . .
> In his untimely death the prop of a Mother is broken
> The hopeful consolation of Sisters is destroyed.

Like Button Gwinnett and Alexander Hamilton before him, James Wilde was the victim of an imported code of honor popular in America between 1750 and 1850, especially in the military. Though prominent Americans such as George Washington and Benjamin Franklin vociferously condemned dueling, and religious and civic officials sought to stamp it out, duelists believed the only way to answer an insult was to point a gun at one's opponent and fire until the offended party was "satisfied."

Colonial Park has a predominantly secular aura. Some of the epitaphs even express the sentiment that life is short, tragic, and meaningless. The tombstone for Hampton Baxter Lillibridge, who "departed this life September 18th 1817 / aged 25 years 3 months and 8 days," contains the following bleak verse:

> Death like an overflowing stream
> Sweeps us away, our life's a dream.
> An empty tale a morning flower
> Cut down and withered in an hour.

Savannah: Laurel Grove Cemetery When Colonial Park was closed in 1853, Laurel Grove became the city's premier cemetery. Since it was from the start divided into two parts — Laurel Grove North for European Americans, Laurel Grove South for African Americans — it contains a rarity: a collection of antebellum black tombstones.

Slave markers that had been removed from earlier burial grounds were planted in a row at the roadside (plate 25). Some stood upright, some leaned forward, and others backward, like a row of crooked teeth. Each spoke for a long-departed soul, one of the millions who had once been considered mere chattel. The single word "August" on one of the stones was probably the name of a slave born in the month of August, since it was a common African practice to give an infant the name of the month or day of the week on which he or she was born (plate 26). As late as the 1930s, one man was recorded as saying: "We hab membuhs in our fambly name Monday, Friday, July an Augus." (In Nigeria, it still is common to name a child Sunday.)

Family plots are set off by stone, wood, or metal posts, and many of the tombstones are made of cement. Some of the inscriptions are deeply personal and heartfelt; for example, this anguished plea echoing the weary tone of Negro spirituals:

> JOHNIE HARRIS
> Born
> April 18, 1883
> Died Oct. 14, 1902
> His Prayer: Oh Father come close
> By my bedside, I am so tired
> Staying here. I want you to take

Me home to live with you in
Heaven.
I am going to fly
With the angels
Good bye mama
Good bye

One large area devoid of tombstones had a single wooden marker that read STRANGER BURIALS. A separate burial ground for strangers was not uncommon in black communities. It was not a friendly gesture, as I had first thought, but one linked more to fear than generosity. Africans carried to coastal Georgia the belief that the dead should be returned to their original homes for interment. Otherwise, in the words of one man recorded by the Georgia Writers' Project, "duh spirit'll jis wanduh roun an nebu be satisfied lessn it brung back home tuh be buried." Whenever possible, bodies were shipped back to their hometowns so that their spirits would not roam the countryside causing mischief among the living. Segregating strangers in ground separate from the cemetery proper was a way of isolating them from the peaceful spirits buried at home who were presumably at rest.

Savannah: Bonaventure Cemetery Bonaventure Cemetery offers a very different scene. Caroline Couper Lovell, she who had played in Colonial Park Cemetery as a girl, also recalled Bonaventure in her memoir as an "idyllic City of the Dead, blazed scarlet with azaleas beneath its gray cathedral aisles of moss-draped oaks." While her recollections of Savannah are known to only a handful of readers, John Berendt's hugely successful novel *Midnight in the Garden of Good and Evil* has made the city and its beloved Bonaventure famous throughout the world. Featured on the book cover, the statue known as the Bird Girl was a familiar sight to Savannah residents. Unfortunately, with all the publicity from *Midnight* and its film version, the statue was subjected to so much attention by crowds of tourists who disturbed the adjacent graves that it was moved to the Telfair Museum of Art.

What visitors will find is a garden cemetery considered by many to be the most beautiful and romantic in the entire South. Overlooking the Wilmington River, filled with red cedars, magnolias, blazing azaleas, and oaks festooned with Spanish moss, Bonaventure is still as striking as it was when naturalist John Muir spent five days camping there in September 1867. In his diary of the thousand-mile walk he took from Kentucky to Florida, Muir described Bonaventure as "so beautiful that almost any sensible person would choose to dwell here with the dead rather than with the lazy, disorderly living." He was awed by the gigantic live oaks draped with silvery moss. Bonaventure struck him as "one of the most impressive assemblages of animal and plant life" he had ever seen. "The rippling of living waters, the song of birds, the joyous confidence of flowers, the calm undisturbed grandeur of the oaks, mark this place of graves as one of the Lord's most favored abodes of life and death." Reflecting upon "the friendly union of life and death so apparent in Nature," Muir was contemptuous of "warped and pitiable" ideas about death, which are "haunted by imaginary glooms and ghosts of every degree." Were children to walk with nature in Bonaventure, they would learn "that death is stingless indeed . . . and that the grave has no victory." Like earlier romantics before him, Muir saw the rural cemetery as an expression of "divine harmony."

John Berendt's take on Bonaventure in *Midnight* focuses less on the foliage than on the people buried there. Early in the novel, the narrator is brought to the cemetery by a society lady who states emphatically: "The dead are very much with us in Savannah." She explains that Bonaventure was originally a large colonial plantation owned by Colonel John Mullryne, an active participant in early Georgia public life.

Mullryne's youngest grandson, Josiah Tatnell Jr., bought the property in 1785. He married Harriet Fenwick there; he was later elected governor of Georgia. In 1802, Harriet died and was buried beside six of her children in the family plot across the lane from the plantation house. In 1846, Commodore Josiah Tattnall III, the last Mullryne descendant to own Bonaventure Plantation, sold its six hundred acres, but with the provision that the family burial ground be maintained. Eventually, in 1907, seventy acres were bought by the City of Savannah.

In *Midnight,* Berendt's narrator is taken to see some of the more recent graves, first that of John Herndon Mercer (1909–1976), the highly popular songwriter known as Johnny to his many fans. The most distinctive feature of the Mercer family plot is the white marble bench with a sketch of Johnny's profile on top along with the names of his best-known songs: "Something's Gotta Give," "Blues in the Night," "Jeepers Creepers," "That Old Black Magic," "Moon River," "Atchison, Topeka, and the Santa Fe," and "You Must Have Been a Beautiful Baby." The epitaph on his tomb, taken from one of his lyrics, reads, "And the angels sing"; the epitaph on his mother's is "My mama done tol' me" — each highly appropriate for the mother-son pair.

In *Midnight,* the narrator also visits the grave of poet Conrad Aiken (1889–1973), who, like Mercer, was born in Savannah. Aiken's monument is carved from granite in the shape of a bench; inscribed on it are the words "Cosmos mariner, destination unknown." Apparently Aiken, who returned with his wife to Savannah for his last years, used to come to this spot overlooking the river and watch the ships go by. Once he saw a ship with the name *Cosmos Mariner* painted on the bow. That evening, checking the shipping news, he found the comment "Destination unknown" beside the name of the ship he had seen. By putting the ship's name and destination together, he came up with his own epitaph — four words of metaphysical verse that resonate cosmically.

If you are lucky enough to go to Bonaventure at the end of March, you will be dazzled by the profusion of pink, red, and white azaleas. The majestic moss-covered oaks add a mournful strain, as if the trees themselves were grieving for all the dead below. I often think of moss-draped trees as southern counterparts to the funereal weeping willow. With its carefully laid-out paths, elegant monuments, Renaissance arches, Greek columns, and statues of angels and personified grief, Bonaventure lives up to its reputation. Irreverent Savannahians have been known to say they don't care if they go to heaven, as long as they are buried in Bonaventure (plates 27 and 28).

Atlanta: Oakland Cemetery Further north, in Atlanta, the Oakland Cemetery has become a pilgrimage destination for admirers of Margaret Mitchell, the author of *Gone With the Wind.* Her grave, although conspicuously indicated near the cemetery entrance, is something of a disappointment. She is buried in the Marsh family plot next to her husband. The inscription on her tombstone reads:

MARGARET MITCHELL
MARSH
BORN ATLANTA, GA.
NOV. 8. 1900
DIED ATLANTA, GA.
AUG. 16, 1949

There is nothing to identify her as the author of the book that defined the Old South for at least one generation of readers, not to mention millions of moviegoers worldwide.

When Oakland was founded in 1850, Atlanta was still something of a frontier town with a population of barely 2,800. Following the rural-cemetery model, it was laid out in the "country" — that is, about a mile from downtown. The original six acres grew to eighty-eight by 1867 and eventually became the final resting place for seventy thousand persons. The last lot was sold in 1884.

In addition to the general burial areas, there are sections reserved for specific groups: a choice area for Civil War soldiers, a wide expanse for African Americans, an outlying potter's field for the indigent, and a marginal space for Jews. Almost seven thousand Confederate soldiers were laid to rest on a beautiful hillside, their military-issue tombstones catching the light of day and casting their shadows in regimental unity. In the silence surrounding their graves, it is hard not to reflect on the colossal waste of life that wars entail.

This, however, was not the view of those who honored their warrior heroes on the first Confederate Memorial Day, in April 1866. Nor was it the position of the Atlanta Ladies Memorial Association, who in 1869 oversaw the reburial in Oakland of approximately three thousand unknown Confederate dead originally thrown into hastily dug trenches during the 1864 Atlanta campaign. In 1894, a massive marble lion statue was erected to honor them; it stands on a verdant swatch that is still cared for by the Atlanta Ladies Memorial Association.

Across the road from the Confederate soldiers, on the edge of the cemetery, are the Jewish sections, one for Reform Jews primarily from Germany, the other for later-arriving Jewish immigrants from Eastern Europe. The difference between the two ethnic groups is immediately apparent. The tombstones of the Reform Jews are generously spread out across several acres; those of the poorer "Russians" are packed together shoulder to shoulder so as to maximize available space. Whereas the Reform Jews had largely abandoned the use of Hebrew on their markers by the 1890s, the more recent immigrants held on to Hebrew inscriptions and to other traditional signs of Judaism.

A large area has been set aside for African Americans, but it contains relatively few tombstones. Perhaps this is because blacks rarely had the funds for permanent markers other than those collectively purchased for well-known community leaders.

A one-of-a-kind carved anvil sits atop the monument to August Thompson (died March 12, 1910), a blacksmith and minister active in local politics.

Nearby, a tall, impressive monument draped with a tasseled veil and carved with a cross and crown was erected:

In Memory of
CARRIE STEELE LOGAN
Died Nov. 3, 1900
Age 71 years.
The mother of orphans
She hath done what she could.

Carrie Steele Logan was an ex-slave who established the first black orphanage in Atlanta, the Carrie Steele-Pitts Home, which still operates today. On the day of our visit, a curly-black-haired rag doll was sitting at the foot of her tombstone.

By far the best-known African American in Oakland is Maynard Holbrook Jackson Jr. (1938–2003). He made national history when he was elected mayor of Atlanta in 1973, becoming the first black mayor of a major southern city. Reelected for a second term in 1977 and a third term in 1989, he became "one of the founding fathers of the New

Atlanta, the New South, and the New America," in words spoken at his funeral.

Before leaving the black section, we wandered into a gently rolling meadow and came upon a few modest stones peeping up between weeds, leaves, and a patch of violets. The marker for Aunt Mary Webster provided a fitting epitaph for all those interred in this historic American cemetery:

AT REST

10

NEW ORLEANS

WHERE IT'S BETTER
TO BE BURIED ABOVE
GROUND

WE WERE SCHEDULED to go to New Orleans the last week of August 2005. Instead, we watched with horror from afar as the city was devastated by Hurricane Katrina. As the floodwaters rose and half a million people were evacuated, we shared the nation's anguish at the loss of so many lives and the destruction of a unique architectural heritage. And we wondered: what has happened to the cemeteries?

Surprisingly, New Orleans's renowned cemeteries survived relatively unharmed. The oldest, St. Louis I and St. Louis II, stood their ground with little damage: fallen plaster, broken crosses, the disintegration one expects after a raging storm. Lafayette suffered felled trees along the walkways and a crumbled wall. The large Metairie Cemetery, located on a slightly higher section of the city known as the Metairie Ridge, was generally in good condition, with losses mainly in the form of downed trees.

The worst hit were the predominantly black cemeteries in the lowlands, Holt in particular, which had been almost completely submerged during the flooding and was scattered with debris. While the poorer cemeteries suffered more damage than the richer ones, on the whole, the dead had fared better than the living.

The survival of the cemeteries as compared with the rest of New

Above: Wrought-iron fence prongs, St. Louis II Cemetery, New Orleans, Louisiana

Orleans can be attributed to the fact that many graveyards and tombs were raised above the ground. Because much of the city is located below sea level, between the Mississippi River and the huge Lake Pontchartrain, elevation has always been a vital issue for cemetery builders. They had learned from hard experience that if a grave was dug in spongy ground, it might fill up with water before the coffin was even placed in it.

Nineteenth-century accounts of coffins rising to the surface and float-ing away offer grisly scenarios. For example:

> In early days burials were all in ground and were terrifying affairs. Caskets were lowered into gurgling pools of water and were sunk into pits of oozing mud. As often as not, the coffin would capsize as the water seeped within. Heavy rains or a storm would cast newly buried half-decomposed cadavers to the surface.

New Orleans masons solved this problem by constructing ovenlike vaults and placing the coffin on an upper shelf inside. Made of brick, then plastered over and whitewashed, these tombs could be closed and sealed and then reopened at a later date to introduce another body. By that time, the earlier coffin and corpse would have disintegrated and the bones could be swept through a small grate into the lower chamber, thus provid-ing space for a new coffin.

Most aboveground repositories are private family tombs, intended to be used over and over again by kin of the original inhabitant. As long as one waits a year and a day — the legal time required before a tomb can be reopened — the next of kin has the right to inter another family member in the same vault. Ultimately, the bones of several generations will inter-mingle. This burial pattern, unique in America, has produced a special ethos among longtime New Orleanians: because they expect to be re-united with their relatives after death, they often experience a deep attach-ment to the family tomb, not unlike feelings that once existed around the parental home. Whereas most American children do not know where or with whom they will be buried — at the most, they hope to lie next to a cherished partner — many residents of New Orleans learn at an early age that they will share their permanent resting place with blood relations. Little wonder that they return annually on All Saints' Day, November 1, to clean up the family tomb, repair the year's damage, and leave behind the yellow chrysanthemums that traditionally mark the days of the dead in European Catholic communities. A national holiday in France, where it is called La Toussaint, All Saints' Day gets municipal recognition in New Orleans; schools and offices are closed, and police on horseback direct traffic near cemeteries. Even two months after Hurricane Katrina, when much of the city was still deserted, some people made it to the cemetery.

One evacuated woman who had been absent from her family tomb on November 1, 2005, for the first time in her life, reported on a radio show that it was "like not having Christmas." She wistfully remembered past years when her family had gathered at the tomb and shared a hearty pot of gumbo as part of the annual cleanup celebration.

Another woman recalled how family members of all ages spent the entire day together. They came to the cemetery loaded with flowers and plenty of food — sandwiches, cookies, and sherry wine. Then the adults sat around the tombs telling stories of the dead while the children got water from the faucets for flowers and cleaned off the tablets bearing the names of the deceased. Because many New Orleans tombs were in the process of sinking into the spongy earth, the last names on several of the tablets were no longer visible, so the children had to dig into the earth to uncover them.

The roots of All Saints' Day in New Orleans go back more than 250 years. It was first celebrated in 1742 at the rededication of the St. Peter's Street Cemetery, which had been operative since the French founded the city in 1718. After St. Peter's Cemetery was filled and closed, the celebration was carried to St. Louis I.

St. Louis I Cemetery St. Louis I is the oldest extant cemetery in New Orleans and the first to institute aboveground burial. It was established in 1789 in the wake of two great catastrophes: the 1788 flooding of the Mississippi River and the subsequent fire that destroyed more than eight hundred homes. Situated at Basin and St. Louis streets, the cemetery was judged distant enough from the residential area.

Today it is in the heart of the business district, a city block crammed full of vaults in the Mediterranean manner without the softening effect of trees or bushes. This miniature city for the dead, with its distinctive pedimented tombs, brings to mind Mark Twain's reputed statement that New Orleans had no real architecture except for what one found in cemeteries!

Many of the names on the tombs recall the city's French inheritance. Throughout the eighteenth century, even during Spanish rule (1762–1800) and long after the United States had acquired New Orleans through the Louisiana Purchase of 1803, French was the city's predominant language. New Orleans's first mayor, Etienne de Bore (1741–1820) is buried here, as is Marie Laveau, the notorious nineteenth-century voodoo queen (1794?–1881).

As the plaque on Marie Laveau's tomb proclaims, voodooism is a mystic cult of African origin brought to New Orleans from Haiti. It flourished throughout the nineteenth century when Marie Laveau captivated audiences with her occult powers, dispensing charms and potions called gris-gris, giving advice on love, telling fortunes, healing the sick, and calling forth the spirits of the dead. As a free person of color and the illegitimate daughter of a rich Creole plantation owner, she enjoyed the fluidity of New Orleans's French-Spanish society, which was more open to people of mixed blood than most Anglo-American communities.

Marie Laveau's tomb is the destination of many visitors from near and far, some of whom leave handwritten messages and small gifts at her door. Two months after Katrina, there were offerings of Mardi Gras beads, eggplants so shrunken they resembled hearts, candles, a wine bottle, a lock, a mysterious circular board, a Christmas tree ornament, even a box of Altoids. On the front of her tomb, hand-scratched Xs, the voodoo sign of good luck, had resisted the flood. Voodoo aficionados taking a cemetery/voodoo history tour regularly visit this site as well as an active voodoo temple. More than a hundred years after her death, Laveau's hold on the popular imagination seems to be as firm as ever.

Other notables buried in St. Louis I include Paul Morphy (1837–1884), the greatest chess master of his day and the first American to establish an international reputation. Growing up in an affluent New Orleans family, Morphy learned chess from his father as a gentleman's game. Even as he prepared for the law, he achieved such mastery in chess that he sent out a challenge to any American player offering conditions favorable to his opponent. Satisfied that he had no American challenger of his stature, he sailed to London before his twenty-first birthday, on June 22, 1858, and defeated the greats of British and continental chess in a series of mind-boggling events.

One of his most memorable feats was an eight-board blindfolded exhibition at the Café de la Régence in Paris — a ten-hour ordeal during which Morphy reputedly never left his chair or took any food or drink. He won six of his eight matches and drew the other two. Lionized in England and France, Morphy returned to such acclaim in the United States that for a while, a veritable chess craze swept his home country. Yet just before the outbreak of the Civil War, Morphy gave up chess and was never able to find his place again at home or abroad. He spent his last years wandering around the French Quarter of New Orleans, depressed and probably psychotic, talking to people no else could see. If there are ghosts hovering over St. Louis I as some claim, Morphy is surely one of them.

In addition to individual and family tombs, St. Louis I contains several benevolent association structures with multiple vaults. During the nineteenth century, benevolent associations were founded to care for the needs of specific ethnic groups, religions, and professions. With thousands of immigrants pouring into ports such as New Orleans, New York, and San Francisco, these societies provided a necessary service long before life insurance became a staple of the American household. By pooling their material resources, members were able to help defray health and burial expenses and offer cost-efficient spaces for the deceased.

St. Louis I contains group tombs belonging to the Portuguese Benevolent Association, the Cervantes Mutual Benevolent Society, the New Orleans Battalion of Artillery, and the Italian Mutual Benevolent Society. The last group's striking tomb, carved in 1857 from Italian Carrara marble, has three magnificent statues — one on top, carrying a cross, and two in niches, representing Italia and Charity. Its most recent claim to fame comes from its use as a site for the 1969 film *Easy Rider*.

Efforts to preserve St. Louis I started even before the Katrina hurricane. In 2001, a $150,000 grant from the Save America's Treasures Preservation Project, along with funds from Save Our Cemeteries, Inc., and the New Orleans Archdiocese Cemeteries, allowed for the restoration of more than eighty-five tombs. Using sophisticated conservation techniques and the latest in archival documentation (including aerial photos), the project has become a model for site preservation at other endangered cemeteries.

St. Louis II St. Louis II, consecrated in 1824, gives the appearance of a miniature city. It is laid out in a more orderly fashion than St. Louis I, with tombs lined up in straight rows like little houses on a treeless street (plate 29). Only the occasional cypress breaks the barren landscape, starkly reminiscent of Greek or southern French cemeteries exposed to an unforgiving sun.

Even more orderly are the wall vaults and cremation niches. These are inserted into brick walls and covered over with plaques bearing the names and vital statistics of their inhabitants. Many French names are still in evidence: Santinac, Pichon, Gouse.

One decorative element that adds an air of distinction to New Orleans cemeteries, and particularly to St. Louis II, is found in the wrought-iron fencing. These fences surrounding individual and family plots have held up remarkably well, even when bricks and plaster have come tumbling down.

Lafayette Cemetery Whereas both St. Louis I and St. Louis II are Catholic cemeteries established under the auspices of the archdiocese, Lafayette was founded in 1833 as a municipal cemetery for the city of Lafayette, a suburb ultimately annexed to New Orleans. It was intended primarily for American Protestants, who began to vie with Catholic Creoles for domination of the city after Louisiana officially became part of the United States. Previously, Protestants had been buried below ground, in a section at the back of St. Louis I or in the Girod Street Cemetery (demolished in 1957), which was located on the site where the post office and the

Superdome now stand. Some fans of the New Orleans Saints football team are convinced that their team has never won a playoff game because their home stadium was built over a deconsecrated cemetery.

Originally part of the Livaudais plantation, Lafayette was laid out as a perfect square in the middle of New Orleans's Garden District, a neighborhood known for its fine houses and lush greenery. Inside the cemetery, one finds numerous aboveground vaults, the Protestants having learned from the Catholics the importance of elevation in New Orleans burials. But unlike St. Louis I and II, Lafayette boasts numerous thick bushes and magnificent magnolia trees, although some were downed by Hurricane Katrina. Katrina was also responsible for the collapse of one of the cemetery walls and for bringing down many plaques from the vaults, leaving behind bare red bricks.

Still, the cemetery was spared irreparable damage. The tall wrought-iron gate proudly announcing LAFAYETTE CEMETERY is still standing; the mausoleums are still sealed.

Many of the early inscriptions mark the graves of German Americans and Anglo-Americans, members of the upstart community that began to rival the older French and Spanish residents in the first decades of the nineteenth century. One of them, Samuel Jarvis Peters (1801–1855), is credited with transforming the wetlands above today's Canal Street into a commercial and residential zone. He was also responsible for founding the New Orleans public school system. The Samuel J. Peters Junior High School named in his honor sends a delegation with flowers to his tomb each year on Founders' Day.

Joseph Uzée (1807–1850) has a French epitaph that sums up the bourgeois ideal of his era: "Il fut bon époux, bon ami and chéri de ses enfants" (He was a good husband, good friend, and was cherished by his children).

In recent years, New Orleans's old cemeteries, and Lafayette in particular, have become famous through the vampire books of the author Anne Rice. Rice grew up within walking distance of Lafayette and developed an affinity for this evocative site; it worked on her imagination and found expression in her writing. Not surprisingly, after Rice's *Interview with the*

Vampire was filmed in Lafayette, her fans have been going there with cameras in hand.

Metairie Cemetery Metairie is the grande dame of New Orleans cemeteries (plate 30). Spread out across 150 tree-studded acres, it was established in 1872 on the model of the garden cemeteries that had been the pride of the Atlantic seaboard since the 1830s. Even St. Louis, Missouri, New Orleans's rival city a thousand miles north on the Mississippi, had boasted a garden cemetery since 1852; it was time for New Orleans to follow suit.

The Metairie grounds had originally been the site of a fashionable antebellum racetrack, but that was closed in the uncertain aftermath of the Civil War. Then, under the direction of the architect Benjamin F. Harrod, trees, shrubs, and bushes were planted, and the landscape enhanced by two artificial lakes. It quickly became the most desirable burial spot in New Orleans.

Indeed, no less a figure than Jefferson Davis, president of the Confederacy, was buried there in 1889. The ceremonies surrounding his burial were spread out over five days. Several Catholic priests and Protestant ministers from various denominations, plus a rabbi thrown in for good measure, officiated at his funeral, which lasted from noon until sundown and was attended by an estimated fifty thousand people.

But Davis was not destined to stay in New Orleans forever. In 1893, his body was moved to Richmond, Virginia, and reburied in Hollywood Cemetery. Like saints whose remains were fought over and sometimes stolen during the Middle Ages, Jefferson Davis was considered too valuable an icon to be kept in New Orleans. Instead, he was laid to rest among three thousand veterans in Richmond, the most permanent capital of the Confederacy during the Civil War. Nonetheless, Metairie has maintained a very tall obelisk in his honor, with Jefferson Davis towering high above the veterans' plots like a patron saint.

Today Metairie is still a desirable place to be buried, despite the noisy freeway that crosses by on one side and the housing projects on the other. Its handsome tombs and statuary compare favorably with other garden cemeteries elsewhere in the United States; its angels are as graceful, and its mausoleums as fanciful. Yet there is something distinctly characteristic of French New Orleans in the rows of vaults lined up with geometric precision.

Hurricane Katrina laid bare the monstrous discrepancies between New Orleans's white and black residents. Though both groups lost friends, relatives, and property to the devastation wrought by wind and water, on the whole, whites got out of the flooded city more easily than blacks and had an easier time finding places to take them in. So too the cemeteries of New Orleans tell a story of harsh difference due to economic and social inequality.

Let me defer to John Gregory Brown's stunning novel *Decorations in a Ruined Cemetery* for a blunt description of the gap between black and white cemeteries. The narrator is a white woman who lived in New Orleans as a child in the 1960s and whose grandfather made cement grave markers for a poor black clientele.

> When I was a child, that cemetery was identified, by whites and blacks alike, as the nigger cemetery. It was reserved by the Catholic church not simply for its black parishioners but for all other blacks within fifty miles. . . .
>
> Even as a child I knew, because my grandfather had told me so, that most people's gravestones were made of marble or granite, not cement, and only the poorest of the poor settled in their grief for something my grandfather had made. Once the blocks had dried, though, my grandfather smoothed the edges and carved them with his own hands just as though they were marble, all those names and dates and whatever Bible verses people wanted beneath them. He told me it was a shame that what he'd taken so much time to carve wore away from the wind and rain sometimes before a wife was even ready to join her husband in the earth.

Later in the novel, the narrator reflects on the difference between the white cemeteries, where bodies were buried above ground in tombs with family names carved on marble doors, and the black cemeteries, where bodies were buried in earth so soggy that the water would collect on the grave and sometimes "gradually force the body to float back up to the surface. The bones would emerge from the mud like dinosaur fossils. . . . Did they simply pull the bones out once they'd risen to the surface?" In 2005, a visit to Holt Cemetery after the hurricane provided a lesson in what can happen to such burial sites.

Holt Cemetery The most distant of the ten graveyards comprising a "cemetery city" on the outskirts of Metairie, Holt Cemetery is intended primarily for people who cannot afford aboveground tombs and is largely black. Most coffins are placed directly in the soil, and many graves have an improvised, homemade look. Some are bordered by bricks, wooden planks, or pipes, the last rounded at the corners with plumbing joints. The markers, like those described in Brown's *Decorations in a Ruined Cemetery*, are often made from cement or other noncostly materials, such as wood. Many bear handwritten, personalized inscriptions.

A white slab with a wooden cross affixed on top carries this message, written in black paint:

> So Sadly Misted
> Mr. Louis Coolie Sr.
> 4-13-27–1-23-77
> Mr. Louis Coolie Jr.
> 8-31-58–6-1-93
> Rev. Johnell C. Coolie
> 6-6-64–7-2-95

Despite the misspelling of "missed," the marker exudes dignity (plate 31).

The marker for two small boys, Abraham Benjamin (died in 1970) and Alfred Benjamin (died in 1984), is even simpler. It is the back side of a yellow street sign, which has been covered over with black paint. The names and death dates, hand-lettered in white paint, stand out against the black background. This makeshift marker is simply stuck in the earth and outlined by bricks forming a rectangle.

Many markers have fallen down, are propped against trees, stand askew, or are half-buried in mud as a result of flooding from Lake Pontchartrain, overflow from the irrigation ditches that run through the cemetery, or both (plate 32). Some of the wooden crosses seem to have floated away from the bodies whose names they bear and may never be reunited with them. Weeds, leaves, and debris cover the terrain, often obscuring the tombstones and lending them a desolate feeling.

Not surprisingly, even in Holt there are distinctions between the poor and the not-so-poor. In one part of the cemetery, about ten feet higher than the rest, there are nicely carved granite tombstones without obvious damage. Apparently, the floodwaters did not reach this level.

A plaque marks the area where five hundred U.S. veterans are interred, each with a standard-issue military tombstone. Many of these are also askew, and the section could definitely use some sprucing up.

Holt Cemetery is unusual among New Orleans cemeteries in that the grave decorations are constantly changing. Visitors leave behind idiosyncratic mementos — toys and found objects, pages from newspapers sealed in plastic, bottles and jars — anything that might have interested the person buried there. In this way, an ongoing relationship with the deceased continues long after the body has decomposed.

Jazz Funerals No discussion of New Orleans burials would be complete without attention to its jazz funeral parades. The jazz funeral is a unique innovation born in New Orleans — like jazz itself — but with roots that probably go back several hundred years in Africa, especially among the Dahomeans of Benin and the Yoruba of Nigeria. Music has always been intrinsic to African celebrations, whether for a birth, a marriage, or a death.

In traditional jazz funerals, the brass band meets at the church or funeral parlor and proceeds slowly to the cemetery, playing a somber dirge, perhaps a Christian hymn like "Nearer My God to Thee." A dignified procession heads through the neighborhood, giving expression to communal grief and mourning. But once the interment is over and the procession has moved respectfully away from the grave, life starts up again with a rousing rendition of "When the Saints Go Marching In" or another traditional favorite. Anyone who is so inclined may fall in behind the band and strut or dance to the music.

The noted jazz musician Ellis L. Marsalis Jr. fears that much of this is changing because younger brass band players are unfamiliar with the traditional music. Instead, they are bringing in popular songs from their own era — pop and funk and hip-hop. But if the older jazz funeral has changed, this does not mean that it is on its way out — only that it is still subject to the honored practice of improvisation.

More troubling are the problems that New Orleans musicians now face in a post-Katrina world. With the musicians of New Orleans, like everyone else, blown to the wind, their return to the city is not a given. Musicians come and go according to the demands of their work, and many have lost both their work and their homes.

At the time of this writing, a few jazz funerals have started up again, organized by undertakers eager to maintain the tradition. A horse-drawn hearse carries the coffin around the city, followed by "second liners" — mourners who join the procession on its way to the cemetery. The fact that many resident musicians were present in New Orleans for Mardi Gras 2007 is a good sign. In that spirit, let us hope that those who were forced to flee their homes to escape death will be drawn back to New Orleans, partly because their dead family members await their return.

WE WERE ON A QUIET hill in St. Louis's Calvary Cemetery. All around us lay the graves of boys and girls buried in a special section reserved for children. Most were Italian Americans, the sons and daughters of immigrants still devoted to their native language. Some of the markers bore porcelain photos of chubby-cheeked offspring carried away too soon.

VICENZO CRIMI

NATO IL 26
SETTEMBRE 1931
MORTO IL 17,
GENNAIO 1933

As I bent over to gaze at Vicenzo's portrait, a car pulled up by the roadside, and a stocky woman with a decided gait headed in my direction. In a minute she was at my side, sweeping up the artificial flowers that encircled the marker. I was so startled that I asked only, "Is this the oldest children's section?"

She answered, "Well, let's see, my brother died in 1933, and that's seventy-two years."

With that she was off, striding briskly up the hill.

Above: Finger pointing to celestial crown, Jewell Family Cemetery, Columbia, Missouri

I stood there amazed. Seventy-two years and she was still tending her brother's grave! Was she an older sister entrusted to care for her brother until she died? Or a younger sister who had never personally known her older sibling? Or perhaps a twin with a sense of attachment to her womb mate? Whatever the age difference, she was the keeper of her brother's stone, a guardian angel in the flesh.

I walked pensively toward my adult son, Reid, asking myself how I could have survived if I'd lost him as a child, or any of my other children. Reid was busily photographing a different tombstone, one that stood out from all the rest — a lone pillar carved with a Jewish star, set apart at the very edge of the children's section. In fact, it bore three Jewish stars, each on a separate side of the pillar, with the photo of a little dark-eyed boy placed in the middle (plate 33).

CARMELINO
MACIOCIA
DIED
FEB 18, 1919
AGED 5 YEARS

Why, we wondered, was this unfortunate Jewish child with an Italian name buried in a Catholic cemetery in St. Louis? Had he been placed in the children's section by an indulgent priest because the boy had nowhere else to go? Carmelino was not entirely alone in his grave, for the name of Nicolino Maciocia — presumably his brother — was added to his marker at the bottom of the pillar, almost as an afterthought. And if Carmelino has had no recent family visitors, nonetheless there is a small rock cemented to the top of his marker — a Jewish token of remembrance.

Clearly, attempts had been made to perpetuate the memory of Vicenzo Crimi and Carmelino Maciocia — one by Vicenzo's sister over a period of seven decades, the other by an unknown visitor represented symbolically by a stone. Of course, the mandate to remember is visible in any cemetery — why else inscribe markers with names and dates and specific epitaphs? Yet a unique poignancy attaches itself to children's tombstones, forcing an age-old question: how can one accept a deity who carries away children? Christianity offers the bereaved parents a set of beliefs intended to make the loss bearable. Reclaimed by God, the innocent child will be counted among the blessed in paradise. The consecrated cemetery can then be understood as an antechamber to family reunions in heaven.

At Calvary, as in other American cemeteries, special baby sections were established at a time when mortality rates for children were much higher than they are today. Some cemeteries created a separate area for children because it was cheaper. You could bury twenty-four children in the space required for six adults. This space-saving format was used in Palo Alto's Alta Mesa Memorial Park for its first baby section, laid out in 1904, with each tiny plot bearing a small uniform plaque. The much larger and much fancier Forest Lawn Cemetery in Glendale, California, established in 1906, became famous for its spacious heart- and oval-shaped grassy areas containing rows of plaques with sentimental inscriptions for darling boys and girls lost early in life. Still other cemeteries buried children in mass graves without the benefit of individual markers. This was the case in Wilmington, North Carolina's Oakdale Cemetery for its first baby section, which came into use between 1856 and 1858 soon after the cemetery was founded. In Conshohocken, Pennsylvania, at the St. Matthew's Roman Catholic Church cemetery, the "baby pit" was eventually covered over with a mausoleum. Recent attention to some of these sites has resulted in belated monuments; for example, a marker at the Miami City Cemetery was erected in 2006 for a group of twenty-four children, only six of whom were named, who had been laid to rest between 1909 and 1939.

Calvary's Italian American children were buried at a considerable distance from the adults. They too have many inscriptions written in Italian and many porcelain photos, in keeping with the practice of their homeland. In that Italians are expected to maintain an ongoing relationship with a dead relative by tending the gravesite for years after death, the relic-like photo helps keep the image of the deceased alive in the memory of the living. A funeral photo had to be above all else an expression of dignity, as well as a sign that the family had attained a respectable socioeconomic status. In this way, Italian immigrants, many of whom had been peasants in their villages, were able to pass on to their descendants an iconic version of the American dream.

Some of the photos have been scratched out or removed. The mutilation was probably caused by vandals, but the removal of photos may have been the work of post–World War II Italian Americans themselves. After the war, many second- and third-generation Italian Americans were eager to distance themselves from Old World practices because they conflicted with the American norm and because cemetery regulations discouraged their use. Today, the surviving photos of mustached men and dark-haired women attired in their Sunday best are priceless mementos of a now-lost world.

But what is truly remarkable about the adults' section is the abundance of angels and Madonnas that rise above the headstones, forming a unique field of celestial statuary. A sensitive visitor might imagine that he or she had already died and gone to heaven (plate 6).

Catholicism was the first European religion to establish itself in St. Louis, a French outpost named for the saintly medieval king Louis IX. Though not the oldest cemetery in the area, Calvary contains the remains of the notable Chouteau family, who were associated with the city's founding. In 1764, a New Orleans merchant named Pierre Laclède established the village of St. Louis as headquarters for his fur-trading company. From Native American and French trappers hunting in the vast territory west of the Mississippi under French rule, he purchased the abundant pelts that Europeans coveted for their coats and hats and luxury items. With his wife, Marie Chouteau — legally the wife of another man, who refused her a divorce — Laclède built a prosperous business and founded a dynasty of enterprising sons. Ironically, because the official name of his common-law wife was Madame Chouteau, their sons were obligated to bear her surname instead of their true father's. One son, Auguste Chouteau, became a prominent figure, remembered not only for his business ventures but also for his uncultivated field that served as a burial ground for the fledgling settlement.

St. Louis grew considerably during the following decades, and in 1815 Chouteau gave notice that bodies could no longer be buried in his field. The land was sold in 1816, and the new owner moved the graves so as to be able to build on the property. The relocation of graves from valuable city land to sites distant from the center was, as we have seen, the fate of cemeteries in most American metropolises.

In 1823, the first of several St. Louis ordinances prohibiting burials within the city limits was passed. Since the city limits were expanded many times during the nineteenth century, new cemeteries kept cropping up, and thousands of bodies were moved from one locale to the next. The body of Auguste Chouteau himself was subject to no fewer than three disinterments before his remains found their final resting place in Calvary. A huge circular complex worthy of nobility reminds passersby of the Chouteau dynasty and its role in the making of St. Louis.

The Louisiana Purchase of 1803 inaugurated the transformation of St. Louis into an American city, with English replacing French as the dominant language and Protestants vying with Catholics for economic and cultural preeminence. St. Louis would become the jumping-off point for the celebrated Lewis and Clark expedition (1803–1806) and for the tens of thousands of pioneers who made the journey to the far west during the 1800s. In the process, Native Americans who had once thrived in the Mississippi region were pushed farther and farther west, forcing them to leave behind the remains of their ancestors.

A striking Calvary monument in the form of two back-to-back stone feathers was dedicated in the summer of 2003 and honors the Native Americans who were buried in these grounds before Caucasians appropriated the land. One of the inscriptions reads, "We Nimiipuu honor these men who gave their lives for all of us. We respect the 15,000 people who share this site with them." Another explains: "Traveling approximately 2,000 miles from present-day Idaho, 4 Nimiipuu (Nez Perce) came to St. Louis in the fall of 1831 to the home of William Clark. Feeling pressure from an encroaching presence in their homeland, these men sought information on white man's culture and a greater understanding of the 'Book of Heaven.'" During their stay, the four men were baptized by the Catholic Church. Two of them — Black Eagle and Speaking Eagle — are buried in Calvary Cemetery.

Many visitors to Calvary come to see the tombstones of noted people. Literary-minded folk make pilgrimages to the graves of Tennessee Williams (1911–1983), author of such world-famous plays as *The Glass Menagerie* and *A Streetcar Named Desire,* and novelist Kate Chopin (1850–1904), whose portrait of an adulterous woman in *The Awakening* has become required reading in many women's studies courses.

Civil War buffs are drawn to the family burial site of General William Tecumseh Sherman (1820–1891). Sherman lived in St. Louis on and off throughout his career, and although he died in New York, his body was returned to St. Louis, where son Willy had previously been buried.

And those concerned with African American history pay homage to the former slaves Dred Scott and his wife, Harriet Scott, coplaintiffs in the historic Dred Scott case. Scott lost his plea for freedom before both the state supreme court of Missouri in 1852 and the U.S. Supreme Court in 1857. Subsequently, he and his wife were purchased by Taylor Blow, who then set them free. Scott's tombstone reads:

DRED SCOTT
BORN ABOUT 1799
DIED SEPT. 17, 1858
Freed from slavery by
his friend Taylor Blow.

Numerous pennies showing the face of the emancipating president, Abraham Lincoln, have been left on the top of his stone (plate 34). Like the rocks and pebbles deposited at Jewish graves, the pennies are palpable symbols of remembrance, in this case testimonials to Scott's enduring presence in the American psyche.

Sections of the cemetery reserved for priests and nuns contain communities of identical crosses differing only in their inscriptions. Three rows of squat crosses dating from the 1850s and 1860s mark the graves of the Sisters of the Good Shepherd. Family names such as Flaherty, Flynn,

Fogarty, Kavanaugh, McCarthy, and O'Connell attest to the vast wave of Irish immigrants who reached American shores during the second half of the nineteenth century. Rising behind them is a larger-than-life statue of Christ as the Good Shepherd, tending his flock of crosses.

On the other side of the road, flat stones laid out on a sloping hill designate the more recent graves of the Sisters of Charity. From their inscriptions giving the year of death, their age at death, and the number of "years of vocation," it appears that these sisters were exceptionally long-lived. For example:

SISTER
FELICITA FARRELL
DIED JULY 19, 1956
AGED 91 YEARS
71 YEARS OF VOCATION
R. I. P.

The ubiquitous "RIP" stands for "Requiescat in pace" — the Latin original we translate as "Rest in peace."

The neighboring tombstones for nuns from the Convent of the Visitation indicate that they too were blessed with long lives, most making it into their eighties and nineties. The oldest of the group seems to have been

SISTER M. ANGELA
DEACY
DIED OCTOBER 18, 1956
AGED 98 YRS
R. I. P.

What accounts for this longevity? Although women who have never borne children have a higher incidence of breast cancer than women who have, the nuns were spared the wear and tear of pregnancy and the dangers of childbirth, factors that contributed to the high mortality rate of the time. Also, as Brides of Christ, the celibate sisters were not vulnerable to sexually transmitted diseases. Perhaps the nuns' longevity is above all due to the fact that they lived carefully regulated lives, free from the stresses of paid employment and marital friction, and they followed the religious road to inner peace long before they entered into eternal rest.

Bellefontaine Cemetery Bellefontaine Cemetery lies directly across the road from Calvary. While Bellefontaine contains less acreage and fewer graves than its neighbor, it became the model garden cemetery for the entire Mississippi region.

Bellefontaine owes its origins to a group of eleven prominent businessmen who purchased 138 acres north of the city limits in 1849 in order to create a nonsectarian burial ground. The cemetery was barely operative when calamity struck. St. Louis's worst cholera epidemic, sent upstream from New Orleans, filled the other metropolitan cemeteries, forcing three to close and four new ones to open. In the course of the summer, one tenth of the population died of cholera.

A month before the epidemic, on May 17, a raging fire had spread from a docked steamboat through a sizable section of wooden houses, killing or destroying whatever lay in its path. The ninety-bed St. Louis City Hospital had been struggling to handle the victims of the fire when the cholera epidemic erupted. Approximately one hundred burials arrived each day at Bellefontaine, sent from various St. Louis churches. During one sweltering July week, more than seven hundred people died, most of whom were small children and recent immigrants. Coffin makers and gravediggers struggled to keep up with the deaths. A lone child's walnut coffin made during the 1849 epidemic has been placed in the St. Louis Historical Museum as a reminder of that fateful year.

With this disaster weighing heavily on their minds, the Bellefontaine directors sought out a competent superintendent to manage and develop the cemetery, which was soon expanded to 332.5 acres. They found the right person for the job: Almerin Hotchkiss, a young civil engineer who had helped design the beautiful Green-Wood Cemetery in Brooklyn a decade earlier. Hotchkiss was responsible for laying out the winding roads and landscaping the tree-filled grounds of what would become one of America's most famous garden cemeteries.

Bellefontaine was officially dedicated on May 15, 1850, and Almerin Hotchkiss remained superintendent for a record forty-six years. When he retired, in 1895, his son Frank took over for the next two decades. The senior Hotchkiss died in 1903 at the age of eighty-seven, and his funeral service was held at his home on the cemetery grounds. A large block of hewn granite inscribed with his name marks his burial site.

Bellefontaine's most prominent inhabitant is probably William Clark, of the Lewis and Clark expedition, who is buried on a hilltop under an obelisk bearing the Masons' emblem. His epitaph honors him as a "soldier, explorer, statesman and patriot." In front of his monument lie the smaller stones of his second wife and descendants, including his oldest son, General Meriwether Lewis Clark, named for his father's partner on the famous expedition.

Unfortunately, William Clark's co-explorer Meriwether Lewis came to a less glorious end than Clark. In a fit of depression, he killed himself on October 11, 1809, in a poor wayside inn along the Natchez Trace, about seventy miles from Nashville, Tennessee. Two years after his death, an associate visiting his grave wrote to a friend: "He lies buried close by the common path with a few loose rails thrown over his grave. I gave Grinder [the innkeeper] money to put a post fence round it, to shelter it from the hogs, and from the wolves." Today a monument in the form of a broken column symbolizing early death marks the site.

Bellefontaine has a plentiful supply of notables: statesmen and brewers, soldiers and authors, industrialists and engineers, merchants and philanthropists, and some very accomplished women. It is the final resting place of Sara Teasdale (1884–1933), the first person to win a Pulitzer Prize for poetry, and of Susan Elizabeth Blow (1843–1916), founder of the country's first public kindergarten. Her kindergarten at Des Pères School in St. Louis, established in 1873, became the model for such programs throughout the nation.

A glass cover shields the face of Charles Balmer from the elements, giving him the spooky quality of a ghost looking through a porthole (plate 35). In life, Balmer (1817–1892) was a substantial figure, a German-born composer and organist who was chosen to conduct the music for Abraham Lincoln's funeral in Springfield, Illinois, in 1865.

A tombstone with the carving of a riverboat captain standing at the pilot wheel of his ship commemorates Captain Isaiah Sellers, who navigated the Mississippi between New Orleans and points north for more than forty years (plate 36). According to Mark Twain in his *Life on the Mississippi,* Captain Sellers "ordered his monument before he died and kept it near him until he did die. . . . it represents a man who in life would have staid there till he burned to a cinder, if duty required it." It was Captain Sellers who originally wrote riverboat articles under the name of Mark Twain, articles that Samuel Clemens burlesqued in *his* very first newspaper publication. When Captain Sellers died, the young Samuel Clemens, needing a pen name, "confiscated the ancient mariner's discarded one" and eventually made it world-famous.

Directly across the road from Sellers's tombstone, one cannot miss the red granite neo-Gothic mausoleum built for Adolphus Busch and Lilly Anheuser Busch, names associated with what is now the largest brewery in the world. (It was Lilly's father who actually founded the brewery.) With its bronze spire at the peak of the roof, two side towers, niches containing reproduction medieval statues on the façade, bronze entry gates, and stained-glass windows, the Busch mausoleum is perhaps the most ornate in the entire cemetery — which says a lot for a cemetery teeming with elegant mausoleums and elaborate statuary. High on its façade is chiseled a proud inscription:

BUSCH

1838–1913

VENI

VIDI

VICI

Bellefontaine's mausoleum row is one of the most impressive in the country. There St. Louis's elite built showcase homes for eternity. No money was spared, no style deemed too ostentatious — as long as it was inspired by ancient civilization. Greek temples abound with Doric, Ionic, and Corinthian columns holding up classic pediments. Egyptian influence is also present, most notably on the Tate mausoleum, with its strange sphinxes sporting big ears and stylized beards. The most original is the Wainwright mausoleum, commissioned in 1892 from architect

Louis Sullivan. Crowned by a large dome that is decorated on the inside with gilded putti and stars, it resembles the style of Byzantine churches found more commonly in Athens or Istanbul.

Like many other garden cemeteries, Bellefontaine is a sanctuary for magnificent statues erected in honor of the dead. There are countless angels and urns, reflecting the Victorian rivalry between traditional Christian symbolism and Greek Revival motifs — a rivalry that British author Tracy Chevalier captures brilliantly in her Edwardian novel *Falling Angels*. Urns, draped and undraped, were the chosen icons of the freethinking cultural avant-garde in England and America, while angels in various postures — standing upright, reclining gently, smiling tenderly — always carried traditional religious associations.

Especially after 1850, angels became as familiar to nineteenth-century funerary settings as death's-heads and soul effigies a century earlier. Both in bas-relief and full-bodied sculpture, angels invaded Victorian garden cemeteries with the mission of guiding the soul to heaven. Sentimental Protestants as well as Catholics welcomed them as symbols of consolation. Whatever their earlier reservations about popish icons, Protestants opened their hearts and their coffers to winged marble figures of various sizes that gave concrete form to the Catholic belief in guardian spirits. Although angels were supposed to be androgynous according to traditional Christian interpretations of the Hebrew Bible and New Testament, in which they appear as God's attendants or messengers, they were usually represented in stone as feminized or frankly feminine. At Bellefontaine, one stands out from all the rest: the seductively nubile angel kneeling on the multi-generational Ames/Semple family plot between the tombs of Jennie Marmaduke Ames (1874–1925) and Henry Ames (1850–1916).

Today's visitor to Bellefontaine enters a realm of gently curving roads, rolling hills, mature trees, man-made lakes, and artistic monuments that realize the fondest wishes of its founders.

New Mount Sinai Cemetery Jews too had made their way to St. Louis by 1849, though obviously in much smaller numbers than Catholics or Protestants. In the 1840s, they were burying their dead in two cemeteries that have since disappeared, but the New Mount Sinai Cemetery, established in 1850 by the B'nai B'rith Society, has survived and expanded from its original one-acre site on Gravois Road to more than thirty acres. Today the site is laid out with roadways, walkways, trees of great variety, lawns, flowers, a Japanese garden, Greek Revival mausoleums, a chapel with stained-glass windows and niches for cremated remains, as well as traditional tombstones. At first view, New Mount Sinai is a miniature Bellefontaine, with the appearance of a nonsectarian rural cemetery.

The oldest part of the cemetery reveals how quickly those nineteenth-century Jewish settlers adapted to mainstream culture. True, they were mostly Reform Jews from Germany, eager to embrace the Enlightenment ideals of assimilated citizenship. Their early tombstones bear no Jewish stars — a symbol that did not become popular until the twentieth century. At a distance, theirs look no different from Protestant markers: obelisks, urns, carvings of flowers, wreaths, vines, doves, willow trees, lambs for children, and Masons' emblems. A typical inscription follows the formula established in thousands of other non-Jewish cemeteries. Many indicate birth in a German-speaking land — Germany, Bavaria, Prussia, Austria — often with the name of the city or town as well. This is a pattern one finds increasingly in the Midwest and West among new settlers who want their European or East Coast origins recorded for posterity.

Despite the overall appearance of a nonsectarian cemetery, many of these early Jewish tombstones are also inscribed with Hebrew letters. The formulaic expression "May his [or her] soul be bound up in the bonds of eternal life" is frequently written in Hebrew under the English data.

One stone is engraved with the symbol of the *kohanim* — the priestly class that confers benediction. It is a striking carving of two outstretched hands with their thumbs touching each other, set above the inscription for Isaac Kahn (1833–1861).

Not far from Kahn's grave there is another equally beautiful carving, that of a large lyre, on the obelisk erected for Charles Dreyer (1845–1882). And in the same section, on a stone bearing the words "In memory of our beloved brother Ernst Frank, 1871–1890," a parting handshake suggests the pain felt by family members at the loss of this young man. Identical shirt cuffs encircling the hands inform us that this is a strictly male handshake. The more standard handshake, often between spouses, usually has clearly identifiable masculine and feminine cuffs.

Hebrew lettering and priestly hands, a lyre and a parting handshake — these are the images that early St. Louis Jews brought together in their funerary arts. They represent an amalgam of traditional European Jewry and contemporary Americana that allowed the Jewish community to prosper in St. Louis.

St. Louis's African American Graveyards: Quinette and Greenwood African Americans were present from the start in Missouri settlements, but since almost all were slaves, they were usually buried in unmarked graves. Researcher Ann Morris writes that the only inscribed marker she has found in St. Louis County for an African American who died before the Civil War is a slate table stone in Mount Olive Catholic Cemetery, which reads:

> Here Lie the remains of
> DICK
> Coloured Servant of John Withnell
> He died of cholera
> 1849

Free blacks were buried in church-owned cemeteries or in potter's fields along with indigents and strangers. The tradition of the potter's field reserved for paupers and unknown persons goes back to the Bible, as evidenced by Matthew 27:7.

After the Civil War, several exclusively African American cemeteries were established in St. Louis, the oldest of which is Quinette, located in Kirkwood. This cemetery has been documented in *Gone but Not Forgotten* by Keith Rawlings, whose interest in Quinette dates back to the 1960s when he photographed its tombstones for his Boy Scouts' merit badge. Many of these stones are now gone — the victims of vandalism and ghoulish greed — but Rawlings's photographs and his research into the history of the people buried underneath the stones help preserve their memory.

It is believed that Quinette was founded in 1873 on land given by the U.S. government to former slaves and free Negroes. The last known burial in Quinette took place a hundred years later, in 1973, for a baby of unknown gender laid to rest by the minister and his wife who lived next to the cemetery.

For much of the twentieth century, the Quinette gravedigger was a man named Henry James, who died in 1981 at the age of ninety-six. His son Richard remembered that most folks were buried in pine boxes, but some were buried in nothing at all. His father was paid in cash, or in food by those of lesser means. Aside from the fees for the services of the grave-digger, burial at Quinette was free for people of African descent residing within five miles of the cemetery.

In 1978, the Kirkwood City Council passed an ordinance for the ter-mination of the cemetery; they eventually sold the area to a restaurant owner, operator of the adjacent Green Parrot. Quinette went into a period of precipitous decline, with headstones overturned and trash everywhere. Then, in 2002, a developer bought the land and, as part of the purchase agreement, deeded the cemetery over to the City of Kirkwood and contrib-uted $50,000 to its future care.

Soon after the founding of Quinette, Greenwood Cemetery on St. Louis Avenue was established as St. Louis's first commercial cemetery for Afri-can Americans. Larger than Quinette and officially nonsectarian, it as-pired to the picturesque vistas that were the hallmark of Bellefontaine and Calvary.

In its early days, Greenwood boasted many Victorian marble and granite tombstones, some enhanced by rosebushes and flowers; several gravesites were outlined with seashells, rocks, or miniature fences. Fol-lowing a practice common among African Americans in the South, per-sonal items belonging to the deceased were often left at graves. Green-wood did so well as a commercial cemetery for African Americans that two others followed suit: the Father Dickson Cemetery, founded in 1903, and the Washington Park Cemetery, founded in 1920.

But with no perpetual-care funds to pay for maintenance, all three became sadly neglected during the second half of the twentieth century, overgrown with weeds and vulnerable to vandalism. Only recently have efforts been made to restore them. A large sign at Greenwood announces:

Greenwood Cemetery Restoration Project
HELP CLEAN-UP THE CEMETERY ANY SATURDAY,
9AM TO 3PM

Although most of Greenwood is still overgrown with weeds, the tombstones in the front have been uncovered, and several are decorated with artificial flowers hung on crook-like holders. The downhill acreage in the back is thick with uncut grass, weeds, cornflowers, climbing clematis, and various other vines that make you think you are in the backwoods. Hidden and half-hidden tombstones, visited only by birds and butterflies, await the cleanup team.

Central Missouri: Cemeteries in the Boonslick Two hours by car west of St. Louis, in the area around Columbia and Boonville, there is a treasure trove of cemeteries dating back to the first half of the nineteenth century. Around 1805, Nathan and Daniel Morgan Boone — the sons of the legendary frontiersman Daniel Boone and his wife, Rebecca — settled on the banks of the Missouri and began to operate a commercial salt lick from a natural spring, boiling the salty water until only the salt was left and then shipping it to St. Louis, where it was in great demand for cooking and preservation. Today, the Boonslick has become an important center for agri-business, education, health care, transportation, and tourists in search of America's past.

We were drawn there by the work of the local historian Maryellen McVicker, whose doctoral dissertation focused on the Boonslick cemeteries. A seventh-generation descendant of central Missouri pioneers, McVicker has dedicated her adult life to preserving the gravesites of her ancestors.

The Red Top Church and Cemetery Two of McVicker's ancestors, Nathan and Priscilla Roberts, donated land to the Red Top (Disciples of Christ)

Christian Church ten miles north of Columbia in Boone County. They set aside one acre from their farm for the original church and cemetery, founded in 1822 and later augmented by nine additional acres. Today, in a lovely bucolic setting, nine hundred people rest in peace, disturbed only by the digging of an occasional new grave. McVicker tends to their stones with proprietary dedication. She has even rescued broken tombstones from abandoned sites and brought them (without the bodily remains) to lie beside their kin.

The earliest stones are among the most unusual to be found anywhere in America. "Anthropomorphic" fieldstone markers about three feet high, carved in the form of round heads with necks joined to tablet-like bodies, look like miniature people. With smaller footstones in the same shape, these abstract effigies give off a primitive energy suggesting the secrets of the dead.

The scratchy writing on one of them reads:

THOMAS ROBERTS
WAS BORN NOV THE
9, 1798 DECEASED
OCTOBER THE 6 1829.

ELIZABETH ROBE
RTS WAS BORN JULY 15TH
1829 + DEPARTED THIS
LIFE APRIL 12TH, 1832

Thomas Roberts was the son of Nathan and Priscilla Roberts, and Elizabeth was probably his daughter. McVicker believes that these stones were carved and inscribed by a slave under the direction of a white overseer, and that they continued a tradition of African art brought to the South. In that Africans believed the dead are always with us, their abstract effigies — like the porcelain photos on Italian markers — forcefully evoke the persons consigned to the earth.

Aside from these two abstractly human-shaped markers, termed "anthropomorphic" by gravestone scholars, the other stones in the graveyard follow familiar American models. A few are carved with a parting handshake or a hand with the index finger pointing upward toward heaven.

Red Top (so called because of the church's red roof) is still very much a nineteenth-century country churchyard.

The Jewell Family Cemetery Nearby, in the city of Columbia, the Jewell Cemetery is a perfect example of a nineteenth-century family graveyard. Started on their farm by George and Mary Jewell, who moved from Virginia to Kentucky and finally to Missouri in 1822, it contains several generations of descendants. McVicker calls Jewell a textbook graveyard because it shows how new-style tombstones emerged throughout the century. Since the Jewells were a wealthy family, they were able to afford the latest funerary fashions, and these are lined up in a row from left to right.

George Jewell (died 1841, at age seventy-six) and Mary Jewell (died 1843, at age seventy-nine) are buried underneath two limestone box crypts. These very heavy, very expensive, and very rare monuments were shipped up the Missouri River from St. Louis and hauled by wagon to the family plot.

Beside his parents' tombstone stands the marble column topped by an urn marking the grave of William Jewell, M.D. (1789–1852). William was a prominent local personality — the mayor of Columbia, a generous contributor to the Baptist Church, and founder of the still-thriving William Jewell College in Liberty, Missouri. His Greek Revival marker is symmetrically positioned between the somber crypts of his parents on one side and his first and second wives, Arethusa Boyle Jewell (who died in 1818) and Cynthia Compton Jewell (who died in 1822), on the other.

Next come the Greek Revival headstones of William Jewell's son and his son's wife, both of whom died in 1844, and then a few of William's grandchildren. One of the marble stones, more elaborately carved than the rest, shows a hand surrounded by a garland of flowers, the index finger pointing upward to a celestial crown. It was erected for Hannah Jewell Hardin (1793–1861) — the mother of a future Missouri governor, Charles Henry Hardin. In deference to Governor Hardin, the state has maintained the Jewell Cemetery in its present immaculate condition.

Amid these elegant marble markers, there is one tombstone different from all the others. It is the anthropomorphic stone made for Angelina Hardin (1827–1829), the little daughter of Charles Hardin and Hannah

Jewell Hardin (plate 37). Because this stone is identical in every way to the two anthropomorphic stones at Red Top — except that Angelina's inscription is written by a very poor hand — it is likely that all three were made by the same person. There is only one other similar stone in Boone County, located at the New Salem Baptist Church graveyard.

Curiously, tombstones in this style were also made for Daniel and Rebecca Boone. Carved by a local blacksmith and paid for by Boone before he died, the markers were left behind in Missouri when the Boone couple's bodies were returned to Kentucky in the 1840s for reburial. These tombstones are now on display in the Central Methodist College in Fayette.

Not only does the Jewell Cemetery display a textbook selection of nineteenth-century markers ranging from the most classic to the most unusual, it also has a feature that's missing in most other cemeteries. Behind the family tombstones but within the cemetery walls lie the unmarked graves of the family's slaves. It is a sobering experience to look out on a scattering of bricklike markers that have no names, no dates of birth or death, nothing but blank six- or eight-inch stones barely emerging from the grass. Here there is nothing to mark the individual identities, nothing to allow for personal remembrance. And yet, on the day of our visit, flowers had been left by one of the stones, either to honor an ancestor whose gravesite had been remembered by successive generations or to commemorate the collective community of slaves.

Walnut Grove Cemetery We had timed our visit to coincide with Maryellen McVicker's group tour of the Walnut Grove Cemetery, Boonville's pride and joy. Established in 1852, it is a splendid example of a nonsectarian rural cemetery in the mode of St. Louis's Bellefontaine, though on a smaller scale. There are 8,000 graves here as compared to Bellefontaine's 86,000. Footpaths curve through the old walnut grove, now planted with cypresses — the Greek symbol of death — and numerous other trees. The most expensive plots were close to the front gate, with the original founders grouped around a fountain. Statues, some highly original, mark the graves of Boonville's elite: a reproduction of the Nike of Samothrace (the original is in the Louvre) commissioned in Italy;

a huge bell on the top of the Bell family monument; an ear of corn decorating the marker of Dr. A. W. Kueckelhan. A life-size mother and daughter holding hands graces the grave of Kate Tracy, who died of cholera in May 1854, at the age of seventeen (plate 64).

The mausoleum of the Leonards, with the graves of several family members underneath, bears the wistful words:

TO LIVE IN HEARTS WE LEAVE
BEHIND IS NOT TO DIE

This affirmation looks to remembrance as a counterforce to death. As long as we are remembered by someone, we are not entirely dead. This is the humanist's answer to belief in a supernatural afterlife. But the hope to be remembered — and positively remembered — has its limits. What happens when the last person who remembers us also dies? Then do we die a second death, more permanent than the first?

And what if we leave behind forms of immortality — paintings, books, musical compositions, buildings, institutions? Will these preserve the memory of our individual identities long after we are gone? History books are crammed with the narratives of outstanding men and women — in the military, in government, in industry, in literature and the arts, even in private life — whose acts have entitled them to a place in our collective memory.

There is no doubt that most people wish to be remembered after they die, especially by family members and friends. Tombstones, with or without photos of the deceased, with or without evocative epitaphs, stimulate remembrance. They call forth images of those we have loved and can even inspire reveries surrounding people we have never known.

ETHNICITY,
RELIGION, AND
CLASS IN
UNDERGROUND
CHICAGO

CHICAGO'S CEMETERIES ARE a sprawling conglomerate of diverse peoples representing numerous ethnic groups. From the first Irish, German, Scottish, Scandinavian, and Polish settlers who built the city's early structures to more recent immigrants from China, Korea, Mexico, Albania, and Croatia, Chicago's multicultural population has created a dynamic metropolis second to none, despite its longtime label as the "second city."

In many other American regions, religion was the sole determining factor in the creation of a cemetery. Burial grounds were Protestant, Catholic, or Jewish, with municipal graveyards available to everyone. But in Chicago, ethnicity has always inflected religion: Roman Catholic cemeteries were known to be predominantly Irish, Polish, German, Italian, Ukrainian, or Lithuanian. Similarly, there were Protestant cemeteries identified as German, Scandinavian, Scottish, Bohemian, Lithuanian, or Dutch. Nondenominational cemeteries often sold part of their grounds to specific ethnic groups, such as Armenians, Latvians, Serbians, Chinese, Japanese, Hispanics, or Gypsies. In the suburbs, two cemeteries, both called Evergreen, are largely Greek.

Blacks, who have lived in Chicago since its earliest days, were origi-

Above: Gypsy tin church, Forest Home/ German Waldheim Cemetery, Chicago

nally buried alongside everyone else. But paradoxically, in the wake of the Civil War, white cemeteries became increasingly exclusive; so much so that in 1911, a black Illinois legislator named Edward Green pushed for the passage of a law to end discrimination in the sale of plots. Blacks responded to discriminatory policies by creating their own segregated spaces, beginning with Mount Glenwood in 1908, and followed by Lincoln, Burr Oak, and Restvale, all located on the south side of the city.

Burr Oak is of special interest because it is the final resting place of Emmett Louis Till (1941–1955) and his mother, Mamie Till Mobley (1921–2003). The murder of the fourteen-year-old boy when he was visiting relatives in Mississippi was a significant moment for the civil rights movement. Refused the right to see her son's corpse, Till's mother insisted on opening the casket, then transported it back home to Chicago, where she placed the body on view. Fifty thousand people came to see the remains. Even though the murderers, Roy Bryant and J. W. Milam, were acquitted by an all-white-male jury, they later described the killing in a story sold to *Look* magazine. Mamie Till spent the rest of her life as a civil rights activist. The epitaph on her tomb proclaims: "Her pain united a nation."

But if ethnicity provides one key to the makeup of Chicago's graveyards, class provides another. "Class" is a category Americans are often reluctant to use outside sociology courses, yet Chicago's cemeteries force the term upon us. How else can we talk about the life-size statues enclosed in glass boxes to protect them from the fierce Chicago wind, which are found in Graceland and Roseland (plate 38), as well as the grand mausoleums erected for the affluent? Compare these to the modest granite markers self-identified as "working class," that are placed near the Haymarket Martyrs' Monument in Waldheim, and the plots that have no stones at all in the Cook County Cemetery for the Indigent. Only by thinking along the lines of ethnicity and class, as well as religion, can we begin to make sense of those green spaces outlined on Chicago city maps.

Early History Chicago's first two official graveyards — one Protestant, one Catholic — were created in 1835, along the shore of Lake Michigan. Since the graves were only three to four feet deep, bodies decomposed rapidly and human remains were sometimes uncovered. This situation was unacceptable to the Irish workers who came in droves to dig the Illinois and Michigan Canal, started in 1830 and finished in 1848. They purchased a tract of higher ground to the south of the city in the township of Lemont, and in 1837 they established what would become known as St. James the Sag — the first of metropolitan Chicago's many Roman Catholic cemeteries. Those early Irish chose their site wisely: despite the proximity of rivers, canals, and minor lakes that all periodically overflow, gravestones dating as far back as the 1830s are still visible on the cemetery hillside.

In the 1840s, with a rapidly increasing population, the city of Chicago needed additional burial grounds. Following a pattern common to many other cities, bodies were removed from the older sites and placed in the new Chicago City Cemetery, at a safe distance from Lake Michigan. Less than two decades later, in 1858, neighbors of the new cemetery signed a petition urging that the area be turned into a park. In 1864, it was transformed into Lake Park, subsequently renamed Lincoln Park, in honor of the assassinated president. Once again, human remains had to be removed and relocated to consecrated sites, such as Calvary in suburban Evanston and to other private cemeteries beyond the city limits.

After the first Jews arrived from Germany in 1845, they purchased nine tenths of an acre in the Chicago City Cemetery, at a cost of forty-five dollars, to use for burial space — which they would be obliged to vacate twenty years later when it became a park. Thereafter, Jewish groups purchased a number of burial grounds, either separate tracts of land or portions of nondenominational cemeteries. One example was Oak Woods, where the Jewish section was enclosed within a wrought-iron fence (plate 7). There one still finds an abandoned small, red-brick building, one of the *bet-taharas* used for the ritual preparation of Jewish bodies before they were laid to rest.

In time, new cemeteries were created farther and farther away from the city center. Historic cemeteries include Rosehill (interdenominational), Graceland (Protestant), Jewish Graceland, Wunder's (Protestant), St. Boniface (Catholic), Bohemian National (interdenominational), and Mount Olive (Scandinavian Protestant) on the north side; All Saints Polish National and St. Nicholas Ukrainian (both Catholic) in the northwest;

and Concordia (Protestant) and German Waldheim /Forest Home (inter-denominational) in the southwest. Far to the south, one finds Oak Woods (interdenominational), Mount Olivet (Catholic), St. Casimir Lithuanian (Catholic), and Burr Oak First Evangelical Lutheran for African Americans. Even farther south, at 159th Street, one finds the Cook County Cemetery for the Indigent.

Today, Chicago and its environs, with a population of three million, contains more cemeteries per capita than any other U.S. city — more than two hundred. By comparison, the New York City metropolitan area, with a population of roughly ten million, has fewer than one hundred cemeteries.

The sites highlighted in this chapter were selected because they best illustrate how ethnic, religious, and class issues worked their way into underground Chicago. But to be truthful, they were also chosen because each is visually compelling, historically rich, and hauntingly memorable.

Forest Home/German Waldheim Cemetery Forest Home/German Waldheim is situated on 220 acres in the town of Forest Park. Among its 190,000 underground residents, there are German Lutheran pioneers, dedicated labor activists, and numerous members of the successful professional class, such as the parents of Ernest Hemingway — he a physician, she a music teacher. Its noted inhabitants include the anarchist Emma Goldman, the evangelist Billy Sunday, and a community of Gypsies.

Originally, long before the arrival of European immigrants, the land was the site of a Pottawatomie Indian village, with burial mounds located along the Des Plaines River. In fact, the first person to receive written title to the land was a half-Indian, half-French trapper named Leon Bourassa, in 1839. When other Native Americans were forced west to reservations under the terms of the 1833 Treaty of Chicago, which ended the Black Hawk War, Bourassa and his Pottawatomie wife stayed behind on the property to care for the graves of their ancestors. In 1851, Bourassa sold a large tract to Ferdinand Haase, a young man recently arrived from Prussia with inheritance money and big ideas.

Haase built a three-room French-style house using stones from the

Des Plaines River, which still cuts through the property. Because the land was picturesque and sufficiently far from the burgeoning urban center, he opened part of it in 1856 as picnic grounds. Haase's Park became extremely popular during the next decade, especially among those of German descent. He even managed to strike a deal with the railroad to build a spur line from the main tracks to the park, which became a selling point when Haase began offering parts of his land for cemetery usage to German religious and secular organizations. German Lutherans established Concordia Cemetery in 1872; a group of German lodges established German Waldheim as a nondenominational cemetery in 1873; and Forest Home was established in 1876 as a nonsectarian cemetery for members of the English-speaking community. Ultimately, in 1968, Forest Home merged with the adjacent German Waldheim, using Waldheim's original entrance as the sole entry to the combined cemetery. Concordia continues to function as a separate entity.

In the old Waldheim section, one finds many stones inscribed in German, such as the red granite marker for Amanda Baumer (1871–1902), which begins "Hier ruhet sanft in gott" (Here lies peacefully with God) and ends soberly "vier lieben kindern" (four beloved children).

Those who visit this part of the cemetery today do not come for Amanda Baumer. They come mainly because this section contains the famous Haymarket Martyrs' Monument, dedicated on June 25, 1893, and recently designated a national historic landmark by the U.S. Department of the Interior — the only cemetery marker in the country to receive such a distinction. The monument commemorates the workers who were killed during Chicago's Haymarket Riot of May 4, 1886. The riot had begun as a nonviolent demonstration to protest the police brutality that had taken place the preceding day at the McCormick Reaper Plant; there, police had intervened in a fight between strikers and strikebreakers and subsequently caused the death of several people. The gathering at Haymarket Square the day after the McCormick incident was peaceful until the police ordered the crowd to disperse. Then someone threw a bomb, and the shooting began. Seven policemen and four workers were killed, and more than sixty people were wounded.

In the aftermath of the riot, police began a roundup of known radicals and labor leaders, culminating in the trial of eight men accused of conspiracy. Despite the fact that the bomb thrower was never identified and no evidence connected the accused men to the crime, they were all declared guilty of having incited mob action through their speeches and publications. Seven of the activists were sentenced to death, but only four were actually hanged. One committed suicide in his cell, two others had their death sentences commuted to life imprisonment, and one was given fifteen years in prison. Several years later, Governor John Peter Altgeld was persuaded by defense attorney Clarence Darrow, among others, to review the case. Darrow was a lifelong crusader against capital punishment, perhaps because he was the son of an undertaker and had seen the grim reality of death close up during his childhood. Altgeld concluded that the trial had been unfair and pardoned the surviving prisoners, which earned him the enmity of conservative forces for the rest of his life. Along with the executed, the pardoned prisoners were eventually buried in German Waldheim.

Waldheim was the only cemetery that would accept the bodies of the convicted men — Adolph Fischer, George Engel, Louis Lingg, Albert Parsons, and August Spies. Their graves became a rallying point for members of the international labor movement. Eventually the Pioneer Aid and Support Association, organized to provide for the widows and orphans of the executed and the dependents of the prisoners, raised funds to erect the Haymarket Martyrs' Monument. It bears a statue of Justice, represented by a woman placing a laurel wreath on the head of a fallen worker. The inscription at its base reads:

> THE DAY WILL COME WHEN OUR SILENCE WILL BE MORE
> POWERFUL THAN THE VOICES YOU ARE THROTTLING TODAY.

Nearby one finds — appropriately — the grave of Emma Goldman (June 29, 1869–May 14, 1939). Goldman was an international anarchist, pioneer feminist, and free-speech advocate. Born in Russia, she lived in the United States from 1885 to 1919, at which time she was deported back to Russia for her involvement in anarchist, socialist, and communist causes. (J. Edgar Hoover, then a special assistant to the attorney general, was primarily responsible for her deportation.) One of the turning points in Goldman's life had been the Haymarket Martyrs' trial, which convinced her to become a revolutionary. Following the model of those who had been executed, for the rest of her life she proclaimed the need for radical change in American society. Although she died outside the United States, in Toronto, Canada, she wanted to be buried in Waldheim with others from the labor movement. Roger Baldwin, founder of the American Civil Liberties Union, gave her eulogy. At the foot of her marker, her admirers leave their calling cards in the form of small rocks, shells, coins, and various political buttons.

Goldman's upright tombstone is edged by a collection of smaller gray granite stones, all in the same style: simple markers tilting upward with polished surfaces giving the names, dates, and epitaphs of activists identified as "working-class heroes, working-class journalists, selfless fighters for human happiness and peace." The rhetoric is solidly left wing: William Z. Foster (1881–1966) is commemorated as a "working-class leader" and "tireless fighter for socialism"; Otto H. Wangerin (1888–1975) as an "outstanding leader for working-class internationalism"; Elizabeth G. Flynn (1890–1964) as "the rebel girl fighter for working-class emancipation"; Eugene Dennis (1904–1961) as a "communist leader and fighter for working-class internationalism"; and Sylvia Woods (1909–1987) as a "heroine in the struggle." The epitaph for Jack Kling (1911–1990) and Sue Kling (1912–) speaks for their joint ideals: "We marched as one to change the world." Such words sound poignantly outdated today.

The labor activists' section is by no means representative of the greater Forest Home/Waldheim population, which covers a very wide spectrum of Chicagoans. Neither are the Roma, or Gypsy, graves, whose plots are adjacent to the cemetery entrance. Gypsy tombs stand out because they are heavily decorated with carved religious images and portraits of the deceased (plate 39). Their memorial portraits, either black-and-white or in color, are often set within a frame that has a protective lid. If you want to see the portrait, you lift the lid. Gypsies look like Eastern Europeans, except for a certain something in their attire — the man's jaunty hat, the woman's prominent jewelry or scarf around her head. Some of the more recent tombstones bear large laser-inscribed portraits of the dead when they were very much alive.

Eastern European Gypsy groups, many from Hungary and Romania, came to Chicago as a part of the great wave of immigration that took place between 1880 and 1914. As coppersmiths and metalworkers, they found employment repairing and refining industrial equipment. Others worked as musicians, entertainers, and fortunetellers. Since 1970, another wave of Gypsies has arrived from Yugoslavia. Known variously as Rom, Roma, or Romany, these groups have different languages, cultures, and religions, as well as different degrees of integration into American society.

At Waldheim, the religious images on Gypsy tombs include crosses — both Roman Catholic and Eastern Orthodox — and carvings of Jesus and the Virgin Mary, especially in her Eastern Orthodox incarnation. There is even a miniature tin church sitting on a tree stump, like a rural mailbox. Epitaphs tend to be unconventional. For instance:

POLLACKO CHRISTO
1923–87
THE MAN WHO
SAW IT ALL AND
DID IT ALL.

BABE CHRISTO
1927–2001
SHE DID IT
HER WAY.

Graceland Cemetery While German Waldheim became the cemetery of choice for Gypsies and working-class activists, Graceland became a haven for their opposites: wealthy industrialists, civic leaders, and other prominent Chicagoans. The reaper inventor, Cyrus McCormick (1809–1884), at whose plant strikers clashed with policemen in the fateful hours leading up to the Haymarket riot, is buried here, as are other members of Chicago's moneyed aristocracy: meatpacking giant Philip Armour (1832–1901); department store king Marshall Field (1835–1906); newspaper publisher Victor Lawson (1850–1925); and five-time mayor of Chicago Carter Harrison Sr. (1825–1893), among many others.

Carl Sandburg singled out Graceland as the subject for one of his *Chi-*

cago Poems (1916), underlining the distinction between the super-rich buried there and the poor buried elsewhere. The poem begins irreverently:

TOMB of a millionaire,
A multi-millionaire, ladies and gentlemen,
Place of the dead where they spend every year
The usury of twenty-five thousand dollars
For upkeep and flowers
To keep fresh the memory of the dead.

The "merchant prince gone to dust" is then contrasted with "cash girls" eking out a pitiful living in bars. With his proletarian leanings, Sandburg had little sympathy for Graceland's lavish mortuary displays.

Graceland was established in 1860 on land bought by Thomas Bryan, a successful Chicago lawyer and entrepreneur. No expense was spared to transform its 119 acres into an idyllic home for the dead. The landscape architect Ossian Simonds drew up comprehensive plans that incorporated buildings into a park-like paradise. Curving roads wind past stretches of green shaded by numerous trees. An expanse of water — more lake than pond — is bordered by generous weeping willows.

But what makes Graceland special, in addition to the beauty of its landscape and the renown of its inhabitants, are its architectural masterpieces. Indeed, one of the monuments is acknowledged as "the beginning of modern architecture in America." Those words on the Getty tomb are part of a tribute, not to the deceased lying under it, but to the man who designed it — architect Louis Henri Sullivan (1856–1924).

The Getty tomb (plate 40) was commissioned by the lumber merchant Henry Harrison Getty for his wife, Carrie Eliza. Later, he too was buried there, along with the couple's only child, Alice. When the tomb was erected in 1890, Louis Sullivan was considered the leader of the Chicago School, known for its innovative use of modern technology. Rather than relying on the Greek or Egyptian shapes that had become the hallmarks of American mausoleums, Sullivan conceived a graceful cube that had no precedent. The lower half is made up of smooth limestone, the upper half is covered with octagons that surround delicately carved arches; an intricately patterned bronze gate stands in the center. The combination of solid limestone and almost lace-like decoration resulted in a masterpiece that continues to draw students of architecture to Graceland.

Sullivan himself is buried in Graceland under a rough granite headstone. On the front, his profile is set into a metal emblem patterned on one of his own intricate geometric designs.

Other noted architects include John Root (1850–1891), also a member of the Chicago School, and Ludwig Mies Van Der Rohe (1886–1969), the German-born Bauhaus innovator whose immigration to Chicago in 1937 inaugurated a career rivaling that of the American wunderkind Frank Lloyd Wright, himself one of Sullivan's early disciples. Root is buried under a stunning Celtic cross intricately carved in Scottish granite. Mies Van Der Rohe's marker is a flat, black, polished granite stone that reflects his architectural commitment to an unadorned geometric style.

But if Sullivan, Root, and Mies Van Der Rohe were proponents of the avant-garde principles underlying Chicago's twentieth-century skyscrapers, their influence at Graceland is overshadowed by that of antiquity. The big spenders continued to be enamored of Greek columns and Egyptian pyramids. The monument to piano manufacturer William Kimball (1828–1904), with its impressive Corinthian columns and kneeling angel, stands across from the single soaring Corinthian column erected for George Pullman (1831–1897), inventor of the Pullman sleeping car. Next to Pullman's column, an exedra (stately bench) completes the ensemble. For a time, the Pullman family had to protect George Pullman's coffin from angry workers; they covered it with tar paper and asphalt and placed it in a huge underground concrete block. The workers' enduring anger resulted from a bitter strike in 1894, quelled only when President Grover Cleveland sent in federal troops. Most of the strikers lost their jobs, and the new employees were required to pledge that they would not join a union.

Close to these two neo-Greek monuments are two neo-Egyptian tombs. The one for brewer Peter Schoenhofen (1827–1893) in the form of a pyramid is guarded on one side by a standing angel and on the other by a reclining sphinx — a fanciful combination that could have issued only from a late-Victorian imagination (plate 41). The other Egyptian-inspired tomb, erected for the lumber and real estate king Martin Ryerson (1818–1887), is quite a different matter. It derives its modern shape from a combination of mastaba (a blocky structure with a flat top and slanted sides) for the base and a pyramid resting on top, like the head on a body. From this pyramid set with three small windows, one could presumably look out into eternity. Ryerson's tomb was designed by Louis Sullivan a year before he did the Getty tomb. Sullivan's third and final mausoleum was the 1892 Wainwright tomb in St. Louis's Bellefontaine Cemetery.

Graceland is proud of its architectural treasures and welcomes the visitors who come to see them, as long as they don't picnic on the graves or attempt to swim in the lagoon.

Roman Catholic Chicago: The Irish Cemeteries Most of the men and women who labored to build early Chicago did not aspire to be buried in Graceland, or in German Waldheim for that matter. A large proportion of Chicago's residents were Roman Catholics committed to burial in consecrated churchyards. Between 1837 and 1849, the Catholic community, which consisted largely of Irish working-class families, had the choice of no fewer than seven cemeteries — all of which still exist today.

Because St. James the Sag was to the south of the city, Calvary Cemetery in the northern suburb of Evanston was established to serve the needs of a second generation of Irish. The first forty acres were bought in 1851 by Bishop Van de Velde for the sum of twenty dollars an acre; Calvary formally opened on All Souls' Day 1859, as the first diocesan cemetery in the area. Its grave markers include not only traditional crosses, crucifixes, angels, and Madonnas but also firemen's helmets, because many of the Irish were employed by the fire department.

With new waves of immigrants continuing to feed Chicago's Catholic population, the diocese became an archdiocese, and new cemeteries — predominantly Irish, Polish, and German — were added. Of these, Mount Olivet on the south side has remained much as it was a hundred years ago, with its row upon row of crosses bearing Irish names and some fine pieces of sculpture that assume an otherworldly air when reflected in the watery ditch that fills up after a rainfall.

At present in greater Chicago, there are forty-two cemeteries under the direction of the Catholic archdiocese, some less than an acre in size, some over three hundred acres. With more than three hundred full-time employees, the archdiocese provides care for an excess of 2.4 million gravesites. In terms of their combined space, these consecrated grounds are larger than "almost any of the communities in the Chicago area, with the exception of the city of Chicago itself."

All Saints Polish National Catholic Cemetery In the second half of the nineteenth century, Chicago's Polish population began to vie with the Irish for ethnic preeminence. Like the Irish, most Poles worshipped in Roman Catholic churches and planned to be buried in consecrated ground. One of these sites, St. Adalbert Cemetery, established in 1872 in nearby Niles, eventually became the largest Polish cemetery in the area. Working-class families could count on Polish mutual aid societies to pay for burial expenses and the Catholic Church to administer last rites.

But not all Poles were happy with the Roman Catholic Church as it was administered in Chicago. They objected to the heavily Irish influence in archdiocesan politics, which, they felt, did not adequately serve Polish needs. In 1895, a group of dissatisfied Polish Catholics organized themselves as an independent parish under the leadership of a renegade priest, laid the cornerstone for a new church, and bought a beautiful tract of land on Higgins Road to be used as a cemetery. For these acts, that Polish priest, Anthony Kozlowski, was excommunicated by the Irish archbishop Patrick Feehan, a decision that engendered bitterness between Polish religious dissidents and Irish Catholic authorities for decades to come.

All Saints Polish National became part of the Polish National Catholic Church, a splinter organization that had a decisive break with the Roman Catholic Church in 1904. Thereafter it followed the regulations established by its own synods, which were made up of clerical and lay representatives. Most significant, like other parishes within the Polish National Catholic Church, it rejected Latin in favor of Polish for its liturgy and no longer required celibacy for its priests.

Today, All Saints Polish National is an unlikely quiet, heavily wooded space barely ten minutes away from the huge O'Hare airport complex. Visitors brought blindfolded to the site could easily imagine themselves in an Eastern European forest. The atmosphere is enhanced by the many crosses and crucifixes, which emit a peculiarly Polish sense of suffering (plate 42). Despite their grievances against the Roman Catholic Church, those turn-of-the-century Poles had no quarrel with traditional Catholic symbols.

St. Casimir Lithuanian National Cemetery Although Lithuanians had been under Polish or Russian domination for about five hundred years before their recent independence, they are not a Slavic people. Descendants of the original races that lived on the shores of the Baltic Sea, they have preserved much of their native culture, including their non-Slavic, Indo-European language.

In 1867, a time of famine in their country, Lithuanians began emigrating. Many of them went to Chicago after the great fire of 1871, attracted by opportunities in construction, factories, steel mills, and the stockyards. By the turn of the twentieth century, there were more than five thousand Lithuanians in Chicago, a sufficient number to establish a cemetery that would be inseparably both Catholic and Lithuanian. St. Casimir, founded in 1903 and named after the patron saint of Lithuania, covers 523 acres; less than half of the cemetery is currently occupied by burial plots.

Initially, Lithuanian immigrants made little effort to carry their native culture into the graveyard. They adopted the early-twentieth-century American manner of making all cemeteries look alike. But beginning in 1949, new political emigrants fleeing Soviet domination called for more ethnic tombstones and a truly Lithuanian style.

Folk art emblems, such as wheat stalks, tulips, sprigs of rue, and peasant embroidery, began to appear on granite, sandstone, and marble slabs. Traditional religious images, such as the crucifix, the Blessed Virgin of Vilnius, Saint George, and Saint Joseph, that adorned Lithuania's wayside chapels were born anew in the hands of skilled carvers. The tombstones got larger and larger and increasingly dramatic. When you stand in front of these monuments in the newer sections of the cemetery, you are amazed by the spectacle; it's as if you were encountering a previously unknown, entirely original school of art.

Many of the tombstones — more than one hundred — are the work of sculptor Ramojus Mozoliauskas (1925–). These often give the impression of a figure emerging from the rock — a gentle Jesus holding a lamb, a suffering Christ with bound wrists, or Jesus in the distinctive Lithuanian pose known as the Worrier, with his head resting in his hand. Other sculptors contemporary with Mozoliauskas also created dynamic markers with asymmetrical shapes and bold contrasts between rough gray granite and highly polished surfaces. They emit a sense of energy very different from the quiet crosses gathered together in the older parts of the cemetery.

In the mid-1970s, when there were enough of these unusual markers to merit attention, members of the Lithuanian community commissioned a book on the St. Casimir cemetery that has to be one of the most soulful publications ever written. The copious photographs and the texts by various contributors tell the story of a unique experience in cemetery history. The moving essays written by Birute Pukeleviciute express a piercing sense of nostalgia for his homeland as well as a grudging appreciation of his adopted land, as seen in the following excerpt:

> Today, having arrived in America as immigrants, having given our energies, talents, and more than once our health, having sworn allegiance to its star-spangled banner, having sent our young men to her wars, we decorate at least the cemetery named after St. Casimir with memorials of Lithuanian tradition.
> . . .
>
> We have but one request to this land: that we be allowed at least to bury our deceased in the Lithuanian manner; that we be permitted to pour three handfuls of earth on the graves of our father, mother, brother or friend and, concluding the burial rites, to sing as was the custom in our land:
> — The Angel of the Lord announced to Mary and she begot from the Holy Spirit. . . .

Mount Olive Scandinavian Cemetery Like others from northern and Eastern Europe, Scandinavians began to emigrate in large numbers during the nineteenth century for a variety of economic and political reasons, including lack of available land and obstacles to social mobility in their home countries. By the 1860s, they could be found not only on the East Coast of America, but also in the midwestern states of Iowa, Wisconsin, Illinois, and Minnesota. During the years of mass immigration that lasted until the outbreak of World War I, more than a million Swedes emigrated, mostly to the United States. The railroad had made it possible for them to travel from their entry point in New York directly to Chicago. By 1880, nearly thirteen thousand of Chicago's half a million inhabitants had been born in Sweden. So many Swedes found farming opportunities in and around Chicago that by the early twentieth century they possessed most of the arable land in Chicago County. Other Swedish immigrants continued on to rural Illinois and Minnesota, where, after the Civil War and the Homestead Act, they had access to considerable acreage.

Still, not all Swedish Americans were farmers. Many immigrants passing through expanding cities like Chicago and Minneapolis found that the urban labor market had greater possibilities than the farm regions. This was especially true for unmarried women ready to abandon the backbreaking chores of farm life for whatever work the city had to offer, which often meant jobs as maids in private homes or seamstresses in sweatshops.

From 1870 onward, Chicago had its own Swede Town, but it did not have a Scandinavian cemetery. The earliest Swedish, Norwegian, and Danish pioneers had buried their dead in the Chicago Cemetery. When that cemetery was closed, they took over sections of Rosehill, Graceland, and Oak Woods. But in 1886, Chicago's Scandinavian churches decided it was time to establish their own cemetery, which they called Mount Olive (not to be confused with Mount Olivet).

Predominantly Lutheran and Swedish-speaking, Mount Olive's early inhabitants bear such names as Hansen, Olson, Thompson, Johnson, Bensen, Rasmussen, and Christensen. Their markers are sturdy and sober — granite slabs and draped obelisks, occasionally adorned with fern or ivy motifs. Many of them are now askew, leaning like the Tower of Pisa or already toppled from their pedestals (plate 43). Few descendants return to tidy up the graves of their ancestors, since so many early Chicagoans of Scandinavian descent have moved away. This is different from the careful maintenance of graveyards in Sweden, Norway, Denmark, and Finland, especially at Christmastime, when they sparkle under the light of countless candles.

Sections of Mount Olive have been sold to Armenians, Latvians, and, most recently, Hispanics. The Hispanic section, with its decorated tombstones and exuberant floral displays, contrasts with the understated, now untended, Scandinavian markers. Crosses and Madonnas, photos of the deceased, and sentimental epitaphs liven up the mournful grounds. We stood silently before the tombstone erected for Juana Iris, adorned with a teddy bear surrounded by a colorful display of artificial flowers. Her epitaph says it all:

WE LOVE
YOU
SADGIRL
2001

Bohemian National Cemetery Step back in time to 1876. Bohemians from Czechoslovakia are adding their numbers to the ethnic enclaves that preceded them. Chicago is beginning to recover from the tragic fire of October 8, 1871, which raged for three days, killed three hundred people, destroyed eighteen thousand buildings, and left ninety thousand people homeless. Rebuilding the city is now the work of first- and second-generation immigrants from the impoverished nations of Europe, alongside laborers pouring in from elsewhere in the United States.

Among the new immigrants, Bohemian Czechs are welcome for their skill as craftsmen, even if some of their liberal ideas are eyed with suspicion. When one of their community — a woman who considered herself a devout Catholic — is denied burial in a Roman Catholic cemetery because she had not made a confession prior to her death, leaders from Bohemian freethinking groups call for a new cemetery, one that is not under the jurisdiction of the Catholic Church. On January 7, 1877, Frantisek

Zdrubek, editor of a Bohemian-language newspaper, delivers a stirring speech that argues for a secular cemetery where any Bohemian could be buried without needing the approval of a clergyman. Twenty groups under the aegis of the Czech Slovak Protective Society buy fifty acres of land on Crawford Avenue (now Pulaski) for ten thousand dollars. The National Bohemian Cemetery becomes the burial site of choice for Chicago's secular Czech population.

Numerous red and gray granite tombstones bear the memorial portraits of men with serious mustaches and women with sober faces. Many inscriptions are written in Czech. Quite a few monuments are erected in the form of trees cut down at six or eight feet, their bark unraveling so as to leave space for a scroll-like inscription. The fallen-tree or tree-stump monuments, made from composite materials, were popular in the Midwest and the West from the 1880s to about 1905. Like the broken column and the inverted torch, they represent loss, especially when death seems to have come too early. Tree-stump monuments could be ordered from the Sears, Roebuck catalog or from local manufacturers specializing in this very American funerary art form. At the Bohemian, as in other secular-oriented burying grounds, they found a ready audience among members of fraternal organizations such as the International Order of Woodmen of the World, the Independent Order of Odd Fellows, and others who embraced the outdoor ethos of America's heartland.

In time, the cemetery housed the grave of the Bohemian community's most illustrious member — Anton Cermak (1873–1933), the thirty-fifth mayor of Chicago. Cermak was born in a village near Prague, immigrated to the United States with his family when he was one, and received only three years of elementary school education before joining his father as a coal miner in rural Illinois. In 1890, Cermak moved to Chicago and found work on the railways, which led to his own haulage business. He became active in Democratic politics, moving up the ranks from the state legislature to the Chicago City Council and eventually, in 1931, to the mayor's office. Cermak helped Franklin D. Roosevelt gain the majority of Chicago voters during the 1931 presidential election. On February 15, 1933, he appeared with Roosevelt at Belmont Park in Miami. An Italian immigrant named Giuseppe Zangara fired five shots at Roosevelt, one of which hit Cermak in the stomach. On the way to the hospital, Cermak told Roosevelt, "I'm glad it was me and not you, Mr. President." Cermak died three weeks later and was buried in National Bohemian at a funeral attended by throngs of mourners.

Long before Cermak made national history, a movement to construct a columbarium at Bohemian National was gaining momentum. (The word "columbarium" is derived from the Latin *columba*, meaning a dovecote. Like a dovecote housing pigeons in compartmentalized shelters, the columbarium houses the ashes of the deceased in separate niches.) Bohemian freethinkers were determined to declare their freedom from traditional prejudices against cremation and to establish their place among the avant-garde. It took several years to obtain agreement from the cemetery leadership; a design competition among Bohemian American architects took several more years and led to the choice of Frantisek Randak (1860?–1926).

At the cornerstone-laying ceremony, in 1915, a leading member of the Bohemian community, Dr. Iska, made this prescient remark:

> Let us remember that this building will survive us, that it will stand when those who speak our beautiful Bohemian language are probably fewer in number. And if, by the cessation of immigration and by the complete assimilation of our fourth or fifth generation into an American nation of one single language, the Bohemians should disappear in this country, this building will remain as a permanent monument to their efforts and to their Bohemian characteristics, the most marked feature of which is courage. . . .

Indeed, today visitors to the National Bohemian Columbarium encounter a world unlike any other in America. On each side of the foyer there are niches containing urns of various sizes and framed photos of the deceased. Each niche is covered over with a piece of beveled glass, giving the impression of a reliquary, but instead of a shrine to a saint, each is dedicated to one or more secular human beings — most often a husband and wife, but sometimes a single person or a whole family. We were overwhelmed by this profusion of humanity, each calling for our attention. And this was only the beginning.

In a few minutes, Bob Trospero appeared. He was the caretaker of the crematorium and, as we later learned, its cremator. He told us that a cremation was taking place right then, under our feet. How long does one take? we asked. About two and a half to three hours. Looking at his watch, he figured this one would be over in about two hours.

In the meantime, Bob answered our questions. Bodies are brought to National Bohemian by licensed funeral parlors, either for burial in the cemetery or for cremation. In either case, a coffin could be raised from the ground floor to the chapel above it, where we were standing, for the purpose of a funeral service, then lowered to the ground floor if the body was to be cremated. Bob performs about three to four hundred cremations a year, those of Hindus as well as members of other religions.

The chapel, with its eight marble columns and stained-glass windows, is decorated with the gilded insignias of all the fraternal organizations that have played a role in National Bohemian's history. Among them are the Czechoslovak Society of America, the Bohemian American Cremating Association, the Ancient Free and Accepted Masons, the Independent Order of Odd Fellows (IOOF), the Veterans of Foreign Wars, and the Knights of Pythias. Although some of these insignias are fairly common iconography — for example, the Masons' plane and compass with the G for God in the center — they take on added radiance as an ensemble illuminated by the clerestory windows. Especially striking is the IOOF, with its central eye radiating beams of light, its three interlocked rings, and the words "Honor the dead."

In addition to those of male-only organizations, emblems for two women's groups are present — the Czech Slavonic Ladies Benevolent Association and the Unity of Czech Ladies. The latter provided aid for its members as other charitable and patriotic causes. All in all, it is a dazzling array of visual signs.

But the major attractions are the niches themselves, which are located in three separate areas. The oldest section is on the reverse side of the foyer wall, to the right as you face the chapel. Opened in 1916, it was completely sold out by the 1920s. The second-oldest section is on the reverse side of the foyer wall, to the left as you face the chapel; it was erected in 1931. The newest area is the central foyer itself, which opened in 1948.

While all of the niches are set into metal frames resembling woodwork, each section has its own style reflecting the period when it was made.

The first has the flowing, ornate lines typical of art nouveau. The metal has a dark brown cast, like walnut or mahogany. On the lower rung of each frame, there is a protruding attachment suitable for holding a vase. In one of these, I saw two long-dead yellow roses with a handwritten note asking that they be placed near the remains of a particular family, whose members had died in 1931, 1951, and 1987, respectively. Someone was still thinking about them. Each niche is upholstered in puffy white satin, like the inside of a fancy casket.

The second-oldest section has a very different aura. Its silvery metal framework and angular lines express the art deco style of the 1920s and 1930s. It also has magnificent lighting fixtures hanging from the ceiling.

The foyer has somewhat smaller niches and the less decorative style that emerged after World War II. The "woodwork" made from burnished copper has a lovely patina. The niches are still covered with beveled glass, but fabric has been banished from the interior.

Words fail to express the feelings these hundreds of niches evoke in an onlooker. Each cubicle represents one or more persons reduced to the size of an urn, a small photo, or a significant object, such as a beaded flower or an ethnically dressed doll (plate 44). Many of the urns in the two older sections are minor works of art; brass and bronze containers in the shape of a sarcophagus, a mausoleum, or a book. Some have classical columns in bas-relief on their sides, statues of symbolic women, or nothing more than the name of the deceased in stark letters. Unfortunately, in the foyer containing niches from the postwar period onward, the fine art nouveau and art deco craftsmanship disappears, replaced by standardized urns that look like biscuit tins. Most of these have a wreath on the side and the name of the deceased in its center. But even here, the desire to distinguish these ashes from all the others is maintained by the photos, personal mementos, religious symbols, and ethnic emblems selected for each niche.

Helen A. Sclair, who has been studying Chicago's cemeteries for more than thirty years, sees a tendency away from nationalistic expressions and toward a greater "homogenization" of burial styles. If this is

true, we are losing unique manifestations of America's immigrant popu-
lations. Yet new foreign groups continue to bring their customs to the
graveyard, in Chicago as elsewhere in the United States. Yesterday's Bohemians and Poles, Swedes and Irish, cede territory to Latinos and Kore-
ans, to Middle Easterners and Southeast Asians, each claiming the right
to bury or cremate their dead according to rites practiced in their homelands. This is the American way: respect for plurality within a shared nation. New citizens are indeed obliged to learn the English language, as
well as a minimum of American history, yet so far there is no overarching
government policy on burial. The American flag is not a requirement at
the graveside, though many miniature flags do appear on Veterans' and
Memorial Days. As long as one adheres to state laws and the regulations
of a chosen cemetery, one can treat the grave like an extension of the
home, a small space marked with familiar words from any language and
decorated with emblems that might hang above one's bed — a crucifix, a
bird, a flower, a wheat stalk. Such symbols carved into stone suggest that
even in the graveyard, America is in no danger of becoming a homoge-
nous stew devoid of religious and ethnic flavor.

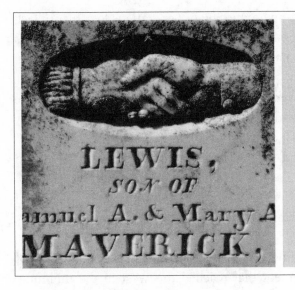

ON DECEMBER 10, 1859, an immigrant to San Antonio named Carl Guenther wrote to his mother in Germany: "Our children are growing rapidly. Fritz [the eldest] speaks very distinctly, but occasionally mixes Spanish, German and English all together." At that time, San Antonio was a polyglot city, one third Hispanic, one fourth German, one fifth Anglo-American, plus a medley of other European settlers. Little Fritz was brought up in three languages, though he spoke German at home, went to Lutheran services in German, and would be buried in San Antonio's City Cemetery Number 1 among a cluster of tombstones with German inscriptions.

A few yards away from the Guenther family plot, the young Lewis Maverick lies next to the graves of his parents and siblings. Dead in 1866 at the age of twenty-seven, he is remembered by San Antonians as the first Anglo-American born and reared in their city.

Both Fritz and Lewis were the sons of legendary San Antonio pioneers — the colossally successful miller Carl Guenther and the soldier, statesman, and entrepreneur Samuel Maverick. Each of these two immi-

Above: Farewell handshake, Lewis Maverick stone, City Cemetery No. 1, San Antonio, Texas

grants to Texas put his stamp on the city for generations to come. In fact, Maverick's "stamp," the brand he did or did not place on his cattle, was the source for the word "maverick." How did this come about? We'll get to that shortly.

The graves of the Mavericks and the Guenthers can be found in the first of thirty-one public cemeteries laid out in the eastern part of the city between 1853 and 1904, all destined to contain the remains of non-Latinos. Latinos were then, and still are, buried on the west side of the city. In essence, San Antonio has a segregated burial system patterned on its residential settlement, with Mexican Americans on one side and people of European and African descent on the other.

San Antonio's Eastside Cemeteries The Eastside cemeteries were part of the rural cemetery movement that reached the West in the mid-nineteenth century. The site chosen by the San Antonio City Council, approximately a mile and a half east of City Hall, was considered sufficiently remote to prevent contagion from the dead. Arranged in a gridlike pattern, one graveyard adjoining and even enclosing another, these rural cemeteries lack the romantic appearance of their famous eastern and midwestern counterparts. More stubble than garden, they have the feel of Texas's dry, flinty expanse.

City Cemetery Number 1, dominated by Germans and Anglos, was followed by numerous other burying grounds suitable to San Antonio's increasingly diverse residents. Between the 1860s and the 1880s, when its population grew from 8,000 to more than 20,000, new cemeteries were laid out for German Catholics (St. Joseph's), German Lutherans (St. John's), Polish Catholics (St. Michael's), Conservative Jews (Agudas Achim), and Confederate soldiers, among other designated groups. In addition, City Cemeteries Number 2 and Number 3 were opened for all comers. By 1904, when the population had reached more than 53,000, all the allotted acreage had been used up.

From the beginning, lots were donated to fraternal organizations providing for the burial of their members, such as the Masons and the Independent Order of Odd Fellows. The Knights of Pythias stated explicitly: "If a member is sick we nurse him, if he dies, we bury him, if he leaves a widow, we seek to help her; if his children are left, we try to educate them."

But since these groups were segregated by race, African Americans could not be buried with them. In the late nineteenth century, several African American fraternal organizations began to request burial grounds for their members — the Grand United Order of Odd Fellows in 1889, the San Antonio Lodge Number 1 in 1894, the United Brothers of Friendship in 1895. Some of the early black cemeteries, which were eventually neglected or abandoned, have recently been taken over for maintenance by the city.

Returning now to City Cemetery Number 1, we pick up the stories of Samuel Augustus Maverick and Carl Guenther, each a legend in San Antonio history.

Samuel Augustus Maverick The gravesite of the Maverick family is a large plot dominated by a Texan pink granite monument erected for Samuel and his wife, Mary. At their feet are the smaller tombstones of some of their ten children, five of whom died as youngsters and one, the aforementioned Lewis, who died in early adulthood. Samuel's inscription reads:

SAMUEL AUGUSTUS MAVERICK

BORN IN PENDLETON S.C.

JULY 23RD 1803

EMIGRATED TO SAN ANTONIO

EARLY IN 1834

DIED SEPT 2ND 1870

Mary's reads:

MARY ANN ADAMS

WIFE OF

SAMUEL AUGUSTUS MAVERICK

BORN IN TUSCALOOSA ALABAMA

MARCH 16TH 1818

EMIGRATED TO TEXAS IN 1838

DIED FEBRUARY 24TH 1898

An especially lovely white tombstone, with carved roses and three oval inscriptions, is dedicated to the memory of the first three children that Mary and Samuel lost to untimely deaths: Agatha (April 12, 1841–May 9, 1848), Augusta (March 30, 1843–April 12, 1849), and John Hays (February 6, 1850–July 19, 1850).

The stone erected for their eldest son, Lewis, bears a standard farewell handshake, a male hand with a buttoned cuff grasping a female hand with a pleated cuff. Lewis had enlisted in the Confederate Army during the Civil War and returned home unwell, dying shortly thereafter.

Anyone assuming that nineteenth-century parents were inured to the death of their children will be disabused of that assumption by reading Mary Maverick's memoirs. She wrote of Agatha: ". . . the poor child breathed her last at two A.M., Tuesday, May 9th, 1848. Even now, in 1880, after thirty-two years, I cannot dwell on that terrible bereavement."

Her husband, who had been away at the time of Agatha's death, was equally undone. "He went to the grave and threw himself down upon it, and remained there until it was dark. No one but God could tell the depth of his anguish. . . . He was ever after a sad changed man." From this point on, Mary was to know many other days of anguish, culminating in the death of her husband, whom she outlived by twenty-eight years.

During his lifetime, Samuel Maverick was an amazingly energetic, innovative, courageous pioneer. Having fought in the Texas revolution that produced the Republic of Texas in 1836 and later the State of Texas, he was intricately involved in the early development of San Antonio — its military defense, its legislature, its real estate, and its finance. After a battle in the heart of San Antonio, he was imprisoned for two months in Mexico by General Santa Anna's army. Accompanying his close friend Colonel Jack Hays, Maverick helped to open a shorter trade route between San Antonio and Chihuahua, Mexico. He and Mary lived through cholera epidemics and Indian raids and endured dangers that most of us have difficulty even imagining. Yet there were also the good times with their family and friends, entertaining and being entertained by some of Texas's best-known figures, including mayors and generals and other members of San Antonio's fledgling upper crust.

As for how the word "maverick" entered the English language to denote an iconoclastic person, it came about in the following manner. In 1845, a neighbor owing Samuel Maverick the sum of $1,200 paid the debt in cattle, four hundred animals at three dollars a head. Maverick was so little interested in his cattle that he was notoriously lax in branding them. Ten years after he acquired the herd, he still had only four hundred head, an unlikely number if one takes into account the many calves that must have been born. Since cattle roamed freely in those days, without fences, neighbors apparently helped themselves to the unbranded calves and put their own brands on them. In time, any unbranded calf was dubbed "one of Maverick's," and the term "maverick" came to be used not only for an unbranded calf, but also for a fiercely independent person who refused to be branded by conventional rules of behavior.

As a business deal, Maverick's cattle were not a total failure, for he sold them in 1856 at six dollars a head, thereby reaping a 100 percent profit.

Carl Hilmar Guenther The German writing on the obelisk for the Guenther family indicates an ongoing attachment to their European origins long after Carl had come to America.

CARL HILMAR
GUENTHER
GEB. MARZ 19, 1826 [BORN]
IN WEISSENFELS SACHSEN
GEST. OKT. 18, 1902 [DIED]

DOREOTHEA GUENTHER
GEBORENE PAPE [NÉE]
GEB. JAN. 8, 1840
IN GADENSTEDT HANNOVER
GEST. JUNE 14, 1898

Like the Mavericks, the Guenther parents are accompanied in death by family members, totaling five pairs that extend from the first burial in 1884 to the last in 1937. It is a solid, orderly arrangement worthy of the family progenitor, a successful German businessman whose flour mill and home — now a combination restaurant, gift shop, and museum — serve as a popular San Antonio meeting place.

Anyone interested in the early history of Texas should read Carl Guenther's letters, conveniently translated from German to English. They describe in minute detail the travails of a man determined to succeed in America after he left his native Germany in 1848, at the age of twenty-two. Always the dutiful if independent son, he wrote regularly to his parents in Weissenfels, in the Prussian province of Saxony, from travels that took him to New York, Wisconsin, New Orleans, and the far West. Working to support himself at jobs ranging from carpentry to loading cotton, he eventually made his way to the German colony of Fredricksburg, seventy miles west of San Antonio, where he built a flourishing water-powered corn mill and found himself a German-born wife. As in the case of Samuel Maverick, Guenther's wife was barely half his age — fourteen years younger — which did not prevent him from outliving her.

The Guenthers had better luck raising their children than the Mavericks; seven survived into adulthood. Perhaps this was due to the fact that the Guenthers belonged to the second generation of San Antonio residents, relocating there in 1859 when life was safer and healthier.

In his letter of December 10, 1859, to his mother, Guenther describes San Antonio as "the busiest city in Texas," its mainstay being trade carried on with Mexico. His family life was happy, even though his wife suffered from homesickness for her parents and siblings in Fredricksburg, then a five-day journey from San Antonio. Today, one can cover the seventy miles by car in little over an hour.

On March 26, 1864, Guenther refers to the Civil War as a time of "uneasiness" but without much personal suffering for his family. As a slave state, Texas had joined the Confederacy and sent many soldiers into battle. Texas Germans tended to sympathize with the Union, and to avoid conscription, many went south into Mexico.

After the war, life became more luxurious for those with means. "Every ball demands new gowns for the ladies. . . . Even I had to buy a new white satin vest, and that is very uncomfortable to wear in this heat." Guenther noted that before the war one drank local beer, but "now that is not good enough, it has to be Bremer beer; English port and ale, and, particularly, Chicago beer," as well as "every kind of wine." He himself had two ice machines, as "people want some at all times to cool themselves." And the new ice cream parlors offered the women a social hour with their friends "while the men are in the bars" (letter of July 5, 1867).

Coming from a German Lutheran background, Carl and Mary Guenther respected the traditions of their heritage — for example, they had their children baptized — but they do not seem to have practiced their religion rigorously. Carl summed up his feelings to his mother in a letter of December 15, 1867, that strikes a remarkably modern, almost ecological note.

> Having passed through so many lands, met so many different people and observed so many different religions, I have acquired a reverence for nature, whose products we are, and I contemplate my end in peace and with confidence. As nature lets nothing be wasted or lost, so I am sure we will not be entirely lost when our end comes, and whether consciously or unconsciously, we will turn up again somewhere and somehow.

Though he was to live until the age of seventy-six, Carl began to set his house in order long before his death. In 1878, he brought his sons Fritz and Arthur into his business as partners. And in a postscript to his letter of May 11, 1879, he announced: "Last week I bought a family lot in the City Cemetery." Always a man to think ahead, Carl Guenther chose a spot that to this day is shady and offers cool relief for visitors taken there on historical tours.

Castroville In the mid-nineteenth century, German-speaking enclaves could be found in several Texas settlements, and one of the most unusual exists to this day about twenty-five miles to the west of San Antonio, in the sleepy town of Castroville. Since the Castroville settlers came from Alsace, they spoke an Alsatian German dialect, which is still used for conversation among a dwindling older population.

Castroville has been described as "a French town with a German flavor growing out of Texas soil." It was French because the founder was French and most of the original settlers were from the Alsace, a region that was officially a part of France in the nineteenth century until the 1870 Franco-Prussian War. It was German because these settlers were essentially German in their language and customs. (Alsatians were obliged to change their nationality, from French to German and vice versa, five times over the course of a hundred years, depending on which country had won the most recent war.) It was Texan in that its inhabitants spoke English as well as German and grew their crops in Texan soil.

Henri Castro, a French Jew of Spanish-Portuguese stock whose family had become wealthy and prominent in southern France, was the sole mastermind behind the settlement named in his honor. An entrepreneur of international proportions, he had lived in the United States and then returned to France before conceiving the idea of bringing settlers to the Republic of Texas.

Having secured French financing and Texan land grants, Castro sent agents to selected parts of France to find willing colonizers. His first success was among the Alsatians, and though others joined the colony in due time, the Alsatians determined the character of the town.

After a sixty-six-day voyage, the first contingent arrived in the port of Galveston, Texas, in January 1843. This was followed by a grueling two-hundred-mile trek inland to the uninspiring flat-roofed village of San Antonio. There they waited, profoundly discouraged and impatient, until the autumn of 1844, when Henri Castro finally appeared to lead them to the promised land.

The early days in the colony were beset by all manner of difficulty — rain, heat, the barrenness of the land, the fear of Indian attacks, and the lack of anything resembling comfort or culture — yet these Alsatian pioneers triumphed in the new land, as had so many other Europeans in America. They built houses of logs and then of stone. They erected a tiny chapel and then a sturdy stone church. Most of all, they farmed the land, producing melons, potatoes, and corn and other vegetables. A glowing letter in the *Galveston News* of August 6, 1847, said of the Castrovillians: "It is impossible to find more industrious people than the Alsatians." Castro, who brought his wife and children to live among them, wrote to the colonists with characteristic brio:

My friends, you have justified my expectation by your patience, your courage and your labor. The continuation of your conduct assures your future, likewise that of your families. Your success is the recompense of my toil.

. . . It is at Castroville that I wish to leave my ashes, to rest eternally among you.

Unfortunately, Castro's ultimate wish was not to be realized. He was in Monterey, Mexico, at the time of his death, leaving a will dated May 1, 1864, that bequeathed his property to his son Lorenzo Castro, with the injunction that he should provide for the senior Castro's wife, Amalia. She lived in the village for another seven years, much reduced in circumstances because her husband's finances had not kept up with his expenditures. Ultimately dependent on the kindness of her neighbors, she died in San Antonio on February 28, 1871, and was buried the following afternoon in the Castroville Catholic cemetery.

Officially named in honor of Saint Louis, the Catholic cemetery was established soon after the settlers had arrived in Castroville, in 1844. Today, surrounded on two sides by a thick edging of trees and shrubbery, on the third side by a highway, and at the entry by a sturdy stone wall, it commands the full slope of an open hillside where its distinctive crosses stand out to full advantage. These are both cast iron and wrought iron, the latter rooted in the craft of Central Europe (plate 45) and transported to American settlements in western Texas, western Kansas, North Dakota, and the Great Plains by Catholics from the Alsace, Bavaria, and other parts of southern Germany. Many cast-iron markers were ordered by catalogue from foundries in St. Louis, while others were shipped to Texas from distant Europe.

Most of the early markers in the Castroville Catholic cemetery have inscriptions in German, many artfully written in the old Gothic script called fraktur. Some begin "Hier ruht" (Here lies) or "Hier ruht in Gott" (Here lies in God) and end with "Ruhe in Frieden" (Rest in peace) or "Ruhe sanft" (Rest gently). "Geboren" (Born) and "Gestorben" (Died) are often abbreviated as "Geb." and "Gest."

Sometimes the inscription is written on the cross itself or on a separate white plaque in the form of a heart. One of the few inscriptions bearing the names of both husband and wife records the union of the Haby family progenitors, whose descendants are residents of Castroville to this day.

Nicolaus und Theresia
Haby
Geboren im Elsasz,
Gestorben zu Castroville
Texas

A crucifix hangs under the inscription, and an angel's head is placed at the base. The Haby cross and several others are coated with white enamel that has invariably rusted in places, producing an exquisite two-tone pattern. Other crosses in cast iron are now entirely rusted to a rich reddish brown. Some of these have Gothic ornamentation at the ends, ogival or fleur-de-lis points that add a distinctly medieval flavor.

One of the most ingenious inscriptions follows the lines of the cross:

REST

IN

PIECE

FRANKSCHMIDT

BORN

SEPT

5

1875

DIED

JULY

18

1878

*

R. I. P.

Despite the signs of Americanization found in the use of English and the Texas star, the writer had yet to navigate the spelling traps of his new language: note "piece" instead of "peace."

Higher up on the hill, newer gravesites in gray or pink granite have gradually replaced the iron crosses so numerous below. These have their own beauty and an occasional inscription worth pondering over. One that speaks for innumerable burials, not only in Texas but throughout the world, is engraved on the slab of three Castrovillians — William Leinweber (1885–1962), Lydia Haby Leinweber (1894–1987), and Alfred Haby (1882–1932). It reads:

> REST IS THEIRS AND
> SWEET REMEMBRANCE, OURS.

Once again we are called upon to remember, as if the dead rest more peacefully when the living continue to care about them. We have come a long way from the Puritan inscription that advised the passerby to think on his (or her) own death. Now the obligation for those above ground is remembrance of those beneath the earth.

Janine Erny, the woman from Colmar who first brought Castroville to my attention, described a trip she took there in the 1990s with a group of Alsatians. She wrote that the cemetery gave them "the greatest emotional shock" and revealed the true sense of their visit. "To see engraved on the tombs the names of families and villages from our homeland was unbelievable. All of a sudden, time and space no longer existed between them and us."

Spanish Spoken Here Long before words were inscribed in German or English on Texan tombstones, the Spanish language had been introduced into the territory by missionaries from Spain and by Spanish-speaking Mexicans. In time, the Hispanic heritage would prove stronger than the German, and would rival even the Anglo culture. San Antonio's cemeteries bear witness to Spanish colonization efforts dating back to the 1700s and to the vibrant Mexican American communities that thrive there today.

Missionary Cemeteries Hispanic missionaries were the first to introduce European-type burial to the Southwest: Jesuits as early as the sixteenth century in present-day Arizona and New Mexico; Franciscans during the eighteenth and early nineteenth centuries in Texas and California.

Previously, most Native Americans in the West had led nomadic lives as hunter-gatherers, disposing of their dead wherever the tribe happened to be. But once the missions were erected, Native Americans who had converted to Catholicism were buried in the *campo santo* — the "blessed field," usually situated next to the church.

Burial under the church or inside its walls was reserved for prominent members of the white community, as evidenced by the human bones found beneath the floors of San Antonio's Franciscan missions (Mission Concepción, Mission San José, Mission San Juan, and Mission Espada). Even a royal edict of 1798 that forbade burial inside churches for reasons of public health failed to stop the practice.

Of the missions that stretch out along the San Antonio River, Mission San Juan is the only one that has preserved part of its original cemetery. Established in 1731, it flourished during its first quarter century, baptizing 847 Indians and ultimately burying 645 of them. But this early success was not to endure. By 1789, there were only 58 Indians in residence at San Juan, and by 1815, only 15. Then, in 1825, with Mexican having replaced Spanish rule, the mission was closed and its lands auctioned off.

It took the dedicated work of a French immigrant lay priest, Francis Bouchu, during the second half of the nineteenth century to bring the mission halfway back to life, and the successive efforts of the Daughters of the Republic of Texas, the San Antonio Conservation Society, and the Depression-era public works programs to complete the process. Today the much-restored Mission San Juan is under the wing of the National Park Service.

What remains of the original cemetery is only half an acre, yet on All Saints' Day and All Souls' Day, November 1 and 2, this cemetery bustles with visitors. They come to honor deceased relatives and friends, whose spirits are believed to return to earth at this time. Officially, only November 2 — a national holiday in Mexico — is called el Dia de los Muertos (the Day of the Dead), but unofficially, the triumvirate of Halloween, All Saints' Day, and All Souls' Day forms a three-day unit enthusiastically celebrated in Latino communities.

People bring offerings to their loved ones' graves, colorful arrange-

ments of freshly cut or artificial flowers and any number of sundry orna-
ments culled from Mexican, Christian, and Anglo traditions: Mexican-
type skulls and skeletons, images of Jesus and the Virgin Mary, and Halloween ghosts and jack-o'-lanterns. In recent years, to the dismay of many
proponents of Mexican culture, Catholic ritual, or both, Halloween has
grafted itself on to the other two celebrations and threatens to eclipse
them.

On November 1, 2005, San Juan's little mission cemetery was already
bursting with flowers. Family members were disposing of last year's
faded arrangements and laying out new decorations. Remembered as a
"beloved husband and father," Jesse F. Zuniga (1939–1993) had not been
forgotten. The green-and-white porcelain photo centered on his tombstone pictures him playing the accordion, and the large image of a button
accordion on the back of his stone sums up his passion for Mexican
conjunto music.

San Fernando Cemetery The minuscule San Juan Mission Cemetery of-
fered us a preview of what was to come the following day at the large San
Fernando Cemetery, the mother of all Dia de los Muertos celebrations.
Located on the west side of the city in a characteristically Mexican section,
San Fernando attracts large numbers of Latinos on November 1 and No-
vember 2.

On November 2, 2005, the cemetery is ablaze with color. Orange
and yellow marigolds, as well as chrysanthemums, roses, gladioli, carnations, and various other flowers, seem to have blossomed overnight. Ingenious displays featuring pumpkins, jack-o'-lanterns, scarecrows, ghosts,
witches, bats, skeletons, skulls, and other familiar Halloween figures
stretch out as far as the eye can see. These vie with religious images of the
Virgin Mary and Jesus, colorful pictures surrounded by crinkly paper and
ribbons mounted on crosses or hearts. Large Styrofoam letters spell out
greetings to dad, mom, grandma, grandpa, brother, sister, son, daughter,
husband, wife. It's a scene of celebration rather than mourning, inviting
the dead to join in the festivities.

By 3:00 P.M. the cemetery roads are jammed with cars, vans, and
pickup trucks. Some families settled in under trees and umbrellas to pro-

tect them from the glaring sun. Fortunately, a little breeze attenuates the heat, setting in motion the plastic skeletons hanging from several trees and activating the delicate wind chimes that are part of one elaborate display. Strains of Latino music can be heard in the distance.

Nearby, a Spanish-speaking woman surveys the basket of artificial flowers she has placed on a flat tombstone as an older woman seated on a folding chair tells her to move it a little more to the left.

Two women with walkers slowly make their way across the field, accompanied by an old man carrying a large image of Jesus and a woman cradling a can of flowers. When they all get to the designated plot, the man takes over one of the walkers, and the walker-less woman, gesticulating with her free hands, decides just where the photo and the flowers should be placed.

A little boy carrying a bouquet of roses circles impatiently as his mother, on bended knees, distributes red carnations on a tombstone.

Four children sitting on the ground take turns putting candy in a plastic jack-o'-lantern, candy they had collected from their Halloween trick-or-treat outings.

A silent man, his arms across his chest and his head bowed, stares at the profusion of flowers heaped on a newly dug grave.

Another man walks among the tombstones bearing a flowerpot in each hand (plate 46).

A Styrofoam bird, stuck in the soft earth of another fresh grave, addresses the dead with a handwritten message: "We love you Daniel Elizabeth. You live in our hearts."

A white-clad nun in calf-length garb is looking for her parents' graves. She is a member of the Salesian Sisters, a teaching order with outposts in eighty-three countries.

A policeman riding a bicycle and wearing a helmet and black Bermuda shorts circles to make sure everything is in order.

In the older part of the cemetery, which dates back to the first half of the twentieth century, there are fewer visitors and hardly any flowers. Many of the tombstones have Spanish inscriptions — "Esposo" and "Esposa" (rather than Husband and Wife) and the phrase "Recuerdo de sus hijos" (A remembrance from their children). Quite a few have black-

and-white porcelain photos of the deceased — a mustached young man or a somber matron. Among Texas Latinos, porcelain photos of the dead never completely died out, and in the past decade, they have been making a comeback, frequently in color.

When night falls, scattered candles reveal the location of a few families who are conducting all-night vigils. The parents and siblings of Mark Anthony, dead at the age of ten, are seated there with his three siblings. Four tall candles placed on the boy's bench-like marker light up a colorful display of autumn leaves, pumpkins, and scarecrows, giving off a strange orange glow (plate 47). Mark Anthony's family decorate his grave on his birthday, at Christmas (which he loved), on the Day of the Dead, and whenever the spirit moves them.

In Mexico, el Dia de los Muertos follows certain ritual patterns. Families go to the cemeteries to welcome the dead and to clean up the graves. They bring enormous picnics consisting of meat dishes, beverages, and *pan de muerto* — a sweet anise yeast bread baked in the form of a corpse with its arms folded across the chest. Gravesites and *ofrendas* (family altars) are decorated with flowers, food, drink, candles, religious icons, photos of the deceased, and a few personal mementos. People write messages to the dead, telling them how much they are still loved and missed.

Ofrendas have come across the border with the Mexicans and are now much in vogue. Whether in homes, schools, the Cathedral of San Fernando in downtown San Antonio, or in cultural centers like the Centro Cultural Aztlán in the mall directly across from San Fernando Cemetery, lavish *ofrendas* are set up in honor of specific people. Their photos, often artfully framed, are graphic reminders of their former presence on earth and their continued presence in living hearts. The goal of both *ofrendas* and cemetery displays is to evoke the memory of the dead and let them know they are not forgotten.

As far back as the Aztecs and other Meso-American civilizations, the Mexican peoples honored their dead in an annual celebration. In the Aztec calendar, this fell roughly at the end of the Gregorian month of July and the beginning of August. Skulls, symbolizing death and rebirth, were used during this month-long ritual, when the dead were believed to return to earth.

Five hundred years ago, when the Spanish conquistadors landed in what is now Mexico, they discovered this ancient ritual and tried to eliminate it. But because the ritual refused to die, they ended up appropriating it. They moved the date so that it coincided with All Saints' Day and All Souls' Day, which were already holy days in the Catholic Church. All Saints' Day was officially instituted by Pope Urban IV in the thirteenth century, though its roots can be traced back to the fourth century. All Souls' Day was established by Odile, the Abbot of Cluny, in the early eleventh century as a special day for prayers on behalf of the faithful in purgatory. Catholic doctrine expresses the belief that prayers for a soul in purgatory can help that soul make its way upward into heaven.

Spanish Church authorities in Mexico offered converts the example of their Lord, who according to Scripture had risen from the dead so as to lead His followers to eternal life. And those authorities did not prohibit the use of skulls and skeletons in popular Mexican culture. After all, these same reminders of mortality — memento mori — had been used effectively in late medieval religious art.

Today, some people don wooden skull masks called *calacas* and dance in honor of the deceased. Some eat sugar skulls that are each made with the name of the dead person on the forehead. During the Day of the Dead season, stores sell fake skulls, skeletons, and other ghoulish figures made in all manner of sizes and materials. These are generally leering creatures who seem to find death funny. From an early age, children play with these ironic corpses, caricatures of death and decay. In the words of Russian filmmaker Sergei Eisenstein, "This is Mexican defiance of death, an affirmation of the vitality of life."

There is nothing in American or European funerary culture that quite compares to the Mexican Day of the Dead. The French may flock to Père-Lachaise with pots of yellow chrysanthemums, and Tyrolean Germans may leave out cakes for the spirits returning to their former homes, but only Mexicans celebrate el Dia de los Muertos with an elemental intensity that incorporates the grotesque. For at least one day out of the year, the dead are brought back into the fold of the living as participants in humanity's ongoing tragicomedy.

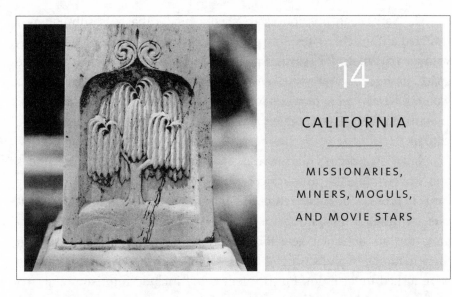

14

CALIFORNIA

MISSIONARIES, MINERS, MOGULS, AND MOVIE STARS

LIKE TEXAS, CALIFORNIA owed its first European-style cemeteries to Spanish missionaries. Between 1769 and 1823, along six hundred miles of El Camino Real (the Royal Highway) stretching from San Diego in the south to Sonoma in the north, Franciscan friars laid out a series of twenty-one churches, each with an adjoining burying ground. The wood-and-adobe structures were part of a master plan to Christianize Native Americans and strengthen Spanish rule in the Southwest. The missions attracted Indians by providing them with lodging, food, clothing, Catholic instruction, and — eventually — burial. In time, more than fifty thousand Indians living in California were baptized, and an untold number were laid to rest in mission churchyards.

Mission San Diego Cemetery The first of the missions, San Diego de Alcado, was founded in 1769 on San Diego Bay by the legendary Father Junípero Serra. For want of water, it was moved inland five years later to its present site in Old Town San Diego. There in the mission courtyard, one finds the remains of hundreds of Indians who had been converted to Catholicism.

Above: Willow tree motif, Uniontown Cemetery, Lotus, California

The San Diego mission established a model that was subsequently imitated at the other sites. The church was part of a central quadrangle, with an apartment for resident padres, visitors' rooms, kitchens, storage space, production areas, and dormitories for Indian girls and unmarried women. Nearby were quarters for soldiers and barrack-like buildings for Indian families. The cemetery was usually situated right next to the church.

Native American children and adults were expected to learn trades and work within the mission complex. In a short period of time, they came to provide the main source of labor for the mission economy. Whatever we think of this enterprise today — whether we appreciate or denigrate the missionaries' zeal for converting "savages" — it is clear that their methods of indoctrination were often coercive. Women and girls were locked up at night. Punishment could include imprisonment, the stocks, and the lash.

A report written in 1797 by the California governor attributed the chronically high mortality rates at the missions, especially among women and young children, to several causes: heavy workload, poor diet, poor sanitation, and the loss of mobility. Venereal disease was also recognized by more than one early observer as largely responsible for the appallingly high death rate of mission Indians.

When they felt death coming, many sneaked away to die in the lands of their ancestors and avoid burial in the churchyard. In these lands, they would be mourned according to age-old Indian practices. A keening or ritualized wail would rise up from the entire community. Widows or widowers would singe their hair and cover their faces with ashes. Messengers would be sent to summon distant friends and relatives to the cremation or burial. Funeral songs would urge the spirit of the deceased to go on its way "to the beautiful trail above" and leave the living alone, since their grief was intermingled with the fear that spirits could do them harm. Even when a Native American died at the mission, the other neophytes would not refrain from keening in the traditional manner.

Mission San Francisco de Asís Cemetery The sixth mission, San Francisco de Asís, popularly known as Mission Dolores, was founded on October 9, 1776. From the start, the mission was handicapped by the Bay Area's foggy climate and its lack of suitable space for agriculture. Yet despite these initial impediments, Mission Dolores has survived for more than two hundred years. Its church, completed in 1791, is the oldest building in San Francisco, and aside from the National Military Cemetery at the Presidio army base, its graveyard is the only burial ground that still remains in the city. At one time, the Mission Dolores churchyard held 5,515 graves, mostly of Native Americans, before sections of the cemetery were overrun by urbanization and the remains moved to the Holy Cross Cemetery in suburban Colma.

In 1900, San Francisco officials decided that no further burials would be allowed in the city; in 1912, they ordered all bodies to be removed; and in 1914, they sent eviction notices to urban cemeteries, branding them "A public nuisance and a menace and detriment to the health and welfare of city dwellers" (Ordinance 2597). Most of the bodies ended up south of San Francisco in the town of Colma, which was already acquiring a reputation as a repository for human remains when Mark Twain visited there in 1866. He wrote a satirical article entitled "More Cemeterial Ghastliness" (*Territorial Enterprise*, February 3, 1866), that berated the "undertaker tribe" for its heartless practices, such as charging a toll for the road that led to the Colma Lone Mountain Cemetery (later Laurel Hill). Today, the town of Colma is a virtual city of the dead, with 1.5 million deceased residents, placed in seventeen cemeteries — Catholic, Jewish, Italian, Greek Orthodox, Serbian, Japanese, and nondenominational.

At Mission Dolores, the tiny remaining churchyard still has almost two hundred tombstones, most designating people who died in the decades following the gold rush. In those years, San Francisco was a boomtown with all the problems caused by unregulated expansion, including frequent epidemics. Among the early notables buried here are Don Luis Antonio Arguello, first governor of Alta California under Mexican rule (1784–1830), and Don Francisco de Haro, first mayor of San Francisco (1792–1849).

A life-size statue of Father Junípero Serra, the man credited with founding the first nine California missions, stands in a central rose garden amid a multicultural community bearing Spanish, English, Irish,

Scottish, and Italian names (plate 48). There are exotic flowers and trees
— Canary Island palms and birds of paradise — rising up next to English
yews and Japanese maples and all manner of flora from distant countries.
It's a cemetery that doesn't seem to know whether it belongs to the North
or the South, the East or the West; or perhaps a cemetery that thinks of itself as an eclectic Garden of Eden, encompassing all regions of the world,
like San Francisco itself.

Mission Santa Barbara Cemetery Most of the missions have kept very
good records of the births, baptisms, marriages, and deaths of their converts. At Santa Barbara, founded in 1786 as the tenth mission, two regis-
ters contain data on all the Native Americans who died there between
1789 and 1872. For each death, the missionaries wrote down both the
Christian and Indian names of the deceased person; the names of the
parents and the spouse; the person's place of origin; the place and date of
death; and the last sacraments administered. Each entry was signed by
the officiating priest.

Converted Indians were buried in the small mission churchyard,
which has remained to this day much as it was in the late eighteenth
century. Burials usually took place on the day of death or on the following day. The Indian dead were wrapped in mats or blankets and interred without benefit of coffins. No headstones or markers were placed
over their graves. After the cemetery grounds were filled up, it was customary to remove the bones to a charnel house so as to make room for
new burials. This is how one visitor described the Santa Barbara setting
in 1840:

> The grounds have long since been filled. In order, however, that no
> Christian Indian may be buried in a less holy place, the bones, after
> the flesh had decayed, are exhumed and deposited in a little building
> on one corner of the premises. I entered this. Three or four cart-loads
> of skulls, ribs, spines, leg-bones, arm-bones, etc., lay in one corner.
> Beside them stood two hand-hearses with a small cross attached to
> each. About the walls hung the mould of death.

After the Mexican-American War of 1846 to 1848 and the American takeover of the Southwest, many of the missions either were abandoned or used for other purposes. Predominantly Protestant Americans were simply not interested in keeping up the missions, most of which fell into a state of neglect for the next half century.

Gold Rush Cemeteries Following the discovery of gold in 1848, tens of thousands of settlers poured into California, creating a strike-it-rich mentality that subsists to this day. Most who came did not strike it rich, but many remained as farmers, merchants, miners, carpenters, housewives, prostitutes, outlaws. Natives of New York, Virginia, Ohio, Illinois, Indiana, Maine, Vermont, Kentucky, Italy, Germany, Switzerland, Austria, England, and Ireland — to name only a few of the birthplaces mentioned on their tombstones — eventually died in California, leaving behind a heroic legacy their descendants inherited with pride.

Highway 49 (named in honor of the legendary year) runs through gold rush country like a major artery. The road leads from one small town to the next, each with its own 150-year-old history and, of course, its own burying ground. Because the terrain has changed little since the nineteenth century and many of the towns still have less than a thousand inhabitants, one can experience the feel of a bygone age (without its hardships!) and recapture the past in numerous graveyards.

Coloma: Where a Sawmill Made History The Pioneer Protestant Cemetery and the St. John's Catholic Cemetery are now part of the Marshall Gold Discovery State Historic Park at Coloma. Within what is now a state preserve covering several hundred acres, gold was discovered in January 1848 by James W. Marshall, a millwright who had been hired to construct a sawmill for Captain John Sutter and to supply the lumber necessary for Sutter's various enterprises. The sawmill in the mountains was never intended to be a permanent structure, but in time, as the secret of Marshall's discovery leaked out and spread across the continent, gold seekers invaded Coloma, and Marshall's sawmill turned out lumber to build the burgeoning village. It numbered two hundred miners and three hundred buildings by the summer of 1849 and swelled to a population of ten thousand over the next two years. From the start, the sawmill also produced lumber for coffins and grave markers.

The Coloma Pioneer Cemetery The Pioneer Cemetery contains the graves of more than six hundred individuals, with a hundred and fifty tombstones still visible. The earliest surviving tombstone reads:

EZRA SCHOOLEY
Of Ovid
Seneca Co. N.Y.
DIED
May 23, 1850
AGED
43 y'rs, 11 mo's,
And 22 days

Ezra had left his wife and nine children in his native state of New York. Like so many men irresistibly drawn to the lure of gold, he fantasized a future marked by success and wealth. He had intended to send for his family after he struck it rich. Instead, he died soon after his arrival in Coloma.

Ezra's grave, surrounded by a white picket fence, now has a new neighbor. Her very different tombstone, made of polished granite and embellished at the top with a bird, reads:

ROBIN LOUISE
MOORE
OCTOBER 8, 1961
APRIL 11, 2001
LOVING MOTHER
OF
BEN AND LOGAN

In the nineteenth century, when the average life span for a white American male was around forty, Schooley would have been considered elderly at the time of his death, but according to twenty-first-century demographics, Robin Louise Moore still had half her life before her, which makes her sons' tribute to her all the more poignant.

Despite a good number of twentieth- and even twenty-first-century graves, the Pioneer Cemetery has retained its nineteenth-century feel. Characteristically, it is situated on a hill with native trees — mostly live oak — shading the graves laid out with some semblance of order. Well-preserved plots surrounded by wrought-iron fences alternate with stones worn with age.

Some of the headstones identify the deceased as a native of a specific state or country, and even when this data isn't given, national origins can often be surmised from the names themselves; for example, Allhoff, Mahler, and Teuscher from Germany; Johnson and Rasmusson from Sweden; Vanderheyden and Veerkamp from Holland. Many potential miners came to Coloma from all over the world by various combinations of sea and land, but by the late 1850s the gold was exhausted, and twenty years after the initial discovery only two hundred residents remained in town.

Near the original tombstones stand quite a few concrete markers with brass name plates that were recently erected by the Coloma Cemetery Committee. Thus we find at the edge of the cemetery a marker for Ellen Wilson, the notorious shady lady known as Texas Ellen. Born in Canada around 1822, Ellen came to California via Texas, where she had learned the brothel trade. In Coloma, she rented a house with seven bedrooms, named it the Lone Star of Texas, and provided employment for five girls plus a bartender and a cook. In time, her place became the most elegant bawdyhouse in the central mining area. In 1852 and 1853, when Coloma experienced serious epidemics of cholera and smallpox, Ellen was exemplary in her care of the sick and dying. While she herself did not succumb to these diseases, her life was cut short by a wildly jealous man named York; he aimed his gun at a man she was dancing with but killed her instead. York fled and was never captured. Although it was not customary to bury prostitutes in consecrated ground, an exception was made for Ellen Wilson. She was given a Christian funeral and laid to rest in an unmarked grave.

A more typical death for a woman was experienced by:

HANNAH SEATER
WIFE OF
Thomas Seater
Of
Adam Co., Ill
Who died
Feb. 11, 1852
Æ 32 ys.

Hannah Seater died in childbirth along with her stillborn son, who was buried with her.

A few "Negro" residents of Coloma, brought there as slaves, were also buried in the Protestant cemetery. Rufus Morgan Burgess came by wagon train with his parents and their owners in 1849. Granted their freedom upon arrival, the Burgesses were able to purchase land near the gold discovery site, where they developed a profitable orchard. Rufus Burgess also opened a blacksmith shop. Married twice, he was laid to rest in 1900 at the age of seventy-three with both wives at his side.

Similarly, the family of Nancy and Peter Gooch were brought to Coloma as slaves. It was 1850 and California had just attained statehood. Since California had entered into the Union as a state that did not permit slavery, the Gooches were freed and then able to work independently. From the wages she earned as a cook, laundress, and seamstress for the miners, Nancy Gooch managed to buy the freedom of her only son, Andrew Monroe, and his wife, who were residents of Missouri. In 1870, the Monroes and their two sons came to Coloma and became successful fruit growers. Eventually they acquired extensive landholdings, including the mill site where James Marshall had first discovered gold.

And James Marshall, what had become of him? Marshall never made any money from his world-famous discovery, except by autographing cards for twenty-five cents each. He died in 1885, bitter and impoverished. Ironically, Andrew Monroe, former slave and subsequent owner of the celebrated mill site, dug Marshall's grave. Marshall now lies under the monument erected in his honor on the hill facing the spot where he first came upon a gold nugget.

The St. John's Catholic Cemetery The St. John's Catholic Cemetery, founded in conjunction with the Coloma Catholic Church in 1856, is much smaller than the Protestant cemetery, as one would expect. Fewer than twenty tombstones remain from the more than one hundred burials estimated within the cemetery grounds.

Immigrants from Ireland, Germany, England, and Sweden are buried there, as well as American settlers from back east. Grave number 3 contains the remains of James J. Murphy and his wife, Catherine, natives of Ireland who were married in New York in 1853 and came to California around the Horn shortly afterward. James engaged in mining and cattle ranching and lived to the age of eighty-two, dying in 1902. His wife was not so lucky. She died in 1870 at the age of fifty-six. The gravestone James erected for her is the most elaborate in this cemetery of otherwise spare, simple stones.

Another woman with the name of Murphy (no relation to James and Catherine) is buried in grave number 18. Also born in Ireland, "Mrs. Elisha Murphy" (as she appeared on the 1860 census) was a chambermaid known to have worked at the Chalmers Hotel in its early days. She managed to buy an orchard, cows, and several pieces of property in Coloma. At the time of her death, in 1894, she had amassed $2,000 in cash, which she had willed to Roman Catholic charities. The main beneficiary was the Magdalen Asylum of San Francisco, dedicated to care of "fallen women" and girls under eighteen years of age. One senses a personal story there that would be worth telling, if it were only known!

Louis Kloepfer and Elizabeth Leusbrock were born in Germany, met and married in St. Louis in 1849, and set off for California in the spring of 1852. Like so many others crossing the country in pioneer wagons, they lost an infant son along the way and buried him beside the road in Nevada. Once they arrived in California, they started another family, eventually producing seven boys and four girls. The Kloepfers share their chain-enclosed cemetery plot with the Lunemans, a family they had known since their days in St. Louis. Francis Xavier Luneman married the daughter of Louis and Elizabeth Kloepfer in 1879, and they became the parents of no fewer than fourteen children. At a time when Protestants were beginning to curb the number of their children through rudimentary methods of contraception, reducing the overall American birthrate from seven children in 1800 to roughly three and a half in 1900, Catholics were still producing very large families into the twentieth century. Eleven Lunemans and four Kloepfers are buried in grave number 17.

In aesthetic terms, the cemetery has little to recommend it. But St. John's Catholic Church downhill from the cemetery is a veritable jewel. Built in 1858 and rebuilt several times since then, it is occasionally rented by couples who want to be married in a beautiful setting evocative of California's colorful past.

Drytown City Cemetery Because most gold rush towns never grew up into full-fledged cities, most of the nineteenth-century cemeteries have remained relatively unchanged. They are sometimes the sole survivors of towns that have virtually disappeared. One of these, the Drytown City Cemetery, about an hour south of Coloma, left us with an unforgettable memory.

The cemetery is not easy to reach, even after you have spotted it from the road. But that should not dissuade the determined cemetery aficionado. First, drive to Drytown and stop at the Dry Creek Bridge. Look for a property with a NO TRESPASSING sign on the entryway. Go up to the house and inquire, nicely, if you can go through the cattle ranch to the cemetery. The owner will unlock the gate on the dirt road that leads to the graveyard, direct you through the cow pasture, and tell you, "Watch out for the rattlesnakes, and shut the gate behind you." It helps to have a rugged van as you face the longhorn cows and the rattlesnakes and inch your way to this landlocked cemetery. When you get there, remember — as you have been told — to shut the gate to the cemetery so the cows won't get in.

And there, on a small knoll, you will find the remains of Drytown's early pioneers, a handful of hopeful souls who migrated to the promised

land from the East and Midwest and even distant Europe (plate 49). Unfortunately, the promised land was not beneficent to all newcomers.

A double grave at the top of the hill tells a silent story of youthful lives
cut short.

MARY E   J HUMMELL

Wife of   Died

J HUMMELL   Nov. 9. 1851

Died   Aged 23 Years

Oct. 24. 1850

Aged 16 Yrs

1 m. & 4 days

HEAVEN IS OUR HOME

A young wife and husband, among the first to reach the gold country,
dead within months of their arrival, she still a teenager, he a few years
older. Where had they come from? Had they married precipitously somewhere in the East or Midwest and then made the arduous overland journey with a team of pioneers? What felled them at such an early age? She
in childbirth, like so many other women? He from an accident precipi-
tated by grief? Or both of them from disease? God knows the risks of in-
fection, pneumonia, and consumption, not to mention frequent outbreaks of cholera, influenza, and smallpox, were enough to slay an army.
What grieving relatives did they leave behind? Why should I feel grief for
them? And yet I do. Their unrealized lives were offerings to the gods of
adventure, progress, hope. If their faith sustained them in their times of
sorrow and if they believed they would find each other again in heaven, let
us all (believers and nonbelievers) say "Amen."

Sutter Creek Immaculate Conception Churchyard Nearby Sutter Creek
is now a small, upscale town with a picturesque church complex right in
its center. Bordering two sides of the Immaculate Conception Church,
the churchyard is exactly what one would want a small-town cemetery to
look like. Situated on a minuscule hill, it houses a bevy of well-kept graves

that pay homage to its early citizens. Most were born in Europe, mainly in Italy and Ireland, and a handful in Germany, Austria, and Poland.

Some of the Italian headstones are extremely handsome, with carefully sculpted crosses, doves carrying olive branches, and dramatic human and divine figures. Far from their native land, Italian immigrants found comfort in the familiar words — "nato," "morto," "misericordia" (born, died, divine mercy) — and artistic icons of a mortuary culture that stretched back to the Middle Ages.

Other plots pinpoint Irish origins down to the county: Dominick Burke, native of County Mayo; Catherine, beloved wife of Martin Tyrrell, native of County Cavan; and all the Mahoneys who came from County Cork. Proudly they recall their homeland, and even more proudly the birthplace of one of their American offspring. The tombstone of Johanna, daughter of Cornelius and Margaret Mahoney, proclaims, "Born May 21, 1860. Died July 3, 1888. A native of Sutter Creek Cal."

Amid all the Irish and Italians graves, one comes upon the unexpected headstone of a lone Slavic soul.

Anton

Sin   [Son of]

IVANA QUSANOVICA

Prestavise

Na 25 Maya 1882

Boze mu daj   [May God give him

Vijecni pockos   eternal peace]

Amen

One stands in wonder at this miniature pocket of multicultural America, where works of art inscribed in English, Italian, and Croatian have survived unharmed in the open for more than a hundred years.

The Cemeteries of Jackson: Protestant, Catholic, and Jewish If one had only a day or even only half a day to see pioneer cemeteries in the gold country, Jackson would be the place to go. Within walking distance of the town center (if you can walk uphill a mile or two), there is a large Protestant cemetery, a medium-size Catholic cemetery, and a tiny Jewish cemetery, all practically touching one another. They are all rich in local lore and represent the fledgling society that was taking shape in rural California during the second half of the nineteenth century.

In 1854, the town of Jackson officially recognized the public graveyard on Church Street that had been used for burials since the first miners set up camp there in 1848. It was alternately called the Jackson Protestant Cemetery, the Jackson Civic Cemetery, the Jackson Community Cemetery, and, in recent years, the Pioneer Cemetery. Soon after this Protestant cemetery was formally established, an adjacent area to the north was consecrated by Jackson's Catholic community and a small parcel to the east for Jewish burials.

Jackson was ideally situated at a ford where two forks of a small foothill creek met. Gold seekers passed through the ford heading south to the Mokelumne River sandbars or north toward any number of fabled sites along today's Highway 49. In the early 1850s, an Irish immigrant named Andrew Kennedy discovered a gold quartz outcropping one mile north of Jackson, and despite numerous setbacks, the Kennedy Gold Mine became, in time, the deepest gold mine in North America, with a shaft reaching a depth of 5,912 feet. It would continue operating until 1942, producing almost $35 million in gold by the time of its closure.

But it wasn't only the mining that drew people to Jackson. Its creek and springs, frame and brick buildings, and, above all, its rich supply of merchandise and services made Jackson a regional shopping center for the area's miners. By the turn of the century, it had about three thousand residents, including eight physicians and two dentists; three churches; three newspapers; four hotels; five boardinghouses; and several candy, cigar, and macaroni factories. Most of the residents found their permanent resting places in the three cemeteries situated on the hill.

The Jackson Protestant Cemetery What emerges from a close look at the tombstones in the Jackson Protestant Cemetery is a collective picture of early life in a California mining town. Christian to be sure, but secular as well, these early citizens of Jackson identified themselves with their families, their community, their fraternal organizations, and the natural world around them.

Compared to their Victorian counterparts in the East, they seem to have been a practical, down-to-earth lot, given less to romantic yearnings than to civic virtues. There are few crosses here, few quotations from Scripture, but many signs of social affiliations, such as the emblem of the Independent Order of Odd Fellows — three interlocking links of a chain — and the Masons' compass and plane with the G in the middle. At a time when 70 percent of American men belonged to fraternal organizations, these pioneers found in all-male groups the solidarity they needed to confront life in a rude and rugged land. There is nothing on the women's tombs to suggest a similar support system for them.

Images of flowers, ferns, ivy, and birds embellish several headstones. A handsome statue of a felled tree with carved ivy leaves wound round it is encrusted with layers of lichens in various shades of green, gray, and yellow. I had to take a second look to make sure the tree wasn't real. The monument was erected in honor of "Daniel McKay / Died Sept 29 1890 / Aged/ 57 Yrs. 7 Mos & 7 Dys / May his soul rest in peace / Native of New Brunswick." And on the side are written four lines of homey verse.

> A precious one from us has gone
> A voice we loved is stilled
> A place is vacant in our home
> Which never can be filled.

A similar sentiment is expressed on the tombstone of "Mrs. Martha A. Phelps, a native of Iowa, who died April 10th, 1883, Aged 47 Yrs 7 Mos & 26 Days."

> MOTHER, THOU
> HAST GONE FROM
> US, FOREVER, MISSED
> AND MOURNED, BUT
> NOT FORGOTTEN.
> HER CHILDREN RISE
> UP AND CALL HER
> BLESSED.

While hardly elegiac masterpieces, both inscriptions convey a plain-spoken sense of loss that would not have been wasted on their contemporaries.

The Jackson Catholic Cemetery In contrast to the Protestant cemetery, the neighboring Catholic acreage is bristling with crosses. Catholics clung tenaciously to the cross as a symbol of victory over death, although European Protestants renounced it during the Reformation, and American Protestants during the colonial period continued to view it with suspicion. In time, Protestants would reclaim the cross for cemetery usage, but never as consistently as Catholics. In the Jackson Catholic Cemetery, almost every grave is marked with a cross.

A large number of tombstone inscriptions indicate birth in a foreign country, primarily Italy, but also Austria, Ireland, France, and Spain. It is curious to come upon small enclaves of Austrians or Italians — a clustering phenomenon that has continued with various ethnic groups into our own day. In death, as in life, people form circles based on common origins, language, and customs.

By now, the most famous grave is that of Jeanne Marie Suize, born in Thônes, France, on July 14, 1824 — the day celebrated by the French for the 1789 storming of the Bastille. Known as Madame Pantalon (Mrs. Trousers), she was an early pioneer, gold mine owner, and probably California's first woman wine and brandy maker. She preferred wearing men's pants to women's dresses, although masculine attire for women was frowned upon in cities such as San Francisco. Buried in an unmarked grave in January 1892, Madame Pantalon was honored more than a century after her death with a marker offered on July 14, 2004, by the communities of Jackson and Thônes.

In both the Catholic and Protestant cemeteries there are memorials to the miners "who died August 28, 1922, in the Argonaut Mine Fire," a disaster that killed forty-seven people. Twenty-one names — all Italian — are listed in the Catholic cemetery, which says something about the continuing presence of Italian Americans in the dangerous mining industry well into the twentieth century. Nine other men of various origins were buried in the Protestant cemetery. Not incidentally, it was the Societa di Unione e Beneficenza Italiana that erected monuments to the miners in both cemeteries.

The Jackson Jewish Cemetery Separated by a service road at the bottom of the Protestant cemetery, a small, enclosed area contains Jackson's early Jewish community. The Givoth Olam (Hills of Eternity) Cemetery was founded in 1857 and served as a burying ground until 1921. Rededicated as a historic site in 1976, it is now under the jurisdiction of the Judah L. Magnes Museum in Berkeley, which oversees the maintenance of seven pioneer Jewish cemeteries in the gold country (Sonora, Mokelumne Hill, Placerville, Nevada City, Grass Valley, and Marysville, in addition to Jackson).

The Jackson Jewish cemetery contains thirty-two visible gravestones shaded by oak trees and surrounded by a wrought-iron fence. Inscriptions in English and Hebrew tell us that some of these individuals were natives of Russia, Prussia, Bohemia, and Bavaria.

A row of three headstones marks the sorrows of Mark and Fanny Levinsky, who lost three children: Rachel, stillborn, August 24, 1857; Alphonse, born October 14, 1861, died October 17, 1864; and Abraham, stillborn October 13, 1862. In keeping with traditional Jewish custom, several rocks marking the passage of visitors had been left at the graves (plate 50).

During the same years that these settlers were living and dying in Jackson, many other Jews were getting their start in nearby towns as miners, saloonkeepers, and businessmen. The tiny old Jewish cemetery in the town of Placerville bears witness to the early history of San Francisco's notable Haas family, relatives of Levi Strauss, who in the 1850s created the first blue jeans. While Strauss struggled to launch what would become an international institution, three Haas children fell victim to the diseases that were endemic in the gold country. Edmond Haas, age two months, and Lucien Haas, age five years — both children of Abraham and Henriette Haas — are buried in the Placerville Jewish cemetery. Little Nelson Haas, born in 1853, died in 1858, lies just a few feet away. A neighbor keeps her eye on this mini-graveyard at the end of a residential street, picking up the odd beer bottle and making sure that visitors treat it with respect.

Where Are the Chinese Cemeteries? Gold country cemeteries are filled with the graves of Protestants, Catholics, and Jews; Italian Americans, Irish Americans, and other European-born immigrants; and a much smaller number of African Americans — but what happened to the Chinese? Although they figured prominently in California during the gold rush years, their cemeteries are almost impossible to find. Where are the graves of some thirty-five thousand Chinese who by 1860 were gold mining in the foothills of the Sierra Nevada and the Klamath and Trinity mountains?

To begin with, most Chinese did not think of California as a permanent resting place. At least half the men had been married in China and hoped to return to their wives and families before they died. Very few women came with the men, since traditional Asian culture frowned on women leaving the land of their birth, and American immigration laws (for example, the 1875 Page Law) discouraged them from entering the United States. In 1890, forty years after the Chinese first came to America, there were fewer than 3,900 Chinese women in the country, compared with almost 104,000 Chinese men! If a Chinese man had the bad luck to die in California, he was buried "temporarily," that is, for not more than a decade. After the decomposition of his flesh, the bones were sent back to China, following the belief that his spirit would not rest until his physical remains had been interred in his ancestral village. (Interestingly, as we have seen, Africans brought to America as slaves shared similar beliefs about restless spirits buried away from their hometowns.)

A retrospective account of the Chinese procedure for reburial noted, "The first thing to be removed from the coffin was the longest bone. This was measured and a box was made of proper length, two feet wide. Each bone was then dipped in a bucket of brandy and water and polished with a stiff brush until it shone." The polishers never touched the bones with

THE AMERICAN RESTING PLACE ▪ 224

their fingers but used two sticks with the same dexterity as they used chopsticks.

Another reason for the paucity of graves is that many Chinese did not stay in the gold country after mining waned, even if they remained in America. Beginning in the 1860s, many relocated elsewhere in the West, becoming railroad workers, factory laborers, farmers, merchants, servants, cooks, and laundrymen. On the whole, they did not return to the mountains to tend the first-generation cemeteries, which quickly fell into a state of neglect.

Then in 1882 the Chinese Exclusion Act greatly curtailed immigration. This victory for racism, reenacted in various bills during the next sixty years, did not end until 1943, when Americans began to look more indulgently upon their World War II ally. Insofar as cemetery history is concerned, it wasn't until 1959 that California forbade the exclusion of Chinese and African Americans from "all-white" graveyards. By this time the mountain cemeteries had been all but forgotten.

A Chinese American cemetery in Nevada City (due north of Coloma along Highway 49) has recently been rediscovered under thick underbrush. Its boundaries and the exact number of graves are still unknown, but the general location of the cemetery on the historic New Mohawk Quart Mining Claim has been determined by three pieces of architectural evidence: an unpainted fence and gatepost; an elaborate limestone monument with a marble headstone dated 1891; and a square burner for paper money.

Funerary burners like this one were used for burning tributes to the dead — facsimiles of money, clothing, houses, and other possessions. The ritual burning of these items was supposed to make them available to spirits in the afterlife. Other hundred-year-old funerary burners have been found in the Chinese cemetery in Auburn, about seven miles north of Coloma, and in the Historic Marysville Cemetery, about forty miles north of Sacramento, as well as in other parts of California and the Pacific Northwest. These exotic objects have inspired an electronic discussion among scholars working on various aspects of overseas Chinese funerary practices. However esoteric, Chinese funerary ritual has attracted a dedicated band of researchers doggedly piecing together its history.

Southern California: Twentieth-Century Innovations Far from the gold rush mountains, Southern California has produced its own version of death and burial. In the early twentieth century, the area around Los Angeles was at the forefront of the memorial park concept, which has since influenced cemetery design throughout the nation. At the same time, the movie industry set out to produce a make-believe reality that would fulfill the hopes and fantasies of ordinary Americans. Together, cemetery designers and cinema moguls projected an optimistic vision of life and death — a happy ending from which the tragic sense of existence was resolutely banished. Death was represented as a transition to a sunny sphere where one awoke amid angels and long-departed family members.

Forest Lawn Memorial-Parks The role played by the Forest Lawn Memorial-Parks in spreading this vision cannot be underestimated. Forest Lawn Cemetery was founded in 1906 on a hillside in the town of Tropico (today's Glendale). It started out as an uninspiring site with typical granite headstones and modest shrubbery and probably would have grown with the population into a conventionally respectable graveyard were it not for the arrival, in 1912, of one Hubert Eaton, who during the next fifty years transformed Forest Lawn into the best-known cemetery in the entire United States.

Hubert Eaton came to California from Missouri with an eclectic work background and a firm belief in the life hereafter. Once he entered the cemetery business, he combined his religious faith with innovative marketing techniques to attract a broad-based, nondenominational Christian clientele.

His religious view, articulated on a huge stone wall tablet, begins with this assertion:

> I believe in a happy eternal life. . . . I therefore prayerfully resolve on this New Year's Day 1917 that I shall endeavor to build Forest Lawn as different, as unlike other cemeteries as sunshine is unlike darkness. It is to be filled with towering trees, sweeping lawns, splashing fountains, singing birds, beautiful statuary, cheerful flowers, in contrast to traditional cemeteries containing misshapen monuments and other customary signs of earthly death.

Upright headstones recalling death were to be replaced by flat bronze plaques that would not destroy the vistas of extensive green acreage. Today, looking down on the slopes striated only with metal markers, one feels the contours of the earth in its elemental splendor (plate 10).

Yet the happy-ending concept with its sweeping landscape design would not have been enough to make Forest Lawn prosper. It was Eaton's salesmanship that did the rest. Customers were offered a 10 percent discount if they would forfeit their "monument privileges"; that is, the right to erect a standing tombstone. Then there was the pay-as-you-go or pre-need sales plan, which allowed people of modest means to prepare for death ahead of time. A permanent endowment plan, the principal of which cannot be expended, appealed to financially savvy individuals concerned with perpetual care. In the 1930s, Eaton came up with an even more revolutionary idea: that of the all-purpose cemetery containing not only burial space but also a mortuary, a flower store, and a chapel situated on the cemetery grounds. Such attention to customer convenience added immeasurably to Forest Lawn's phenomenal success.

In addition, Eaton began a collection of statuary intended to enhance the landscape. Many statues were replicas of Western masterpieces, such as Michelangelo's *David* re-created from the same Carrara marble that had been used for the original. Dedicated in 1939, this sixteen-foot statue stands atop a hill in front of metal panels made especially for the site by sculptor Ermenegildo Luppi (1877–1937). Adjoining the *David* courtyard, a Garden of the Mystery of Life contains life-size statuary available for "placement as a family memorial." In this way, individuals who want something other than a flat plaque have the opportunity to commemorate themselves or their loved ones with a statue deemed appropriate to the Forest Lawn schema.

A monumental example of such statuary is found on the hillside of the Great Mausoleum (itself a replica of the *campo santo* in Genoa). Three larger-than-life groups under ogival arches represent Enduring Love, Father Love, and Family Love. Each of these academic-type clusters suggestive of biblical figures is marked at the base with the name of the family thus memorialized — Cottrill, Schmid, Witkower.

Hundreds of white marble and bronze statues are placed strategically within the confines of Forest Lawn–Glendale, as they are at its sister cemeteries established in other parts of Southern California (Long Beach, Cathedral City, Hollywood Hills, Cypress, Covina Hills, Palm Springs).

But Forest Lawn has not been without its detractors, beginning with Evelyn Waugh's savage novel *The Loved One,* in 1948. Casting his British eye on the culture of Hollywood, Waugh satirized Forest Lawn in the guise of Whispering Glen — a sanctuary for guileless Americans all too eager to deny death and accept the phony reality offered in its place. Morticians and cosmetologists passionately devoted to creating the appearance of life in the corpses entrusted to them felt the bite of Waugh's mordant wit. More than half a century after *The Loved One*'s publication, it continues to be read by those with a taste for the comically macabre.

Others in the 1940s and 1950s also found the Forest Lawn model unappealing. A 1959 *Time* magazine review of *First Step Toward Heaven,* a biography of Forest Lawn mogul Hubert Eaton (still alive at the time), was titled "Disneyland of Death." Eaton's philosophy of death was clearly too much for the reviewer, who wrote: "Forest Lawn is a cemetery in which nobody calls a spade a spade. Here the loss of life is known as 'leavetaking,' a corpse is 'the loved one' or 'the revered clay,' the dead are merely 'out of sight.'" America circa 1960, especially its heartland, took a dim view of Southern California's rosy picture of death. Yet over the next four decades, memorial parks inspired by Forest Lawn increased exponentially, and so did, with them, a further distancing of death.

Hollywood Forever The cemetery now known as Hollywood Forever is intricately connected to the movie industry. No other cemetery backs up against a movie studio (Paramount), and no other cemetery boasts a list of 135 cinema personalities interred or inurned on its grounds. With the *Hollywood Forever Official Directory* in hand, we set out in search of Marion Davies, Cecil B. DeMille, Nelson Eddy, Douglas Fairbanks, Douglas Fairbanks Jr., Peter Finch, John Huston, Peter Lorre, Adolphe Menjou, Paul Muni, Eleanor Powell, Tyrone Power, Rudolph Valentino, and Clifton Webb. We found them, and much more.

According to the *Directory,* the legendary Rudolph Valentino (1895–1926) is probably the most visited celebrity at Hollywood Forever. Following the unprecedented success of his 1921 films *The Four Horsemen of the Apocalypse* and *The Sheik*, Valentino became America's most famous silent-film star, beloved by millions of adoring fans. They were certainly unprepared to lose him when he died suddenly at the age of thirty-one from peritonitis caused by a perforated ulcer. Riots broke out in New York when more than thirty thousand people lined up in front of the funeral parlor to view his body. Thousands more, including Hollywood's most visible stars, came out to greet his remains after they had been transported by train to California and deposited in Hollywood Forever's Cathedral Mausoleum. Evidence of continued adulation exists to this day in the cut flowers placed regularly at his site, eighty years after his demise. Every August, a memorial service for Valentino is held in the Cathedral Mausoleum (plate 51).

Outdoors, in the section called the Garden of Legends, the twin sarcophagi erected for movie mogul Cecil B. DeMille (1881–1959) and his wife, Constance Adams DeMille (1874–1960), stand amid other notables. DeMille's gleaming white tomb could have served as a prop in one of the many films he directed, perhaps *The Ten Commandments* (1923 and 1956) or *Sunset Boulevard* (1952).

The monument for Marion Davies (1897–1961) is even more impressive. Constructed in white marble and bearing only the word "Douras" (Marion's true family name), the mausoleum contains her body and that of the daughter she secretly had with William Randolph Hearst, her lover for more than thirty years. It was he who masterminded her career after her 1917 film debut and kept her at his side during the gilded years of their relationship, despite his ongoing marriage to another.

The monument to matinee idol Tyrone Power (1914–1958) is a white marble bench buttressed by an upright slab in the shape of a book, with masks of comedy and tragedy on the spine. Engraved on the top of the bench is the passage from *Hamlet* that begins "There is a special providence in the fall of a sparrow," and ends with the oft-quoted lines "Good night, sweet prince: / And flights of angels sing thee to thy rest!" Three white calla lilies placed in an upright container indicated that Power still lived in an admirer's heart.

As a repository for the film industry's early elite, Hollywood Forever is a unique shrine. But during the latter part of the twentieth century, it fell into disrepair for want of endowment money. Families actually paid to have their loved ones *removed* from the cemetery. At this point, in 1998, a young mogul stepped forward and saved the property. The new owner, Tyler Cassity, invested millions of dollars for repair, improvement, and beautification, creating thousands of new outdoor spaces and mausoleum crypts. Hollywood Forever once again became a booming enterprise.

An indication of the sea change occurred on October 26, 1999, when a pink granite cylinder was dedicated to Hattie McDaniel (1895–1952). Though Hattie McDaniel had won an Academy Award for her performance as Mammy in *Gone With the Wind* (1939), she had been refused burial in the old Hollywood cemetery because she was African American. Many white cemeteries, including Forest Lawn, refused burial to blacks and Chinese Americans until 1959, when they were compelled to accept them by state law. The 1999 cenotaph honored McDaniel's wish to be with her cinematic contemporaries. Her epitaph reads:

> AUNT HATTIE. YOU ARE A CREDIT
> TO YOUR CRAFT, YOUR RACE
> AND TO YOUR FAMILY.

Another indication that Hollywood Forever is moving with the times is found in an unusual marker for two men who are still alive. A bench fashioned from pink and gray granite bears two colored ceramic photos of the not-yet-deceased:

> GENNARO ANTHONY DE VITO
> BORN: JUNE 17, 1940
> DIED:
>
> MERRILL JOHN MELTZ, JR.
> BORN: FEBRUARY 9, 1944
> DIED:

In one photo, De Vito is alone; in the other, he is pictured with Meltz. Clearly, the two men think of their relationship as a marriage, binding until death. Given the increased visibility of gay and lesbian unions, we shall probably see more same-sex couples buried together in the future.

Since its early years, Hollywood Forever has also had a significant population of regular folk, whether they were related to the film industry or not. In particular, there is a large Jewish section dating from the 1920s onward. During the last fifteen years, both Jews and Armenians from the former Soviet Union have been choosing big, highly polished black marble monuments often engraved with laser portraits of the deceased. The Armenian stones sometimes bear Armenian as well as English script, while many of the Jewish monuments are marked with the Cyrillic alphabet. As I contemplated the group of oversize Russian Jewish monuments, I thought back to those other Russian Jews squeezed together more than a hundred years ago in Atlanta's Oakland Cemetery. There the poor Russians seemed like pariahs on the edge of the German Jews. Here, as in the Jewish cemeteries in Colma, California, the Russians come across as affluent and avant-garde.

Another distinct grouping is found against the back wall. Without knowing what we were looking at, we were drawn there by the profusion of flowers, toys, pictures, scarecrows, Santa Clauses, pinwheels . . . and then it dawned on us that this was the baby section. Behind a row of miniature white picket fences lay the remains of babies, mostly Latino, whose families had heaped upon each grave tangible offerings to the child they had lost. Somehow a tradition had been established among the mourners to distinguish this section from all the rest. We thought of the expansive Babyland section at Forest Lawn, a heart-shaped enclave marked only by flat markers from the twenties, thirties, and forties. Those mourners of an earlier era had enshrouded their pain in words such as "Good night angel," "Our darlin baby," "Our precious boy," "Our darling tootsie," "Our treasure in heaven." With their parents long since gone, their babies no longer receive cut flowers and plants, which are the only kind of offering permitted at Forest Lawn. At Hollywood Forever, a different ethos prevails. Artificial flowers outnumber cut flowers twenty to one, plastic toys are piled up next to metal cars, stuffed animals, dolls — anything a child would have enjoyed. These gifts affirm the parents' connection to their offspring and, possibly, help soothe grieving hearts.

The most recent addition to the cemetery is the Thai Buddhist stupa garden located next to the Rotunda Columbarium. Stupas are upright Buddhist shrines with knobby tops; made of stone or ceramic, they are soberly unadorned or brightly decorated with geometric patterns. Here they are covered with colorful tiles and mirrors and often bear a ceramic picture of the deceased. There are three Thai Buddhas that greet visitors as they enter the garden and one large Buddha seated in a pond in the back. The sound of fountains adds to the peaceful atmosphere. Since Buddhists are usually cremated, it is geographically convenient for their ashes to be moved from the crematorium on the right side of the columbarium to the stupa garden on the left. Cremation traditionally occurs on the fourth day after death. During the first three days, Buddhist corpses remain in a temple, where ceremonies for the dead include water blessings and chanting by monks. After placement in the garden, a few yards away from Caucasian Protestants, Latino Catholics, Greek Orthodox, Armenian Christians, and Russian-born Jews, Thai Buddhists now have their own place in the neighborhood.

Hollywood Forever turned out to be wildly more interesting than we had anticipated. After a full day on its grounds, we had barely scratched the surface of its multifaceted riches. As we drove out, we spotted along the roadside the headstone for Mel Blanc (1908–1989), the voice behind Bugs Bunny, Daffy Duck, and Porky Pig. Its epitaph provided a fitting farewell: "That's all, folks."

15

WHO OWNS THE BONES?

SITES AND RITES IN HAWAII

ALL THE ISSUES INCARNATE in American cemeteries are intensified under the Hawaiian sun. The tensions between an indigenous people and their Christian colonizers, the efforts made by successive waves of immigrants to preserve their foreign customs, and the sustenance provided by various religions in the face of death — these considerations and more confront the visitor to Hawaii's burial grounds.

At the same time, Hawaiian graveyards are unlike anything found in the continental United States because the landscape and seascape are so powerfully present that they impose themselves on cemetery design and maintenance. Often, nature undermines the memorials created to honor the dead; it covers grave markers with rampant foliage and even washes tombstones out to the sea. Added to this natural undermining of man-made mementos, bulldozers have obliterated sacred sites, leaving in their wake concrete monoliths and other questionable signs of progress. Little wonder that burial grounds figure so prominently in contemporary debates about land use in Hawaii.

The oldest Hawaiian burial sites go back some fifteen hundred years, when the first Polynesians arrived from the Marquesa Islands and Tahiti. For centuries, Hawaii was isolated from would-be conquerors, but even-

Above: Hawaiian ring of stones, County Cemetery, Lahaina, Maui, Hawaii

tually, in the early nineteenth century, the islands were appropriated by Euro-Americans destined to efface many age-old practices, including traditional ways of burying the dead. Yet Native Hawaiians have not given up the struggle to preserve their heritage, and in recent years, they have enjoyed several surprising victories.

Ancient Hawaiian Burial Sites Nowhere is the clash between Polynesian and Western customs more evident than in the quarrels over ancient Hawaiian bones. These controversies erupted over human remains unearthed at two burial sites: Honokahua, on the island of Maui, and Mokapu, on the island of Oahu.

Before the arrival of white men in Hawaii, sand dunes were common repositories for corpses. Exceptions were made for the bones of chiefs and kings, which were often sequestered elsewhere, in caves or at sea or in some other hard-to-reach place where they were unlikely to be found and disturbed. At Honokahua, after some eight hundred ancient human remains had been excavated during the building of a new hotel, Hawaiian citizens staged protests and succeeded in halting construction. In time, new architectural plans were drawn up that situated the hotel farther back from the beach and allowed for the reburial of the bones more or less where they had been found. With chants, prayers, and laying of *ho-okupu* (gifts), nearly one thousand ancient Hawaiians were re-laid to rest and promised they would not be disturbed again. Today, on the beach side of the Ritz-Carlton Hotel overlooking Honokahua Bay, 13.6 acres surrounded by a hedge and segments of an ancient stone-paved spirit trail (plate 52) contain the remains of an estimated two thousand Hawaiians, dating from 850 CE to the 1800s. Registered as a state historic place, this site is now reserved exclusively for Native Hawaiian ceremonial practices.

The controversy on Oahu was even more convoluted. Fifteen hundred skeletons found in the Mokapu sand dunes at the Kaneohe Marine Corps Base were sent to the Bishop Museum for study and "safekeeping," starting in 1938. There they remained for decades, but during the passage of the Native American Grave and Burial Protection Act (NAGPRA), in 1990, various individuals and groups came forward to claim them. In 1999, the Bishop Museum drew up an agreement to give the bones to an ethnic Hawaiian group called Hui Malama Na Kapuna O Hawaii Nei, founded to care for burial sites, ancestral remains, and sacred objects.

For Europeans, who habitually lease cemetery plots for a limited time, knowing that eventually the bones will have to be removed and placed elsewhere, and for many Americans unruffled by construction over abandoned graveyards, it may be difficult to understand the passions invoked by these decaying Hawaiian remains. But for a Native Hawaiian, the bones of one's ancestors (*iwi na kapuna*) are considered sacred for eternity.

It is significant that the Hawaiian word for burial — *kanu* — is the same as the word meaning "to plant." For centuries Hawaiians believed, and some continue to believe, that ancestors were "planted" in the earth in a specific place to convey their *mana,* or spiritual power, to their descendants. The removal of bones from that spot is seen as defiance of the ancestor's wishes and augurs no good.

Charles Maxwell, a Native Hawaiian from Maui, remembers an incident from his childhood where he had no choice but to oversee the relocation of human remains from a plot where some of his ancestors had been interred.

> When I was seventeen years old, Wailuku Sugar Plantation contacted my father and asked if they could relocate eleven burials from two grave plots in the cane fields of Waikapu. My father asked me to witness the removal of the coffins and contents to the Memorial Park. My father told me that whatever was found in the grave, it was *moepu* [burial objects] and had to accompany the *iwi* [bones] because it was personal property of the family that died. Most of them had died in the 1800s and some at the turn of the century. It was amazing that most of the graves were L-shaped with the coffin lying on the bottom. The place where the ground had sunken in contained their personal belongings, including objects such as old chairs and bowls; and in two babies' graves, there were baby carriages. That was their "moepu" and had the same meaning as the ancient ki'i and other items that were found. There were twenty-dollar gold coins all fused together, watches and jewelry; and I personally saw that these items went with my kapuna [ancestors].

Maxwell's ancestors had been laid to rest with a combination of Western and Hawaiian rites: bodies were placed in separate coffins, following the Christian mode; and personal items were placed beside the deceased as a form of protection for the soul's afterlife journey, following the ancient Hawaiian mode. To separate the burial items from the bones would be, in Maxwell's words, "a spiritual and cultural slap in our faces and a denigration of what we believe."

During the congressional hearings that led to NAGPRA, the Hui Malama group stated that Native Hawaiians treasured the bones of their deceased so fervently that they sometimes found ways of "secretly exhuming the body of a beloved, removing and cleaning bones, and keeping them in a calabash in the home or near bedside when sleeping." If this sounds far-fetched, one has only to read the testimonial of David Malo, a Native Hawaiian born around 1793 who learned English, converted to Christianity, and recorded what he remembered of this venerable necrophilic practice. "Sometimes a person would secretly exhume the body of a beloved husband or wife, and remove the four leg bones and the skull, washing them in water until they were clean. They were then wrapped up and enclosed within the pillow, and the friend took them to bed with him and slept with them every night."

Malo described in detail the mortuary ceremonies that prepared the dead body for burial and protected the living from contamination by the corpse.

> The body was first cut open and the inner parts removed, and it was then filled with salt to preserve it. . . . A rope was attached to the joints of the legs and then being passed about the neck was drawn taut until the knees touched the chest. The body was then done up in a rounded shape and at once closely wrapped in *tapa* and made ready for burial.
>
> Sepulture was done at night, so that by morning the burial was accomplished. Then in the early morning all who had taken part in the burial went and bathed themselves in water, and on their return from the bath seated themselves in a row before the house where the corpse had been.
>
> The priest was then sent for to perform the ceremony of *huikala*, or

purification. . . . The *kahuna* [priest] then sprinkled the water mixed with turmeric on all the people, and the purification was accomplished, the defilement removed.

This manner of dealing with the corpse was probably restricted to *alii* (persons of high rank), as was burial in caves and other secret places known only to priests. If anyone revealed the site, the grave would have been vulnerable to robbers in search of *moepu* or, even worse, the bones themselves, for it was believed that by acquiring a person's bones, one could add their *mana* to one's own.

The core argument presented by Hui Malama at the 1990 congressional hearings was that keeping Hawaiian bones "in cardboard boxes in the basements of museums, in the private collections of grave looters and body snatchers" amounted to "past and present desecration." It took fifteen years, but finally, in 2005, the bones that had been stacked in cardboard boxes in the Bishop Museum were given to Hui Malama for reburial.

The Bishop Museum and the Hui Malama group were also involved in another major quarrel, this one referred to as Forbes Cave because the items in question were collected by district judge David Forbes in 1905. These objects — carved bowls, feather capes, tools, gourd water bottles, a game board, and other artifacts including two nude female figures made of wood — were discovered in the lava-formed chambers of a cave in Honokoa Gulch in the Kawaihae district of the Big Island, Hawaii. Since they were found near the remains of Hawaiians thought to be chiefs, they were considered *moepu* of the highest order. Purchased by the Bishop Museum in 1907, they remained in its possession until the year 2000. That year, in a decision that became a major headache for the museum, those artifacts were turned over to Hui Malama, to be reunited with the human remains in the cave where they had been found. Other groups and individuals rose up to protest this decision — why should these objects worth millions of dollars be awarded to Hui Malama just because they claimed to represent all ethnic Hawaiians?

Not everyone believed that the artifacts *should* be reburied. Why not leave them in the safekeeping of the Bishop Museum so that future generations can see them, learn from them, and be inspired by them? After seven years of rancorous litigation, the Bishop Museum recovered the contested items.

The Kawaiahao Mission Church and Cemetery The tension between Native Hawaiian and Western culture goes back more than two hundred years, to the arrival of the English explorer Captain James Cook in 1778. Cook was at first received like a god, with chants and generous offerings of food and women, but when he returned to the islands in 1779, the climate had changed. Exactly who was to blame for the disaster that ensued is still hard to determine. What is certain is that Cook lost his life at the hands of his hosts; his body was burned, and his bones removed. Some were distributed to high-ranking Hawaiian chiefs, but most were returned to Captain Clerke, co-commander of Cook's ship, the *Resolution*. A book published a few years after Cook's death described the formal delivery of these bones:

> . . . the King came on board, bringing with him two bundles of cloth, which contained the bones of their unfortunate Commander. The upper part of the skull, the scalp with the hair and the ears, the bones of the thighs, legs and arms, together with the hands. . . . In the afternoon of the next day, being Sunday the 21st of February, the whole of these sad remains were committed to the deep, with all the honours due on such an occasion.

This did not discourage subsequent explorers, traders, and adventurers from stopping at "Owhyhee" on their way to China, exchanging the coveted wares of iron, muskets, and gunpowder for the provisions that King Kamehameha I was willing to sell. But commerce with occasional traders did nothing to prepare the islanders for the white men who arrived with the intention of converting them. Between 1820 and 1848, the American Board of Commissioners for Foreign Missions of Boston sent twelve companies of Congregationalist missionaries to Hawaii. Because the board insisted that the pioneer missionaries be married, they came with their wives and intended to stay. Many of the couples had scarcely known each other before they set sail, marrying quickly so as to be allowed to join the mission. The Reverend Hiram Bingham, the newly ordained leader of the First Company, was hurriedly matched up with Sybil Moseley, a schoolmistress, and married six days before they left for Hawaii.

Along with their Bibles, their long-tailed coats, and their coverall dresses (forerunners of the Hawaiian muumuu), the missionaries brought with them Christian funerary rituals — namely, burial in churchyards under tombstones inscribed with individual names, dates of birth and death, and often some sign of their faith. When the members of the First Company arrived on the island of Oahu in March 1820, they set aside space for a cemetery on the church grounds, a two-minute walk from their homes. The impressive stone church we see today was constructed later, over a five-year period between 1837 and 1842, from fourteen thousand blocks of coral reef quarried by Native Hawaiians. But a burial ground had to be ready from the start. That consecrated space can still be found at its original location in what is now downtown Honolulu, at 553 South King Street. With real estate in that area selling for hundreds of millions of dollars, it is amazing to find so many open acres sparsely populated by three nineteenth-century houses, a church, a mausoleum, and scattered tombstones.

The small chapel-like mausoleum houses the body of the Hawaiian king Lunalilo I, notable for having been elected to office. Unfortunately, after such an auspicious beginning, he reigned for only one year, from 1873 until his untimely death in 1874. Though he could have been entombed in the Royal Mausoleum in Nu'uanu Valley, he preferred burial with his Christian brethren in the structure erected for him beside the church where his coronation had taken place. The inscription above the door of his tomb reads:

> LUNALILO
> KA MOI   [The King]
> 1874

The small cemetery behind the church reserved for pioneer missionaries and their descendants has been preserved like a sacred shrine by the Hawaiian Mission Children's Society, still an active organization. In this quiet, shady spot, the stones clustered together in family groups speak silently for the dead. Each name chiseled into a tombstone presupposes a tale of courage, commitment, and, above all, faith.

The arduous journey undertaken by the missionaries who came from New England to Oahu involved travel around Cape Horn and across the Pacific, and lasted from six to nine months. Some of the missionaries were sent even farther, to other Hawaiian islands or as far away as Micronesia and Japan. One senses the geographical reach of their lives in many of the inscriptions.

Reverend Hiram Bingham and his wife stayed in Hawaii for two decades, he the indefatigable leader of a stalwart community, she the eventual mother of seven children. They lived in a small house shared with other missionary families — as many as twenty people at a time. Although the Binghams ultimately returned to the United States because of Sybil Moseley Bingham's poor health and found their permanent resting place in New Haven at the Grove Street Cemetery, five of their children are buried in the mission cemetery. Two of them continued their parents' missionary work, as indicated on their tombstones:

ELIZABETH K. BINGHAM
DAUGHER OF REV. HIRAM AND SYBIL M. BINGHAM
BORN MARCH 8, 1829, DIED, NOV. 27, 1899
SHE WAS A TEACHER OF HAWAIIAN GIRLS
LOOKING UNTO JESUS.

Elizabeth's brother, named Hiram like his father, and his wife, Clara, are both identified as pioneer missionaries to the Gilbert Islands.

SHE LABORED 47 YEARS DOING MUCH IN PREPARING
GILBERTESE CHRISTIAN LITERATURE
SHE LED MANY TO CHRIST
1834 1903

HE LABORED 52 YEARS FOR
THEIR ENLIGHTENMENT
GIVING THEM A WRITTEN LANGUAGE
A BIBLE AND A DICTIONARY

FAITHFUL UNTO DEATH
1831 1908

Unlike most tombstone inscriptions in the past, which identified a woman only as the "wife of" or the "daughter of," these headstones credit the missionary wife or the single missionary woman for her long service. Whatever deference they paid to men during their lifetimes, these pioneer women were honored in death as missionaries, teachers, and translators.

Among the oldest cluster of stones, Elizabeth Edwards Bishop is remembered as "the first of the missionary band to enter into rest." The second wife of the Reverend Artemas Bishop, she came to the islands with him in 1823 and died five years later, at the age of thirty-one. Her husband did not join her in the grave until he had attained the venerable age of seventy-seven, in 1872. His tombstone records for posterity that he was "for fifty years a missionary and a leading translator of the Hawaiian Bible." These pioneer missionaries were the ancestors of future Bishops destined to play key roles in Oahu's commercial and cultural history.

The Castles and the Cookes are also there in impressive numbers. Amos Starr Cooke and Samuel Northrup Castle, members of the Eighth Company of missionaries, started a business together that eventually became a huge real estate empire. Since many descendants of missionary families still own large tracts of land, a common saying in Hawaii about the missionaries goes like this: "They came to do good, and they did real well." Samuel Castle's obelisk towers over the small stones of the other Castles — his wife, children, various descendants — all surrounding him like the subjects of a king. In contrast to the vertical thrust of Castle's monument, the Cooke genealogy is laid out horizontally on three very large flat slabs, starting with the progenitor, Amos Starr, and listing at least fifty other names down to the present.

It is not surprising that many of the epitaphs carry quotations from the Bible or other expressions of confidence in Jesus as Savior.

NOTHING IN MY HAND I BRING
SIMPLY TO THY CROSS I CLING.

THANKS BE TO GOD WHO GIVETH US
THE VICTORY THROUGH OUR LORD JESUS CHRIST.

BLESSED ARE THE DEAD THAT DIE IN THE LORD.
TRUSTING IN THE LORD JESUS CHRIST.

Congregation members who did not belong to missionary families are buried in the larger, minimally tended grounds situated between Church and Queen streets. Yet despite the aura of benign neglect, the air is fragrant with the scent of plumeria blossoms and the smell of the ocean. In season, huge fruit-laden mango trees tempt visitors to ignore the signs reading PLEASE DO NOT PICK MANGOS.

Many of the tombstones in this section bear Hawaiian names. One of the earliest wastes no words:

KAMOKUIKI
DIED 1840

Another that is slightly more prolix reads:

JUNIUS KAAE
SEPT 17, 1845
DIED AT HONOLULU
DEC. 19, 1906
MOE IKE KAPU   [Taboo to disturb his slumber]

Combinations of English and Hawaiian names attest to the policy of intermarriage that the missionaries condoned, at least for their men. Many a story has been passed down of beautiful Hawaiian women married to Anglo men, especially when the women were of the *alii* class.

On the whole, there are fewer religious inscriptions here than in the missionaries' cemetery, replaced instead by such matter-of-fact epitaphs as "Our work is done," "Gone home," or "At rest." But this secular tendency wavers when confronted with the death of a child. Children are remembered as beloved by Jesus, often with the much-used Scripture quote "Suffer the little children to come unto Me . . . for such is the Kingdom of God." In their belief that dead children lived in a spiritual realm where they would eventually be reunited with their families, nineteenth-century Anglo-Hawaiians were no different from seventeenth-century New England Puritans, except that Puritans were considerably more anxious about whether they would make it into the Kingdom of God.

At the far end of the cemetery, near the intersection of Queen and Punchbowl streets, a large monument carved from coral reef has been erected "In memory of our beloved friends of yester year found in unmarked graves during the excavation of Queen Street. These 102 beloved souls are committed unto Almighty God, our Heavenly Father, and their remains tenderly laid to rest in peace in this place. November 20, 1988." Conveniently, these ancient bones had been found in a street bordering the cemetery. After considerable deliberation, they were subsequently reinterred as close as possible to their original resting place, with joint Hawaiian and Christian rites.

Catholics on Oahu and Molokai The Congregationalist missionaries were not the only Christians who wanted to convert the "heathen." In the 1820s and 1830s, Roman Catholic priests from the French Order of the Congregation of the Sacred Hearts of Jesus and Mary, popularly known as the Picpus Fathers, also tried to establish a base in Hawaii. For a dozen years after their arrival, they were fiercely opposed by Protestants and by the newly baptized Queen Regent Kaahumanu and King Kamehameha III. Some Catholic missionaries were even forcibly put aboard outbound ships. But on June 17, 1839, Kamehameha III, under the threat of a French naval assault, granted Catholics the same privileges of worship afforded other Christians.

The Catholic cemetery in downtown Honolulu, at the intersection of Ward Avenue and King Street, is a comparatively small space dominated by an iron cross in the center and several giant trees in the back. In fact, one of them — a massive ficus — towers over the great cross and lends its shade to a considerable number of tombstones, like a huge protecting umbrella (plate 53).

Early Catholic missionaries are honored in two special sites. At the center of the cemetery complex, an iron cross — its base in a sad state of decay — commemorates four early bishops who served successively as

Vicars Apostolic of the Hawaiian Islands. Nearby and less obvious, a mass grave marked by a pink and gray granite stone contains the remains of the "Fathers, Brothers and Sisters of the Congregation of the Sacred Hearts of Jesus and Mary, 1850–1928."

Many of the other tombstones attest to the migration of sugar plantation workers who came from the Portuguese islands of Madeira and the Azores in the late nineteenth and early twentieth centuries. Carved names such as Viera, Souza, Dias, Oliveira, Carvalho, Medeiros, Romao, and Faria are often accompanied by porcelain photos of the deceased. A husband and wife — Manuel and Maria Pavao — stare out from youthful photos that belie their threescore years at the time of death, he at 73 and she at 76.

The prize for the most peculiar-looking stone goes to the small lava obelisk with metal inserts reading:

AQUI   [Here]

JAZ   [lies]

EMILIA

DE

ALMEI=

Was there more to come? We shall never know.

And the prize for the most unusual placement must be awarded to a white marble stone swallowed up by the roots of the giant ficus tree. Remarkably, its inscription is still readable.

Sacred to the Memory of
LOUIS PERRY
Born in Terceira Azores
Died in Honolulu, H.I.
May 5, 1892
Rest in Peace

Standing there contemplating the tree's embrace, I thought of Tennyson's reflection on a similar scene in a very different graveyard:

Old Yew, which graspest at the stones
That name the underlying dead,

Thy fibres net the dreamless head,
Thy roots are wrapped about the bones.

[From "In Memoriam"]

Indeed, whether in nineteenth-century England or Hawaii, as elsewhere throughout the world, one cannot escape the realization that nature feeds on human remains. Gravestones may be just one more fragile bulwark in our ongoing battle between being and nothingness.

Not far from the giant ficus tree, in the Buckle plot enclosed by a wrought-iron fence, there are eight white headstones, all but one (a baby's) sporting polished kukui nut leis. The names of the family progenitor, William Wahinepio Kahakuaakoi Buckle (1843–1924), and several of his descendants bear witness to proud intermarriage between Anglos and Hawaiians.

Other stones with inscriptions in Spanish perpetuate the memory of the many workers who came from the Philippines after the United States gained possession of those islands in 1898. It is one of the ironies of history that Spanish-speaking Catholics from the Pacific and Portuguese-speaking Catholics from Europe met on the Hawaiian Islands and were buried together far from their original adjacent homelands.

The most famous Catholic in Hawaiian lore is not buried on Oahu but on the island of Molokai. Father Damien, the son of a farming couple in Belgium, entered the novitiate of the Congregation of the Sacred Hearts, became a Picpus Brother in 1860, and went to Honolulu as a missionary in 1864. There, he was ordained to the priesthood at the Cathedral of Our Lady of Peace. After nine years of service on Oahu and the Big Island, he volunteered to go to the leper colony at Kalawao on the island of Molokai.

At that time, Kalawao was the home of six hundred lepers, who were isolated from the rest of the island by an impregnable mountain ridge. The Royal Board of Health provided them with supplies and food, and nothing else. Damien brought hope to the hopeless. He served as their priest, doctor, coworker, friend. Under his direction, they constructed a church, schools, homes, beds. Together they built coffins, dug graves, and buried the dead.

Though Damien himself contracted Hansen's disease (leprosy) in

1884, that did not stop him from continuing his work till the end of his life. By the time of his death, in 1889, news of his superhuman efforts had filtered beyond the colony, which then began to receive support from around the world. Father Damien was buried in the cemetery of his beloved Kalawao church, St. Philomena.

But the bones of saintly individuals do not always get to rest in peace. Because the lepers' settlement was so isolated, Damien's remains were exhumed in 1936 and sent to be reburied at Louvain, Belgium. At the time of his beatification, in 1995, a relic composed of the remains of his right hand was returned to his original grave on Molokai. The people of Kalawao were grateful for even such a small piece of their hero. Perhaps the relic will someday be moved to the altar of St. Philomena, if Father Damien's sainthood is formally approved.

Today it is possible to visit the graves in the leper colony, but you have to have exceptionally strong legs to negotiate the long, steep, sometimes treacherous descent and the arduous return climb. Failing that, you can pay the hefty expense of a commercial plane. It is definitely worth the effort, for as you stand among the outcast dead, you will surely be inspired by the man who has become the patron of lepers, people with HIV and AIDS, and the State of Hawaii.

Oahu's Civic Cemetery Whether Protestant or Catholic, the missionary cemeteries in Hawaii were designated for Christians. But what about the rest of the population — where were they to be buried? In 1844, the Oahu Cemetery in Nu'uanu Valley was established as a public graveyard open to people regardless of their faith. These would include nineteenth-century sailors set ashore during the heyday of the whaling industry, residents from the continental United States and Europe, and adventurers from all over the world. The Chinese and Japanese, who arrived in large numbers during the second half of the nineteenth century, usually established their own separate graveyards.

The Victorian-style Oahu Cemetery covers eighteen beautifully landscaped acres. A number of tombstones feature the classical motifs that became popular in the early nineteenth century. Urns — the traditional symbol of death in funerary iconography — abound in all sizes. The willow tree, a ubiquitous symbol of mourning in Western art, has also been transplanted to the tropics, at least in stone.

An elegant reproduction of an ancient Greek tombstone (stele) was commissioned by Caecilie A. Alexander in memory of her husband, John, who had taught Greek history and literature at the renowned Punahou School. The image shows John standing and bidding farewell to his seated wife, with two observers included in this mournful scene. Generally, but not always, on ancient Greek steles the dead person is the seated figure while the family members stand in positions of mourning. The newly deceased party and the mourners share a farewell handshake, the *dexios,* meaning "I give you my right hand," which encapsulates the classic Greek meaning of death. Dying was not about going to a better world — the Greeks abhorred the idea of death and a nebulous afterlife — it was about leaving this earth and especially beloved family members and friends.

Elsewhere in the cemetery there are numerous crosses, including several stunning Celtic ones, and hundreds of angels, particularly over the graves of children. Although the cemetery's dominant religion is Christian, there are members of other faiths, such as the Baha'i religious teacher Martha Root (1872–1939). A spokesperson for Baha'i beliefs, which included world unity and gender equality, Root died in Honolulu on a stopover from a two-year tour of India, Australia, and New Zealand. Her tombstone inscription, written in a beautiful Arabic script, praises "God the Most Glorious" and the Baha'i founder, Bahaullah. Members of the Baha'i faith believe that the soul separates from the body at the time of death and continues in the next world as a spiritual entity. The corpse should be wrapped in nineteen sheets of silk or cotton or, if one has limited means, a single sheet. Like Muslims and Orthodox Jews, Baha'ists prescribe burial in the ground and are opposed to cremation.

Since 1942, there has also been a Jewish section, now deeded to the nearby Temple Emanu-el. As in many other Jewish American cemeteries, the tombstones are inscribed in both English and Hebrew and are often marked with the six-pointed Jewish star.

There are many lots for secular organizations, such as the Masons, the Independent Order of Odd Fellows, and the Benevolent and Protective Order of Elks. The Knights of Pythias have two group plots, one belonging to a men's lodge and the other to a women's. In the past, such fraternal groups were extremely popular, but today their numbers have diminished, replaced by newer community organizations such as the Kiwanis and the Lions Club.

A number of plots have been provided by the Honolulu Sailors Home Society, which attends to the burials of seamen dying in the islands without family or friends. There is even a special lot for British seamen. Their headstones or cenotaphs (memorial stones) tell tales of young men perishing from accidents, illness, or simple pleasures like bathing. In the nineteenth century, it was common for sailors to purchase cenotaphs for their deceased shipmates.

Two of the most evocative sites are reserved for the Honolulu Fire Department. Since 1865, firefighters have been buried in these plots, the first marked by a fifteen-foot-high white marble obelisk, the second containing the graves of two dozen firemen killed by Japanese strafing on December 7, 1941.

For anyone interested in Hawaiian history during the last 150 years, the Oahu Cemetery offers a stone archive commemorating the lives of thirty thousand individuals. One of the most famous was Alexander Joy Cartwright Jr. (1820–1892), known as the Father of American Baseball because he established the first standard set of rules for the game. His tomb is regularly visited by baseball aficionados, who often leave tributes in the form of baseballs, bats, or gloves.

There are many fine artistic monuments, none more impressive than the bas-relief made for Walter F. Dillingham by the Brazilian sculptor Victor Brecheret. This stunning art deco masterpiece depicts the building of Hawaii's first railroad by Dillingham's father, Benjamin. Many Dillingham family members have come to rest in this plumeria-shaded grove, including Joseph Campbell (1904–1987), the noted mythology scholar, who is there by virtue of his marriage to Jean Erdman, a Dillingham relative. Campbell's tiny corner has become something of a pilgrimage site for spiritual seekers from around the world.

Hawaii Memorial Park, the Japanese Cemetery Across the road from the Oahu Cemetery is the Hawaii Memorial Park, consecrated to people of Japanese descent. In the 1880s, the first wave of plantation laborers came from Japan to the islands; by 1907, they would number approximately 144,000 and constitute a significant force in Hawaiian commercial, professional, and political life. The Japanese immigrants carried with them a preference for Buddhist cremation, but as there were no crematory facilities on the backwater plantations, many Japanese deaths entailed body burial until the turn of the century, when cremation became available in Honolulu.

Urns containing ashes are placed either in vaults below the ground, which hold up to eight urns, or in larger aboveground vaults, which hold up to fifteen. Almost all of these sites are topped with highly polished black or gray tombstones bearing the name of the deceased in both Japanese and English, the dates of birth and death, and the family crest. With their bold kanji characters, family crests, and lotus blossoms — a Buddhist symbol for eternal life — Japanese stones have an extraordinary aesthetic presence.

The Hawaii Memorial Park is notable for its two columbaria — sepulchers for cremated remains. One is a replica of an ancient Japanese temple, the other has the form of a pagoda. Unfortunately, since the cemetery has been suffering serious financial problems, there has been talk of tearing down the pagoda rather than spending a million dollars to repair it.

Japanese cemeteries receive an influx of people during the Obon season, celebrated in July and August. Family members go to the cemeteries to sweep the graves of their ancestors. They bring symbolic offerings of foods, such as rice, oranges, sake, and tea. They hang paper lanterns on the graves and burn incense to welcome the spirits. An important part of the Obon festival is dancing, which takes place outside the cemetery in Buddhist temples and community centers. Both young and old enjoy the Japanese-style dancing, with many wearing traditional kimonos.

When the Obon season comes to an end, the living place candlelit lanterns on the water to help guide the spirits back to the netherworld. Each lantern has the name of a deceased person written on it. It is a beautiful, colorful, moving ceremony that occurs in the evening after an Obon dance session. The sadness of closure is mitigated by the thought that the spirits of the dead will come back again the following year.

The Japanese in Hawaii are known for spending considerable time in cemeteries, not only during the Obon season but at other times of the year, such as Christmas, Easter, Memorial Day, and the anniversaries of births and deaths. Like the Chinese, they use their annual festival honoring the dead to strengthen their sense of community and to impart cultural traditions to the young.

Royal Mausoleum Up the hill from the Oahu and Japanese cemeteries, a splendid mausoleum contains the tombs of nineteenth-century Hawaiian royalty, from King Kamehameha II to Queen Liliuokalani. They are housed in the crypt of a churchlike building surrounded by a palm-lined circular driveway. Descending an outdoor stairway, the visitor can peep through a wrought-iron door to see the busts and feather standards of two Hawaiian sovereigns — King Kalakaua and Queen Kapiolani — whose names stand out in gold letters against the white marble wall.

Other royal tombs have been placed in the side walls, including that of Queen Liliuokalani, the last sovereign of Hawaii, deposed by an American-led coup in 1893. Hawaii was then annexed as a U.S. territory in 1898 and eventually admitted to statehood in 1959. The much benighted last queen lived until 1917, the relic of a royal family that had embraced Anglo-American Victorian society only to be betrayed by it.

Lin Yee Chung Chinese Cemetery Walking through the Spirit Gate at the entry of the Lin Yee Chung Cemetery in Manoa Valley, one enters a different world. It is a verdant knoll in the center of a beautiful valley, with pleated mountains as a backdrop and foliage made lush from frequent rain (plate 8).

This remarkable site was chosen according to the principles of feng shui, an ancient Chinese system used for laying out cities, villages, houses, buildings, and graves. Feng shui has its origins in the Taoist reverence for nature, and its practitioners aim to achieve harmony among man-made structures and the environment. They believe that a favorable feng shui locale will bring good fortune, peace, and a longer life to the inhabitants.

The dead, as well as the living, need to be situated according to feng shui because their souls are thought to be linked with the sites of their tombs. If the tombs are located favorably, the spirits will not only be happy but also will derive power from the elements — especially from the earth energy, known as chi — which they can then use to aid their descendants. The best cemetery site is a hillside that's surrounded by mountains on at least two sides and is situated near a visible body of water. The spirits of the dead should have no complaint about the locale, and if they want to follow their natural tendency to wander (as many Chinese believe they do), the Spirit Gate will keep them inside the cemetery.

The Lin Yee Chung Society was established in 1851 to accommodate the first influx of Chinese plantation workers. Its mission was to purchase burial land, preserve traditional funeral rites, and arrange for the return of bones to China whenever possible. During the next half a century, some fifty-six thousand Chinese came to Hawaii, about half of whom returned to China after their work contracts expired. When the society bought the cemetery land, it was considered a temporary resting place for the dead, since most Chinese hoped their bones would eventually be dug up and sent home. Individually and collectively, laborers and organizations saved up funds to send Chinese bones back to China, along with the boat fare for someone to accompany the package and see to it that the bones were properly reburied.

But many were not so fortunate. Instead, their bones were disinterred and placed in porcelain containers that were then stored in bone houses — separate structures on the grounds of the Lin Yee Chung Chinese Cemetery. Today, there are approximately one hundred jars, suitcases, and boxes containing bones that never made it back to the homeland.

The Lin Yee Chung Chinese Cemetery comes vibrantly alive during the monthlong Ching Ming festival, in April. Ching Ming — the Clear-Bright festival — is a Taoist observance that goes back three thousand years. In Chinese communities throughout the world, families gather at cemeteries to honor the dead. As the oldest and largest Chinese cemetery in Hawaii, Lin Yee Chung ushers in Ching Ming with a lengthy ceremony consisting of thirty-two steps, performed at the top of the knoll before the

Grand Ancestor's tomb. The Grand Ancestor was the first to be buried in the cemetery and as such is considered the common father of all who share his resting place. Nearby is a smaller altar dedicated to the Sovereign Earth Mother, representative of the female principle symbolizing the return of the body to the earth. Since the full ceremony can last an hour or more, it is usually much abbreviated at other local cemeteries.

After the communal ceremony, individuals gather around the tombstones of their family members. Unlike conventional Christian headstones, Chinese stones are placed at the feet of the corpse and face away from the grave. Typically, they are inscribed with three rows of data giving the dates of birth and death, the name of the individual, and the place of origin. In several instances, the birthplace listed was Zhong Shan, a city in Guandong Province in southern China (plate 54). Apparently, many members of the original Chinese Hawaiian community came from this area and preserved their ties even in death.

During Ching Ming, family members clean and decorate their ancestors' graves. They offer them wine, tea, and food, such as rice, fish, or meat (especially pork), roasted duck, vegetables, sweet buns, and fresh fruits. They place flowers in front of the footstone. They light candles and incense. They burn paper money, often in a chicken-wire frame. Firecrackers are set off to chase away any evil spirits that might be haunting the cemetery. And at the end of the ceremony, on the footstone they leave a special piece of red, white, and gold paper held in place with a rock. Most of the ritual items — incense, candles, grave money, and the special piece of paper — are sold together in a Ching Ming packet by vendors in Honolulu's Chinatown.

The Ching Ming rituals are rooted in an age-old belief that long-departed ancestors have a direct influence on the living. If you take proper care of your ancestors, they will take care of you. The respect you show them through offerings of food and drink is based on the assumption that the dead continue to have human needs. Even if many of today's Chinese Americans no longer believe their departed ancestors have these needs in a literal sense, they perform the Ching Ming ceremony to honor them and to impart to their children and grandchildren the notion of respect for one's elders. As one woman was quoted as saying during the 2005 Ching Ming celebration, "If they become too Americanized . . . at least they will remember their grandparents taking them to the grave on Ching Ming."

A Side Trip to Maui The dead beneath Oahu's soil — whether Native Hawaiians, Euro-Americans, Chinese, Japanese, Filipinos, or any combination thereof — have a good chance of being remembered by successive generations of descendants. On the outer islands, where no metropolis like Honolulu exists, some cemeteries have been neglected and even abandoned. The burial grounds on Maui, the second-largest island, are typical of this backcountry tendency. Curiously, they are among the most evocative to be found anywhere in the world.

On Maui's northernmost point, the remains of ancient Hawaiians have been re-interred at the burial ground of Honokahau, as discussed in the first part of this chapter. Somewhat farther south, the town of Lahaina boasts several cemeteries that recall its history as a major nineteenth-century whaling port. The nondenominational Pueheihueiki Cemetery, more than a hundred years old, is notable for its unidentified Hawaiian graves, each surrounded by a ring of bright white stones.

The Chinese/Japanese cemetery, situated right on the beach, is losing many of its graves to the surf, with the result that headstones are sometimes separated from the persons they once commemorated (plate 55), and bones often poke through the sand. Local Hawaiians come upon skull fragments in the water, which may spook them, but not enough to prevent swimming there.

The Hale Aloha Cemetery of the Episcopal Church, founded in 1863, advertises itself as "a place of serenity for all faiths." In addition to the older graves, there is now a structure for ashes, its post-office-box-like appearance much enhanced by the presence of colorful leis.

Crossing the island and traveling along the tortuous Hana coast, one discovers still more treasures, each surprising in its own way. At the St. Mary's Catholic Church cemetery, the graves are scattered between ocean and fields. Crosses made from stone, concrete, and pipe are adorned with shell and floral leis, flags, artificial flowers — everything in a state of decay, except for the horse that looked quizzically at us from beyond the lava rocks heaped together as a makeshift boundary. A squat cross incised with only the word "Aloha" captures the spirit of this place and many others in the islands.

The picturesque town of Pa'ia — itself in a time warp from the 1960s — is home to the Pa'ia Catholic Cemetery, where each of the children's graves is accompanied by a stuffed animal. Sometimes the animal is attached to the headstone by a string or shell lei; sometimes it simply stands or lies beside the headstone, as if a child had absentmindedly left it there before going to sleep. Like the miniature horses excavated from ancient Greek tombs, these stuffed animals were intended to bring comfort to dead children.

Pa'ia is also the site of the remarkable Japanese cemetery at the edge of the ocean, maintained by the Manto Kuji Sato Zen Mission. Alongside the stunning temple guarded by a huge Japanese bell, the tombstones rise silently in honor of long-departed ancestors. While most of the stones have been carved into conventional rectangles or squares, a few of the oldest are upright slabs of roughly hewn natural stone smoothed by the ocean into something resembling a gigantic thumb. Covered with lichens, they have a mysterious hoary presence, as if they were primitive beings from a mythical past. These may reflect Shinto as well as Buddhist traditions, since Shinto — the official religion of Japan, dedicated to the worship of ancestors and nature spirits — believes such spirits inhabit rocks as well as living things. All of the tombstones, except the most recent, are covered with kanji, some using the old-style system of dating from the Meiji period.

In the early years, when Japanese immigrants worked the Maui sugar cane plantations, families carefully cremated their kin and tended their burial sites. In later generations, many Japanese Hawaiians moved to metropolitan areas and took their family ashes with them, usually leaving the stones behind. Some of the stones that once stood atop Japanese urns had been piled up in a safer place to protect them from erosion by the sea. One dramatic pile, captured in a 2005 photo, was no longer there a year later, its stones having tumbled onto the sandy beach below.

The Buddhist priest and volunteers who care for the cemetery have their work cut out for them. Surprisingly, there are still occasional interments here, both cremations and non-Buddhist coffin burials.

It takes a truly adventuresome spirit to continue on the tortuous Hana coast road, but those eager to see Hawaii as it once was — with its lush vegetation and unspoiled beauty — count that trip among their most memorable excursions. At the end of their three-hour drive, many stop at the town of Kipahulu, a pilgrimage site for admirers of Charles Lindbergh. World-famous for his historic New York-to-Paris solo flight in 1927, Lindbergh chose to be buried on the Hana coast, where he had made his vacation home for many years. Knowing that he was about to die from lymphatic cancer, he spent the last weeks of his life planning his funeral. When the time came, he was dressed in simple work clothes, and his wooden coffin, built by the workers from neighboring cattle ranches, was brought to the small Congregational church in Kipahulu, established by missionaries in 1863. This spectacular setting overlooking a rocky coastline could not be more appropriate for the famed pilot, whose ledger stone inscription reads:

CHARLES A. LINDBERGH
BORN MICHIGAN 1902 DIED MAUI 1974
"If I take the wings of the morning
And dwell in the uttermost part of the sea . . ."

Made from polished Vermont granite, Lindbergh's stone is centered within an eight-foot-square plot, which is covered over with smooth ocean stones and framed by lava rocks, according to Hawaiian tradition.

While there are other graves in the churchyard that adhere to this style, several stand out from all the rest — six slabs decorated with enigmatic lichen-covered rocks. These are the graves of chimpanzees that were kept by one of the Kipahulu residents during the 1970s. According to their inscriptions, Keiki (dead in 1976 at the age of six) and the other chimpanzees were loved by all.

Surely this is one of the strangest cemeteries anywhere in the world. A major American hero shares his burial ground with chimpanzees in a nineteenth-century missionary churchyard. Even without his primate neighbors, Lindbergh is attraction enough for the many visitors who navigate the sinuous Hana road and pay him homage in the form of tropical flowers, shell leis, and face-up Lincoln pennies.

The Hana Japanese Cemetery Unlike the cemetery where Lindbergh is buried, the Japanese cemetery at Hana is known only to the locals, and it takes a hardy hiker to reach it. On a hillside trail leading down to the Red Sands Beach, a hidden cemetery is overgrown with vines and dense foliage. There are no written signs here, only the stones themselves, partially or fully buried under the encroaching jungle. Nature seems to be overtaking everything, crawling up the markers, surrounding gray stones with variegated greenery, effacing names with leaves and lichens. Here and there, Japanese characters peeping out from the underbrush reveal the carver's hand. Never was a place more eloquent in speaking for nature. It seems to be saying that whatever pride we humans take as creators and perpetuators of culture, we are nonetheless part of a vast natural order that, in the end, will claim us all (plate 56).

16

NATIONAL MILITARY CEMETERIES

BEFORE THE CIVIL WAR, American soldiers killed in battle were buried in cemeteries on or near the sites where they had fallen. No separate burial grounds existed for the military, other than those set up on army posts and frontier reservations. But the magnitude of deaths caused by the Civil War — around 620,000 soldiers by the war's end — called for a radical new solution. In 1862, Congress passed legislation "to purchase cemetery grounds . . . for soldiers who shall have died in the service of the country." By the end of the war, there were seventeen national military cemeteries stretching from Annapolis, Maryland, to Springfield, Missouri, and by 1870, after an extensive reburial program, that number had increased to seventy-three. Two that have mythical significance for Americans are Gettysburg and Arlington, established in 1863 and 1864, respectively.

Gettysburg National Cemetery No name in Civil War history is more evocative than Gettysburg, the site of a ferocious battle between 75,000 Confederate troops led by General Robert E. Lee and 90,000 members of the Union Army. It has been estimated that more than 51,000 were killed, wounded, or went missing during the savage fighting that took place on

Above: Unknown/December 7, 1941. "Punchbowl" National Memorial of the Pacific, Oahu, Hawaii

July 1, 2, and 3, 1863. Ironically, the men lost their lives on a field already called Cemetery Hill by virtue of the municipal Evergreen Cemetery at its summit, founded in 1854.

For weeks after the battle, the smell of the dead overwhelmed the nearby town of Gettysburg, not only from the corpses on the battlefield, but also from those who died in makeshift hospitals. In addition, there was the fetid odor arising from the carcasses of three to five thousand horses and mules that had been soaked with kerosene and burned. The stench of death was everywhere.

A few days after the battle, Andrew Curtin, governor of Pennsylvania, inspected the site on the battlefield where the bodies of the slain soldiers had been either hurriedly buried or not buried at all. Supported by legislators from the Northern states, he initiated the creation of a national cemetery on the hillside, and beginning in October, bodies were interred in an orderly fashion.

On November 19, 1863, before the work of reburial at Gettysburg was complete, twenty thousand individuals — government officials, veterans, and private citizens — gathered to dedicate the site to the slain Union soldiers. Edward Everett, former governor of Massachusetts, gave an oration that lasted for two exhausting hours. Then President Abraham Lincoln delivered his address in two minutes. Never has a cemetery been dedicated with such unforgettable words: "We have come to dedicate a portion of that field as a final resting place for those who here gave their lives that this nation might live." And giving a new twist to the words "dedicate" and "consecrate," Lincoln eloquently argued: "But in a larger sense, we cannot dedicate . . . we cannot consecrate . . . we cannot hallow . . . this ground. The brave men, living and dead, who struggled here, have consecrated it far above our poor power to add or detract."

The words are so familiar that many Americans know them by heart. Whenever we hear them, many of us join silently in the final resolution "that these dead shall not have died in vain; that this nation, under God, shall have a new birth of freedom, and that government of the people, by the people, for the people, shall not perish from the earth."

Lincoln took full advantage of the moment to strengthen the Union's sense of resolve after the bloody slaughter. In times of war, ordinary citizens look to their leaders for elevated discourse to give meaning to their losses. Lincoln's stirring address would have meaning not only for those then gathered at Gettysburg but for generations to come.

Like Lincoln's dedicatory remarks, the Gettysburg Cemetery design is inspirational. A column in the central space soars upward toward the statue of Liberty at its pinnacle, with figures representing War, Peace, History, and Plenty situated at its base. In front of this Soldiers' Monument, two rows of large square stones representing the eighteen Union states, the U.S. regular army, and the unknown soldiers are laid out in a semicircle. These large markers give a body count for each group.

U.S. REGULARS	NEW HAMPSHIRE
138 BODIES	49 BODIES
MARYLAND	RHODE ISLAND
22 BODIES	12 BODIES
MINNESOTA	DELAWARE
52 BODIES	15 BODIES
CONNECTICUT	WEST VIRGINIA
22 BODIES	11 BODIES
WISCONSIN	ILLINOIS
73 BODIES	6 BODIES
NEW JERSEY	UNKNOWN
78 BODIES	143 BODIES
VERMONT	
61 BODIES	

The outer row of large markers continues:

UNKNOWN	NEW YORK
425 BODIES	867 BODIES
INDIANA	MICHIGAN
80 BODIES	171 BODIES

OHIO   MAINE

131 BODIES   104 BODIES

MASSACHUSETTS   UNKNOWN

159 BODIES   411 BODIES

PENNSYLVANIA

534 BODIES

Presented in this stark manner, the small flat stones inscribed with individual names or numbers that fan out behind the group markers produce a powerful cumulative effect (plate 58). They speak for the men of eighteen different states who, despite their differences in background and accents, rallied round a national cause. They wore the uniforms of their respective states, which was how they were identified after death even when their individual names were unknown. Today, many of the visitors leave pennies, nickels, and dimes on the group markers as tribute to fallen heroes from their state. I heard one woman remark to another: "Look, we lost a hundred and seventy-one." She was from Michigan.

The Gettysburg Cemetery, we must remember, was intended for Union soldiers exclusively. This was true of all the national military cemeteries set up during the Civil War, even if Confederate soldiers were occasionally buried in them. Given the Northern officials' prohibition of Rebel burials, many Confederate dead wound up in trenches or mass graves. Sometimes Southerners themselves actively opposed burial of their heroes in cemeteries that also held Union soldiers. The residents of Marietta, Georgia, demonstrated the extremes to which such sectarianism could go. During the bloody Atlanta campaign of 1863 to 1864, a prominent Marietta citizen offered a few acres of land for the burial of both Union and Confederate soldiers. However, most of the good people of Marietta did not want Confederate dead to be buried near Yankee dead, so they established the separate Marietta Confederate Cemetery.

During the hostilities, federal monies were allocated to dig, mark, and tend Union graves and, following the war, to locate and rebury Union soldiers from the all-too-numerous battlefields. By 1870, more than 90 percent of the Union casualties — 45 percent of whom were unidentified —

were interred in national cemeteries, army post cemeteries, or private plots.

Such was not the case for Rebel soldiers. Given the demise of the Confederate government and the absence of a central agency, search-and-recovery efforts fell primarily into private hands. Tales told by Southern visitors to Gettysburg after the battle indicated that many of the Confederate bodies were lying in surrounding pastures used for farming, and that soon all traces of them would be gone.

In 1871, an official report shocked the South into action. The investigator claimed that by following a trail of bones "which had been ploughed up and now lay strewn about the surface," he had found the trench where the men of General George Pickett's famed division were lying. Subsequently, a massive reburial effort was undertaken to return the Gettysburg dead to the South. Virginia claimed the largest number of corpses, collecting roughly three thousand during 1872. These were re-interred in the Confederate section of Richmond's Hollywood Cemetery, where Jefferson Davis — the Confederate leader — would also be reburied, in 1893, four years after his first interment in New Orleans. Hollywood Cemetery was already known as the South's premier resting place because it harbored two deceased American presidents — James Monroe (1758–1831) and John Tyler (1790–1862).

During the Reconstruction period, when Union and Confederate soldiers were still being identified and reburied in proper cemeteries, the animosity between the North and the South spread to their respective graveyards. As shrines for Union soldiers, national military cemeteries were largely unconcerned with the Confederate dead — indeed, many Northerners continued to feel that Rebels should not share common ground with those who had died to preserve the Union. Southerners, too, wanted to make sure their heroes did not lie alongside "the enemy." Not until President William McKinley in the final years of the century took the lead in spearheading a space for Confederate dead in Arlington National Cemetery would these tensions be resolved.

Arlington National Cemetery Arlington National Cemetery is much more than the final resting place of American servicepersons and their families. It is a national icon meant to inspire feelings of patriotism and pride, even in times of profound sorrow and mourning. When we hear the words "Arlington Cemetery," we think of the massive marble Tomb of the Unknown Soldier or the eternal flame burning over the grave of President John F. Kennedy or the rolling green slopes covered by thousands of white headstones, lined up like soldiers standing at attention (plate 57). Arlington is an integral part of our heritage because it honors those who have been willing to give their lives in defense of their country or who have served as outstanding national leaders. More than 368,000 veterans and their family members, two presidents, eight chief justices, and many other dignitaries have been laid to rest in this bucolic Virginia setting, where around thirty burials are still conducted every weekday. There is no other place like it in the United States.

Two hundred years ago, the 624 acres that now comprise Arlington Cemetery were mostly virgin forest. The property was acquired in the early nineteenth century by George Washington Parke Custis, grandson of America's first president (in the line descending from Martha Washington's first marriage). Between 1802 and 1818, Custis, his slaves, and hired craftsmen built the home known as Arlington House that still stands atop the hill overlooking the Potomac River and the nation's capital.

Custis's daughter, Mary Anna, married Lieutenant Robert E. Lee at Arlington House in 1831, and they spent much of their married life traveling between army posts and the plantation. The Civil War changed everything. When Virginia seceded from the Union in 1861, Lee resigned from the U.S. Army and took command of the Confederate Army of Northern Virginia, a position he filled until the defeat of the Confederacy, in 1865.

After the war, Lee could not go back to Arlington, since it had been confiscated by the Union Army. In 1863, part of the property had been used to resettle African American freed people, including — ironically — some of Lee's former slaves. When some of them died, they were buried haphazardly on the grounds alongside white Union soldiers, as well as hundreds of Confederate prisoners of war who had perished in Union hospitals.

Official use of Arlington as a national military cemetery began in

June 1864. The first sixteen thousand graves, many from General Ulysses S. Grant's Richmond campaign, were dug directly behind Arlington House on forestland cut down by Union soldiers. Paradoxically, the creation of the national cemetery resulted in racial segregation: white people were interred on the heights, while African Americans — both soldiers and civilians — remained at the northeast corner of the estate, which was also the section where many of the Confederate dead were buried.

When the hostilities had finally ceased, this arrangement came under heavy criticism. Black leaders in Washington requested "the removal of the remains of all loyal soldiers now interred in the north end of the Arlington cemetery, among paupers and rebels, to the main body of the grounds." Southerners, too, were dissatisfied with the location of the Confederate graves and the lack of respect shown their heroes.

The continuing divide between the North and the South as well as the tensions between blacks and whites were galvanized by the postwar celebration first known as Decoration Day, then as Memorial Day. Memorial Day was officially proclaimed on May 5, 1868, as a day of remembrance to honor the Civil War dead, and first celebrated at Arlington on May 30, 1868, with flowers placed on both Union and Confederate graves. The South refused to acknowledge the holiday and honored their dead on different days until after World War I, at which point Memorial Day began to honor not only Civil War victims but all military personnel who died fighting in every American war.

Today, Arlington is not the largest national cemetery — Calverton National Cemetery in New York has more acres and buries about fifty servicemen a day, as compared to Arlington's thirty — but it is certainly the best known. It is the only one to use horse-drawn caissons as a routine part of its burials. Arlington superintendent John Metzler, whose father was an earlier superintendent, sees to it that full-honors funerals are conducted with one-of-a-kind treatment, despite the large number of burials and the limited space; the cemetery is now available only to long-serving servicepersons, highly decorated veterans, and soldiers who have died on active duty. The new Section 60 receives the bodies of those killed in Iraq and Afghanistan.

Since the late 1950s, on the Thursday before Memorial Day, twelve hundred soldiers of the Third Infantry Division of the U.S. Army place small American flags at each of the gravestones. Then they patrol twenty-four hours a day during the weekend to ensure that each flag remains standing.

Arlington's large Memorial Amphitheatre, bedecked with flags and wreaths, is the setting for other observances where leaders pay tribute to America's servicemen and servicewomen. Nearby, visitors gather around the Tomb of the Unknown Soldier, not only on Memorial Day but 365 days of the year. Here a sentinel from the Third Infantry maintains an around-the-clock vigil. The sentinel paces twenty-one steps down the mat before the tomb, pauses twenty-one seconds, and returns. The changing of the guard takes place every half-hour. "Here rests in honored glory an American soldier known but to God," reads the inscription on the Tomb of the Unknown Soldier, which was erected in 1921 as a tribute to all the unidentified fallen soldiers of World War I. Since then, unknown servicemen from World War II and the Korean War have been placed in crypts beneath the terrace paving, which accounts for the change of name to Tomb of the Unknowns.

National military cemeteries created because of the Civil War were not limited to the mid-Atlantic and southern states, where most of the battles took place. Military cemeteries were also established in the Midwest and the West, sometimes near a prisoner-of-war camp or a hospital in which soldiers from both sides had perished.

For example, the Crown Hill National Cemetery in Indianapolis, founded in 1864, was used to re-inter Union soldiers who had died in the city's hospitals and who had initially been buried in the city cemetery. A 1.4-acre site of gently sloping hillside was purchased by the U.S. government for $5,000 from the privately owned Crown Hill Cemetery, thus creating a cemetery within a cemetery. The encompassing Crown Hill Cemetery was to become Indianapolis's premium resting place, with such celebrated residents as U.S. president Benjamin Harrison (1833–1901); poet James Whitcomb Riley (1849–1916); and novelist Booth Tarkington

(1869–1946). The small military cemetery received 707 Union soldiers, each grave marked by a painted wooden headboard that was later replaced by a marble headstone. Confederate dead from the Camp Morton prisoner-of-war camp north of Indianapolis were also moved to the Crown Hill National Cemetery, but unlike the Union soldiers, the Rebels were deposited in a mass grave. Today, there are 2,135 soldiers on the grounds, representing every war since the Civil War: the Spanish-American War, World War I, World War II, and the Vietnam War, among others.

Each new war required new cemeteries. Now established throughout the nation, and some abroad, all bear witness to America's traumatic military history.

Custer National Cemetery The site of Custer's Last Stand, in southeastern Montana, is one of the legendary locales. It was here at the Battle of the Little Big Horn on June 25 to June 26, 1876, that the flamboyant U.S. cavalry officer George Armstrong Custer was killed, along with five companies of the Seventh Cavalry under his command. The victors were bands of Sioux and Cheyenne Indians led by such warriors as Crazy Horse and Lame White Man. The great chief Sitting Bull, too aged to fight, protected noncombatants in the Indian village. In Custer's eagerness to take the enemy by surprise, and perhaps to enhance his own personal glory, he began the attack the afternoon of June 25, despite the fact that a second column of troops was scheduled to join him the next morning. Instead of waiting, he led more than two hundred men into what proved to be a spectacular slaughter. Four miles away, the other Seventh Cavalry companies survived two days of combat and would bury the Custer dead on June 28, 1876.

Burial of the bodies — decomposing, bloated, mutilated — was a gruesome ordeal. With only a few spades at their disposal, the living covered the dead with a few shovelfuls of dirt. An exemplary burial was given Custer, only eighteen inches deep but six feet long. His name was written on a piece of paper and placed into a spent cartridge, which was then pounded into the head of a wooden stake for later identification. All the officers received a stake with a name, but none — except George's brother, Tom — received as good a burial as their commanding officer.

The enlisted men under Custer were essentially left exposed to the elements. Afterward, Colonel John Gibbon recorded that "dotted about on the ground in all directions are little mounds of freshly turned earth showing where each brave soldier sleeps his last sleep."

When the soldiers left, the wolves and coyotes took over. Eventually the battlefield was strewn with the gleaming bones of cavalry soldiers and their horses. Although some of the horses survived the battle, only one of them — Comanche — became famous; for years after, he appeared at Seventh Cavalry parades, always without a rider.

Despite the fact that Custer — a Civil War hero and renowned Indian fighter — could have been held responsible for the carnage, the cemetery was named in his honor. On an official visit to the site three years later, Captain George Sanderson and the Eleventh Infantry reburied all the horse and human bones that had subsequently been unearthed.

Another reburial of the Seventh Cavalry remains took place in 1881, when a permanent granite monument was placed at the site. First Lieutenant Charles F. Roe of the Second Cavalry expressed his satisfaction in an official report: "I feel confident all the remains are gathered together and placed at base of monument, stone put immediately on top of remains, and then earth, so that now they are well buried and will never be exposed again." In addition, so that future visitors would have a better understanding of the battle, Roe planted stakes in the ground "where the men actually fell." Those stakes were replaced in 1890 by marble markers. At that time additional remains were found on the battlefield, and a century later, during the archaeological digs of 1984 to 1985, still more bones turned up.

Fast forward to the late twentieth century for a sea change in the American mentality. The Indian victors of Little Big Horn are no longer seen as vicious enemies. Their rights and dignity are acknowledged in a 1991 bill, signed into law by the first President Bush, stating, "The public interest will best be served by establishing a memorial . . . to honor and recognize the Indians who fought to preserve their land and culture." The new, striking memorials in wrought iron and stone at Little Big Horn belatedly legitimize the claims of the Sioux and Cheyenne, who triumphed in the historic battle even if they eventually lost the war. Custer himself had long been re-interred, at his widow's request, in the West Point Cemetery.

Overseas Military Cemeteries Like Gettysburg and Little Big Horn, most early military cemeteries were laid out on American soil, either on the battlefield itself or near it. Yet even before the Civil War, some soldiers were buried abroad in land set aside for American military personnel. The oldest of these is in Mexico City. Established in 1851, it contains the graves of soldiers who lost their lives in the Mexican-American War and, specifically, the battle for Mexico City that took place between September 8 and 15, 1847. More than a thousand identified and unidentified soldiers lie in this two-acre site.

At the time of the Mexican-American War, it would have been unthinkable to imagine the enormous numbers of American servicemen and -women who would die in Europe and the Pacific during the two World Wars. Many found their final resting places in American military cemeteries in France, Germany, Italy, England, Belgium, and Holland. One of the most famous is the World War I cemetery in Waregem, Belgium, known as Flanders Field. Generations of schoolchildren once knew by heart the following poem written by Major John McCrae (1872–1918):

In Flanders fields the poppies blow
Between the crosses row on row,
That mark our place; and in the sky
The larks, still bravely singing, fly
Scarce heard amid the guns below.

We are the Dead. Short days ago
We lived, felt dawn, saw sunset glow,
Loved and were loved, and now we lie
In Flanders fields.

Take up our quarrel with the foe:
To you from failing hands we throw
The torch; be yours to hold it high.
If ye break faith with us who die

We shall not sleep, though poppies grow
In Flanders fields.

The Americans slumbering here lost their lives in 1918 as part of a multinational effort to force the Germans out of Belgium. After the armistice was declared on November 11, a grateful Belgium granted America these six acres for use as a permanent cemetery, free of charge and without taxation.

Today, the best-known overseas military cemeteries are undoubtedly those connected with the World War II Normandy Beach landing of June 6, 1944, especially the huge 172.5-acre Normandy American Cemetery at St.-Laurent-sur-Mer, France, also known as the Omaha Beach Cemetery. On the first day of the invasion — referred to as D-day — Utah Beach was taken with relatively few casualties, but nearby Omaha Beach, with its steep bluffs and heavily fortified German defense, turned into the worst possible nightmare. There were 2,400 casualties on Omaha Beach on D-day, most in the first few hours, though eventually the beach was taken by the Allies.

Americans slain at both Utah and Omaha were buried in temporary graveyards until their next of kin requested either return of the body to the United States or permanent interment overseas. The American Battle Monuments Commission repatriated approximately 60 percent of military remains, with the rest re-interred in two main cemeteries — one in Normandy at St.-Laurent-sur-Mer and the other in Brittany at St. James, Manche. At the Normandy cemetery, a viewing platform overlooks the former bloody battlefield, now a peaceful beach bombarded only by the Atlantic winds.

The Normandy cemetery has 9,387 burials, including 307 unknown servicemen, 33 pairs of brothers buried side by side, and 4 women. It is the largest World War II overseas cemetery, but not the largest American military cemetery in Europe; the Meuse-Argonne American Cemetery from World War I contains more than 14,000 burials.

Over the past decades, hordes of Americans have visited the military cemeteries in Europe. Often, they are returning veterans retracing the routes they had taken through France, the Lowlands, and Germany. They stop at the cemeteries to remember their slain comrades. Before the rows and rows of white crosses, punctuated occasionally with a Jewish star, they experience anew the pain and pride of soldiers who magnificently defended their country and their country's beleaguered allies.

National Memorial Cemetery of the Pacific Far from the fields of Europe, on the other side of the American continent, U.S. servicemen and -women were also killed in the horrendous Pacific battles of World War II. The National Memorial Cemetery of the Pacific on the Hawaiian island of Oahu was established to receive their remains. It was officially dedicated on September 2, 1949, on the fourth anniversary of V-J Day, for veterans who had given their lives in the Pacific between 1941 and 1945. Later it also welcomed the remains of servicepersons from the wars in Korea and Vietnam. Today it contains more than thirty-five thousand bodies, with almost no unused plots except for those set aside for spouses of the dead.

Known as Punchbowl because of its shape, it lies in the middle of an extinct volcano, the Puowaina Crater, a name that translates roughly as "Consecrated Hill" or "Hill of Sacrifice." Long before it was appropriated for its recent inhabitants, the crater was the site of secret royal Hawaiian burials, and it was also the place where offenders of certain taboos were executed.

As you drive through the entry, you are struck by the huge expanse of consecrated ground. Row upon row of flat stones embedded within acres of grass stretch out under large protective trees (plate 59). Pink plumeria blossoms scent the air and fall upon the gravestones like sacred offerings. Dramatic bouquets of cut flowers — orange lobster claw, red anthurium and ginger, and orange and blue birds of paradise — attest to the continued devotion of family members and friends.

Everything in this site honors the fallen warriors on a grand scale. Some 112.5 acres extend upward to a mammoth memorial set back against the bowl wall. The memorial consists of monumental stairs flanked by ten Courts of the Missing. On the walls of these courts, in alphabetical order and by service branch, are the names of 28,778 servicemen and servicewomen missing, lost, or buried at sea. And at the top of the stairs, towering above the amphitheater-like ensemble, a thirty-foot-tall female figure with a laurel branch in her hand stands on the symbolic prow of a U.S. Navy carrier. Engraved below her are the words that President Lincoln extended to the mother of five sons who had all died in battle: " . . . the solemn pride that must be yours to have laid so costly a sacrifice upon the altar of freedom."

For all the overarching grandeur of the memorial, the most wrenching experience is to be found in the carpet of grass stretched out below. Moving slowly along a row of 130 flat stones marking the graves of servicemen who had died in World War II (one row among hundreds!), I was struck by the wide range of their origins: almost every state of the Union was represented in that single line of rectangular markers. Most of the stones bore crosses, a few were marked with Buddhist lotus motifs or Jewish stars, and a very few said only:

Unknown
Pearl Harbor, Dec. 7, 1941

Hawaiians do not forget their veterans, and they honor them in a special Hawaiian way. Every year before Memorial Day a call goes out asking residents to make leis to be placed on graves at Punchbowl and at all the state's veterans' cemeteries. In 2004, the City of Honolulu posted this request:

LEI NEEDED FOR MEMORIAL DAY

Fifty thousand lei are needed for placing on the graves of veterans, in memory of their service to our country. . . . Each year, the graves are decorated with lei by the Boy Scouts for Memorial Day. The lei have been provided through the generosity of individuals, schools, and organizations in our community.

INSTRUCTIONS FOR SEWING LEI:

All lei must be made of fresh flowers or ti leaves and must measure 20–24 inches before tying. All lei must be tied. Floral sprays such as ti leaf and anthurium bouquets are also welcome.

Compared with the service at the Arlington National Cemetery, Memorial Day at Punchbowl has a distinctly Hawaiian flavor yet also follows conventional military rites. Like Punchbowl itself, it reflects the American ideal that regional character can enhance a sense of national unity.

The war in Iraq has also offered up to Punchbowl its victims. When the ashes of Sergeant Deyson K. Cariaga were brought there on July 22, 2005, a service was held in the best military tradition. Three loud reports from a rifle, posthumous awards (the Purple Heart and the Bronze Star), and the playing of Taps honored the young man's memory before an audience of some 250 people. Two uniformed soldiers carried Cariaga's ashes during the ceremony then carefully placed them on a pedestal draped with leis made from pikake and maile. Cariaga's mother, dressed in black and wearing a mourner's open lei, stoically received a folded U.S. flag and her son's medals. A minister from the New Hope Christian Fellowship at Diamond Head assured the mourners that Cariaga was now in a better place and that they would see him again in heaven.

At present, there are more than two hundred military cemeteries created by the federal government and the states for the burial of veterans and their dependents. The Veterans' Administration, which manages most of these cemeteries, permits one of almost forty symbols to be inscribed on each government-issued marker, ranging from commonly recognized symbols for Christianity, Judaism, Islam, and Buddhism to, as of 2007, the Wicca pentacle. (Wicca is a nature-based religion.) All veterans of the United States Army, Navy, Marine Corps, Air Force, and Coast Guard have the right to be buried in a military cemetery. When their time comes, if they so wish, they may choose to spend eternity among their comrades in arms.

17

OLD AND
NEW FASHIONS
IN DEATH

AT THE START OF the twenty-first century, hospitals, funeral parlors, traditional cemeteries, memorial parks, and crematoriums follow uniform procedures that tend to distance the dead from the living. But a burgeoning countermovement seeks to give death a more personal face. Hospices, home deaths, pre-planned funerals, celebrations of life, idiosyncratic eulogies, highly individualized grave markers, do-it-yourself burials, and green burials are all attempts to blunt the trend toward standardization. Whether one prefers cremation or body burial, dying people and their families are looking for ways to resist nondifferentiated obliteration. This tension between the quest for personalization and the forces of anonymity — like the tension between ethnic identity and blanket Americanization — can be felt in the various funeral options available to Americans today.

Cremation Consider cremation, an option in the United States since the late nineteenth century. During the post–Civil War period, when innovations of all kinds burst on the national scene, cremation was viewed as something more than a mere advance in technology. For its partisans, it was a messianic creed grounded equally in sanitary and spiritual con-

Above: Inverted marble torch deformed by acid rain, Laurel Hill Cemetery, Philadelphia

cerns. As Yale president Timothy Dwight had proclaimed at the beginning of the nineteenth century, many cremationists felt that cemeteries were outdated; they had become grotesque depositories for putrefying corpses and overblown Victorian statuary that bore no resemblance to the spiritual domain. The purifying process of cremation offered an alternative.

The debate that raged over cremation a hundred years ago pitted progressives against traditionalists, cosmopolitans against regionalists, the city against the country, intellectuals against the uneducated. There were also divisions among religions, with all Catholics and Muslims, most Jews, and even some members of the Protestant clergy opposing cremation. The fledgling funeral industry, with its emphasis on viewing the body, was, of course, particularly hostile to the procedure. But city planners worried about limited space for corpses, citizens concerned about sanitation problems, and others wanting a quick, efficient, relatively inexpensive means to dispose of their own bodies eventually put cremation on the thanatological map.

Today people choose cremation because (1) it is generally cheaper than burial, costing about half the price, (2) it saves land, and (3) it is simpler than burial. Some religions, most notably Hinduism and Buddhism, have always permitted cremation; Protestants have generally accepted it; and Roman Catholicism has allowed it since 1963. Islam and Orthodox Judaism still forbid it.

Currently, about one in three people who die in the United States are cremated, though statistics vary widely according to region. Considerably more people in the West choose cremation than those living elsewhere in the nation. In 2004, more than 60 percent of the dead in Hawaii, Nevada, Oregon, and Washington were cremated, followed by more than 50 percent in Arizona, Alaska, Montana, Colorado, and California. Rhode Island, with a 54 percent cremation figure, was the only non-western state to figure among the top ten preferring cremation.

Cemeteries throughout the nation market themselves as appropriate repositories for cremated remains (cremains), regardless of whether those remains are placed in burial sites or columbaria. Because many cemeteries are running out of space, and because cremains take less room than caskets, cremation is allowing some cemeteries to have a longer sales life than they would have otherwise. "It's been a boon for a lot of places that thought they'd be out of space in five years," says a spokesman for the International Cemetery and Funeral Association, which represents 7,500 facilities.

Some old cemeteries have found ingenious ways of placing cremains on their grounds. The Episcopal church in St. Michaels, Maryland, founded around 1677, inserts them into the cemetery walls. The small colonial churchyard still used by St. Michael's Episcopal in Charleston, South Carolina, has laid out its cremains under a pathway. Even the venerable Burton Parish in Williamsburg, Virginia, has set aside an area for cremains in its churchyard and a few inurnments within the church. Mount Auburn in Cambridge offers several indoor and outdoor possibilities, including a garden where cremains are placed directly in the ground without containers. Like many other establishments, the 150-year-old New Mount Sinai Jewish Cemetery in St. Louis now maintains a special section inside its chapel for urns. The Bohemian National Cemetery in Chicago has a hundred-year-old columbarium with beautifully encased niches, each filled not only with an urn but also with mementos of the dead. Hollywood Forever boasts an elegant two-story columbarium built in 1928 with a circular dome design, as well as newer, streamlined mausoleums containing thousands of niches and vaults.

Most definitely, cremation is here to stay. In all likelihood, it will eventually become as popular in the United States as it is in certain European countries, where cremation is by far the preferred method of bodily disposal (76 percent of deaths in the Czech Republic, 75 percent in Switzerland, 73 percent in Denmark, 71 percent in Sweden, 70 percent in the United Kingdom, 52 percent in the Netherlands). Two European exceptions are Italy, with only 6 percent of the population choosing cremation, and Greece, which still prohibits cremation altogether.

A major objection to cremation is that it happens too quickly. One moment there is a body resembling the person you knew; the next moment (well, two to three hours later) there is only pulverized bone. Many bereaved people do not attend the incineration, preferring to pick up the cremains after it is over. Then, if inurnment in a columbarium or cemetery is not on the agenda, there is the question of what to do with the ashes. Some are carried away in boxes or jars or urns and stay within the home, on a mantel or in a closet. Some are buried in the garden under a rosebush. Some are scattered in the ocean or on a mountainside, following the deceased person's request. In most states, the scattering of cremains is legal. Sometimes the ashes are divided, half sent to a birth-family plot, the other half given to a spouse or children. The partition of ashes can become more complicated when the deceased has been divorced, and the children of different marriages claim their share. Cremation, despite its factorylike mechanization, often requires a good deal of individual thought on the part of the living.

And now there is an artistic movement producing receptacles for cremains in one-of-a-kind models. Urns made from terra cotta, wood, metal, and glass, and in the form of statues, pets, prayer wheels, and various abstract shapes, are being marketed for placement in homes, though they may also find their way into columbaria and cemeteries. Responding to the demand for personalization, an art gallery in Graton, California, is promoting this "new aesthetic of death."

San Francisco's venerable columbarium run by the Neptune Society has space for more than 7,500 urns. Built in 1897, its historic main building is a handsome circular structure with vaults that can cost thousands of dollars; those in a newer building on the grounds are considerably less expensive. As in Chicago's Bohemian National Columbarium, the San Francisco niches allow for individualized decoration. It is not uncommon for future inhabitants to specify the type of urn they prefer — classical Greek, Oriental, book-shaped, even a cookie jar — to be accompanied by a telling object, such as a champagne glass or a Hawaiian figurine.

In 2006, the San Francisco Columbarium held a party for its future residents. More than a hundred people showed up to eat hors d'oeuvres, drink beverages, listen to harp music, and discuss plans for decorating their vaults. Such an event may appear bizarre to many Americans, who generally think of death in less entertaining terms. Yet it is not a freak San Francisco phenomenon but part of a larger, nationwide trend to make resting places more "user friendly."

Cemeteries as Learning Sites To my knowledge, no cemetery has as yet invited the pre-deceased to meet their future neighbors, even if many of them do offer various events open to the public. Mount Auburn in Cambridge and Laurel Hill in Philadelphia, the two oldest rural American cemeteries, have taken the lead in specialized tours featuring their distinguished dead, nature walks, and other site-related themes.

Laurel Hill's 2007 scheduled events were advertised with these intriguing titles: The Victorian Celebration of Death; The Spirits and Spiritualists of Laurel Hill; The Ladies of the Hill: Commemorating Women's History Month; RMS *Titanic*: 95 Years Later; Birding Amongst the Buried; Designing for the Dead: Art and Architecture; Dead White Republicans; In Their Own Words: Laurel Hill in Letters and Diaries; "Free at Last": A Tour Commemorating Juneteenth and the Civil War; White Bronze Monuments; Philanthropic Philadelphians; A Kid's-Eye View of Laurel Hill; Twilight Performance of *Spoon River Anthology*; Classy Broads and Daring Dames; Gravediggers' Ball; Sinners, Scandals and Suicides; A Hallowed Halloween: Flashlight Tours with Re-enactors; Dining with the Dead; and Fall Fun for the Family.

Clearly the attempts to draw people to Laurel Hill reach far beyond the conventional use of the cemetery for burial and commemoration. In an odd way, Laurel Hill has returned to its nineteenth-century origins, when its bucolic setting was a choice destination for Sunday outings. Now, one can not only admire the landscape and the architecture but also enjoy customized tours packaged to the interests of the entire family, children as well as adults. "We're rebranding ourselves as a heritage tourism destination," said Laurel Hill's executive director in 2007.

Other American cemeteries have followed suit. Chicago's Graceland specializes in architectural tours; New Orleans's St. Louis I attracts spiritualists and parapsychology devotees; the Oakwood Cemetery in Troy, New York, stages a gourmet daffodil brunch set within the marble walls and Tiffany windows of its memorial chapel; Hollywood Forever hosts an outdoor classic film series with movies featuring some of the stars buried there projected on the mausoleum wall. California's Forest Lawn offers "entertaining education programs, flag-waving patriotic ceremonies, fun-filled contests for kids, inspiring religious programs, and more," all free to the public. Forest Lawn also prides itself on its art collection, housed in a separate museum, and once a year it assembles a group of actors to re-create famous Christian works of art, such as Michelangelo's *Pietà*, in a theatrical production known as *The Pageant of Our Lord*. Promoting themselves as sites of learning, these cemeteries simultaneously showcase their wares and collect revenues for maintenance and restoration. By entering the cemetery grounds for pursuits other than the mournful experience of burial, thousands of visitors who might not otherwise choose to venture among the dead are becoming familiar with graveyards and will think of them as something other than spooky places.

Yet there are reasons to fear that some of these activities will desacralize the cemetery and make it a form of fun park, unsuitable for the feelings of reverence and solemnity traditionally attached to burial grounds. Distancing the dead is one thing — distorting their resting places for commercial ends is another.

Less-commercial enterprises do take place through the schools. Teachers focusing on cemeteries for their historical value have devised programs that involve site visits, study guides, and specific exercises. A leader in this movement is W. Dean Eastman, a high school history teacher in Beverly, Massachusetts, since 1970. Students in his history course spend approximately two weeks visiting four historic cemeteries. They examine colonial gravestones, especially those with death's-heads, cherubs, urns, and willows, charting their evolution according to the time in which these images first appeared, when they reached their height of popularity, and when they finally faded out. Then they try to relate this method of dating, called seriation, to the larger cultural context — to changes in religious beliefs or to differences in class such as I have examined in this book.

Religious Traditions and Secular Innovations One cannot spend time in cemeteries without reflecting on the big questions. Is death final? Do humans have souls that persist beyond the body's decay? Is there an afterlife, and if so, what kind?

According to a 2005 Harris poll, about seven in ten Americans do believe in heaven and life after death, whether they be Protestant, Catholic, Jewish, Muslim, Hindu, Buddhist, or Baha'i. But the concept of an after-life is not the same across religions. The traditional Catholic heaven pre-sided over by God and nine choirs of angels feels different from the gar-den of sensual delights depicted in the Koran. Adherents of the Church of Jesus Christ of Latter-Day Saints (Mormons) posit three degrees of heaven, with the highest represented on earth by the Celestial Room in the temple; only a small percentage of Mormons have access to that room, but all good Mormons whose marriages have been sealed in the temple look forward to eternity with their families somewhere in para-dise. Jews range from the ultra-Orthodox, who believe 100 percent in God's embrace of the righteous after the coming of the Messiah, to secu-lar Jews, who focus primarily on this life and give scant thought to the next. Many Native Americans, even those who have been Christian for generations, hold on to spiritual beliefs particular to their tribes — for ex-ample, that the deceased return as ghosts, or that they are reincarnated in both human and animal forms, or that they depart as spirits to another world.

Other Americans with faith in an afterlife do not necessarily envision heaven in a literal sense but as a communion of spirits bound together by the love of God. Still others speak of an altered state of being without knowing exactly what that state entails. Only atheists, about 5 percent of Americans, consider God and the afterlife to be pure figments of the hu-man imagination.

For most Americans, then, the cemetery is not the end of the line; it is the gateway to some other realm, however ill defined. We have come a long way from the dogmatic pronouncements of seventeenth-century Pu-ritans, with their tragic sense of election and damnation. Many Christians today believe in a less selective God, one who does not close the door of eternal life, even to non-Christians.

If heaven continues to be a viable concept, hell, on the other hand, has morphed mainly into metaphor. Few express public belief in an un-derworld where evildoers are endlessly tortured by devils. Instead, hell is often understood as a psychological experience manifested in madness, depression, and despair, or as a political reality, such as war or imprisonment. These are forms of suffering visited upon the victim, rather than forms of punishment meted out to the wicked. Though the fate of the wicked no longer commands center stage in the American theological discourse as it once did, nevertheless, it is still part of orthodox Protestant and Catholic belief and carries weight — if only silently or unconsciously — with many Catholics and evangelical Christians. Foremost among those who reject mainstream America's liberal interpretation of heaven and hell, evangelical devotees of Rapture literature, based on the Book of Revelation, are convinced that Jesus will take His people to heaven while all nonbelievers will be left behind to face the Antichrist.

Religion is still the leading force behind the rituals of death. Many people who do not necessarily call upon a priest or minister or rabbi at the birth of a child or for a wedding turn to a religious leader at the moment of death. At a time of great sorrow, when the angel of impermanence casts its shadow over life, people look to traditional rites for consistency and comfort. Funeral directors, family, and friends do indeed play important roles, but they usually take a back seat when a religious figure is present. Moreover, religion acts as a counterforce to the secular fads that frequently clash with traditional rites.

A case in point is the eulogy. It has become increasingly common for friends of the deceased to offer eulogies, but when these are too casual or even irreverent, they offend the clergy. In response to what was apparently becoming a popular tendency to eulogize a dead person's fondness for alcohol, in January 2003 a New Jersey archbishop ordered priests in his archdiocese to forbid the laity from giving eulogies at funeral Masses. This did not stop one family: after the Mass, pallbearers carried the casket out to the sidewalk where, with the aid of rented loudspeakers, family members shared their memories of the dearly departed. Funeral directors report that not only Catholic but also Protestant, Jewish, Muslim, and Hindu religious leaders have had problems with nontraditional eulogies.

Nontraditional eulogies are one more way of personalizing death. Another is the obituary. During the past two decades, according to author Marilyn Johnson, the boring old obituary has been revitalized. A good obituary now seizes upon those specifics that distinguish one individual from the masses and tells us, quickly, what we are losing with the death of that particular person. Those interested in writing more lively obituaries can attend the annual International Conference of Obituary Writers or visit such websites as www.blogofdeath.com.

Funeral homes too are being pressured to add a more personal touch. According to the publisher of the trade journals *Mortuary Management* and *Funeral Monitor,* requests for unusual services, while still in the minority, have stretched the creativity of funeral directors. Like party planners, they are being asked to provide receptions that reflect the lives and tastes of the deceased, and all this, of course, on short notice. Some of the twenty-two thousand funeral homes that bury more than two million Americans each year have stepped forward with concierge services that orchestrate everything — location, flowers, food, drinks, speeches, and seating arrangements — all in keeping with the personality of the deceased. Forest Lawn offers the services of certified celebrants, people trained to help plan and create "a personalized memorial, or funeral service" that "may or may not be religious in nature."

Personalization has led to a form of funeral service now called a celebration of the life. Whether orchestrated by professionals or by family and friends, the celebration usually includes personal memories recounted by those who were close to the deceased. Pictures displayed on tables and walls or slides projected onto a screen bring back the loved one at points throughout his or her life. Such events go beyond conventional tributes; they attempt to provide a mini-biography, sum up the life experience, validate it, and lay it to rest. For the mourners, they provide a sense of completion, allowing them to go on with their own lives.

Funeral directors have noted another trend among consumers: people are planning their own funerals. It is possible to choose the type of service that fits one's beliefs and aesthetic preferences, to decide whether one will have an open or closed casket, and to specify the flowers, music, readings, and speakers at the ceremony well before the actual event.

The owner of Lights Out Enterprises, a business n Venice Beach, California, that helps people plan their own funerals, specializes in the tribute video. The tribute video, shown at the funeral or at any time before or after, is a short documentary based on the life of the person so honored. Some clients take comfort in the thought that even after death, their grandchildren and great-grandchildren will be able to see them as if they were alive.

The cemetery began to manifest more personal tombstones as early as the eighteenth century, though such examples were relatively few in comparison with the huge majority marked with conventional motifs. In early America, religious inscriptions and symbols provided the canon for most mortuary markers, not only among Euro-Christians but also among many ethnic and religious groups who wanted to adopt American ways. The Latin-derived "RIP," or "Rest in Peace," was and still is among the most common inscriptions found in American graveyards, even for those who do not claim European Christian ancestry.

Religious symbols — Christian crosses, crowns, and doves; Jewish stars and menorahs; the Islamic crescent and star; Buddhist lotus flowers — were once considered all one needed to know about an individual other than his or her name and life span. Today such religious markings often cede primacy to secular motifs that evoke the idiosyncrasies of a specific person — for example, the words of a beloved song or the image of a favorite sport. Every cemetery has unique markers, not only for the wealthy and famous but also for ordinary folk, who may be represented for all eternity by a tennis racket, a truck, or a violin.

"What people did in life is now coming through on the stones," says the manager of a cemetery on Marco Island, Florida. This growing trend toward personalization has spawned numerous tombstones engraved with hearts, wedding rings, and marriage dates; with the nicknames, occupations, and hobbies of the deceased; with pictures of children and their pets. One Key West, Florida, epitaph identifies the deceased as a "Devoted fan of Julio Iglesias." Such an epitaph isolates a key feature and uses it to represent the entire person.

After a hiatus of half a century, photos on small ceramic ovals have returned to the graveyard. No longer limited to black-and-white, as were most early Italian, Portuguese, Czech, or Mexican American portraits, these are frequently in color and extraordinarily vivid. When I stare into the eyes of a child or young adult, I wonder how the parents can bear looking at such a lifelike picture, yet one woman told me that the faithful photo allows her to remember her daughter as she was before she wasted away.

Even more dramatic are the life-size photos scanned onto stone with laser technology. This method, popularized in Russia, is now widely used in the United States for immigrants from the former Soviet Union, especially Jews, but also Lithuanians and Armenians. Even Muslims within the Russian sphere have been known to adopt this format, though it clashes with the traditional Islamic prohibition against graphic human representation. Such laser-etched, exquisitely detailed arresting faces can now be found in American graveyards from coast to coast.

And going one step further, a few innovative cemeteries are beginning to offer videos based on the life of the deceased that can be inserted into a headstone and played upon request! A recent patent issued to a California inventor envisions a tombstone with a hollowed-out compartment designed to accommodate complex equipment. People will be able to get remote-control devices from the cemetery office to operate the video equipment, as if they were in their living rooms. These video tombstones, with their delicate electronics, weatherproofing, and protection against theft, will not be inexpensive: estimates range as high as $20,000. Is this the wave of the future, or just another California fad?

At the other end of the country, in Barre, Vermont, both traditional and nontraditional grave markers are still made from the granite quarries for which the city is famous. Known for their fine grain and long endurance, granite monuments are produced in Barre in greater number than anywhere else in the United States. Since the late nineteenth century, artisans trained in Europe, most notably in Carrara, Italy, have been coming to Barre to ply the stonecutter's trade. Today around fifteen hundred workers in fifty-seven stoneworking companies operate in the area, down from twice that number in the heyday of the past. Competition from workers in Asia has made a sizable dent in Barre's workforce and production. Foreign imports from India and China are a lot cheaper than those manufactured in Vermont and, as one Barre spokesman admitted, they're also of very high quality. Whereas Asia used to send only slabs, now they are offering finished products for half the American price.

Cremation too has contributed to the reduction of monuments produced in Barre. Because cremains are disposed of in so many different ways, and because cost is often a factor in the choice to cremate, survivors of the deceased often bypass the expense of a monument, although as another Barre spokesman insisted, there is no good reason for the cremated to be denied a proper tombstone.

Barre's arm reaches as far as the Vietnam War memorial and the World War II memorial in Washington, D.C. Its own Hope Cemetery in Vermont, one of three graveyards managed by the city and surely one of the most unusual in the United States, has become a tourist attraction, especially in the autumn when the leaves are in full color. Its 10,500 graves are marked by any number of traditional crosses and angels, but also by one-of-a-kind memorials that symbolize the life of a specific person. There is a beautifully crafted biplane for an early pilot, an oversize soccer ball for a sportsman, a racecar for a driver. The statue for stonecutter Louis Brusa, who died in 1937, is one of the most moving. It shows him leaning back against a rock, his grieving wife standing over him, as he dies from silicosis, an illness caused by the inhalation of granite dust. Sadly, stonecutting establishments did not begin to take measures to protect their workers against dust inhalation until the year of Brusa's death.

One recent stone seen in a Chicago-area cemetery uses the gravestone as a form of advertisement. Under the name DeZara, a circle containing a moon crescent and the word "luna" call attention to a local carpet company. And if one has any doubt as to what these motifs represent, a phone number (773-202-LUNA) is inscribed below. So far, this commercialization of the tombstone has not become a national trend.

Pet Cemeteries Pet cemeteries are not a recent innovation. The first pet cemetery in the United States was founded in 1896 in rural Hartsdale, New York. Now advertising itself as the "oldest operating pet cemetery in the world" and "serving all religions," the Hartsdale Pet Cemetery is the final resting place of nearly seventy thousand pets buried on a shady hillside only thirty minutes north of Manhattan. Having recognized the intense emotions people often feel about their animals, an estimated one thousand pet cemeteries have by now sprung up throughout the fifty states.

The one at the Presidio in San Francisco, surrounded by a white picket fence and shaded by Monterey pines, holds hundreds of animals that once belonged to army families stationed on the base. Markers for dogs and cats date back to the 1950s (plate 60), and there are also graves for other beloved pets — hamsters, rabbits, rats, lizards, mice, birds, and goldfish. Now closed to new burials, the Presidio pet cemetery is looked after by a nonprofit organization.

San Franciscans desirous of a proper burial for their pets can drive thirty minutes south of the city to Colma, a haven for human remains since the late nineteenth century and for animals' since the mid-twentieth. Founded in 1947, Pet's Rest Cemetery now holds thirteen thousand animals, not only dogs and cats but monkeys, cheetahs, and goldfish as well. It claims more media attention and visitors than the seventeen other Colma cemeteries containing people. Burial in Pet's Rest under markers of granite and marble, some imported from Italy's famous Carrara quarries, can be an expensive affair, with lots ranging in price from $550 to $850 (depending on the animal's size), pine boxes costing between $90 and $145, and caskets anywhere from $350 upward. A few graves are marked with freestanding marble statues of St. Francis, the patron saint of animals and the nearby city. Loving pet owners are not known to stint on their wards, even after death.

In that spirit, many newer pet cemeteries, including the Bit of Heaven Pet Cemetery and Crematorium in Houston, Texas, offer a full range of products, such as standard and custom-made caskets, urns, jewelry, headstones, and memorial plaques, as well as the services necessary for cremation and burial. The Tucson, Arizona, pet cemetery adds to the basic costs of the plot, coffin, interment, and perpetual care the optional services of a private or open coffin viewing, a graveside ceremony with a soloist, a catered buffet, and membership in a pet-loss support group.

And some cemeteries go one step further — they make it possible for you to be buried near your pet. Animal burials in a segregated part of the grounds of a human cemetery seem to be the latest fashion. One cemetery in the Milwaukee area, part of a consortium called Companions Rest, has already buried about sixty cats and dogs and sold plots to at least a hundred families for the future disposal of their aging animals. Who knows what the twenty-first century will bring in the way of other novel cemetery developments!

Grave Offerings During the first half of the twentieth century, when pet cemeteries were still rare, the human cemetery was intimately connected to everyday life in many parts of America. One of my friends who grew up in the 1940s and 1950s about ten miles north of Buffalo, New York, remembers going with his family to the Church of Christ on Sundays. Afterward, he and his brother would accompany his mother to the White Chapel Memorial Park in Niagara County, where his maternal grandparents were buried. These visits were "never the least bit morbid or upsetting, rather occasions to hear about my mother's family and the lives of two people I adored as a small child." The outings were "pleasant affairs," part of a Sunday ritual that started with church attendance and ended with a family meal.

Another friend from New York City whose family was of Italian origin recalls going regularly in the 1960s to the St. Raymond's Catholic cemetery in the Bronx with her aunt to visit her uncle's grave. It was such a regular ritual that even when this friend moved away to Chicago and then to California, she continued, on every visit to New York, to go to the cemetery with her aunt. My friend remembers these visits as a natural part of the cult of the dead that Italian American families were expected to observe.

During the second half of the twentieth century, with increased mobility and the rise of megacities, visiting the graveyard on a regular basis became less common for most Americans. The rural cemetery was not close enough to the city where one lived or to the part of the country where one had relocated. And since the new memorial parks were "under professional care" with mechanized mowers and sprinklers, there was less need to go there regularly to tidy up the grave.

And yet, people do go to the cemetery on special occasions — on the deceased person's birthday or death day, on Memorial Day, at Christmas, the Fourth of July, and various other holidays. In the northern California cemetery where my mother is buried, I recognize the regulars who, like me, come there frequently to pluck weeds from the grave, arrange pots of flowers, and talk to the dead. The following observations from my cemetery diary kept during the past few years are examples of how various individuals maintain their ties with loved ones they can no longer see face to face.

The young doctor (1966–1997), with a caduceus next to his handsome dark-eyed portrait, is once again bathed in flowers. Each time I come here, there are new flowers — some cut, some in pots. Today a black-haired woman — presumably his mother — stands bereft before his headstone. She is accompanied by a second woman who seems to be there to comfort her. My heart goes out to that mother. Can there be anything worse than losing a child? As many have said before me, the death of a child goes against the natural order of things.

The cemetery has sprouted flags for the Fourth of July. On the broad lawn where all the stones are flat, small flags have popped up here and there like miniature sentinels assigned to watch over designated graves. The splashes of red, white and blue lend a patriotic aura to the entire landscape.

In the section with headstones, American flags adorn the upright names of Foster, Hatch, Mee, Nichols, and Schultze, among others. Two generations of Schultze family members, all marked by one tombstone, have not been forgotten on Independence Day, though they have been dead for decades. The others, more recently deceased, were men who died before their wives, judging from the empty space on the right-hand side of their stones. I imagine their widows planting the flags because they knew their husbands would like to be remembered as patriots.

In the late afternoon, under a blazing sun, a heavyset, dark-skinned woman sits down on the grass by an unmarked grave. She reaches her hand out to the flowers in the center of the plot — orange spikes intermingled with blue and white agapanthus, with a plastic American flag stuck in the middle. Tears fall from her eyes. She is grieving the loss of her thirteen-year-old son, killed six years earlier in an accident. She tells me he was her youngest child, the one who never got into trouble — it's not easy to bring up a boy in East Palo Alto where you find too many drug dealers. He died so young he never had a chance to see her country of birth, Tonga. His death was a blow to the whole family. His older brother never got over it — still can't seem to get his act together. At least his sister finished school and has a decent job. She would like to think that her dead son is in heaven, but that's a mystery, a mystery. No one knows for sure. As long as she thinks about him, he's still alive.

Three middle-aged people are arranging potted marigolds before a tombstone marked by a large menorah. The grave contains their mother, who died several years ago at the age of ninety-two. This is the anniversary of her death, the day on which Jews traditionally visit the grave of their parents and recite Kaddish, the mourner's prayer. I wonder if they will light a Yahrzeit candle at home in her memory. Before leaving, they place a large stone on the tomb, marking their visit according to Jewish ritual. My mother lying not far away was also ninety-two when she died.

A large man with Polynesian features is watering a row of four or five graves. At one end is an imposing black marble tomb inscribed with a verse from the Gospel of John, written in both Tongan and English. It was made for the man's brother-in-law and cost $7,000. At the other end of the row is an unmarked grave with a bouquet of fresh flowers. This grave is for his wife, who passed away several months ago. They had been married for thirty-two years and had four children. When she died, he was completely lost. He said to me, "You're never really prepared for it. Even if you believe in God and Jesus Christ. Only people who've lost a wife know what it's like." Sure, he could find another woman — there's a lot of mileage left in him — but if you've had a good marriage, it's hard to start over. And he wouldn't want new expenses that would take away from his children. His daughters talk to him every day, but it's not the same as talking to your wife. Only after she died did he realize all the things she did for him, and how much he depended on her. "If you're lucky," he said to me, "you'll die before your husband."

Larry's grandfather and grandmother, his aunt Grace and his uncle Verne (not married to each other) are buried in the same family plot, but his mother and father are not there because they wanted to be cremated and have their ashes scattered over the ocean. Larry doesn't go to the cemetery very often, but recently his Japanese girlfriend wanted to see where his family was buried. She has not lost the traditional Japanese reverence for the dead, and brought an armful of flowers to lay on Larry's relatives' graves. As there were too many for one small plot, they decided to distribute the extra flowers to several nearby markers.

Larry grew up within five miles of the cemetery. He has memories of a happy childhood, with frequent family gatherings, numerous friends, and lazy summers. Baseball was his favorite sport. He thinks affectionately about his family members, especially his gentle mother, and he never forgets his grandfather's birthday, on October 1. Though raised as a Christian, Larry is not a believer. He does not think of life after death along the conventional lines of heaven and hell. If anything, because of his long experience as a yoga practitioner and teacher, he believes firmly in the fundamental interrelationship between mind and body. When one dies, one is, at best, reintegrated into the cosmos.

Rima stood with her mother's coffin before the vault inside the mausoleum, which already contained her father's remains. She and a few family members read aloud from the Koran one after the other in the original Arabic. The solemnity of the occasion weighed upon everyone present.

Afterward, several friends and relatives congregated for a sumptuous tea at the hotel where Rima and her husband were staying. They had flown in from London with her mother's body, returning to the community where they had lived for so many years and where Rima had tended her bedridden mother with a devotion rare among daughters, even with the numerous duties that devolved upon her as the wife of an international businessman.

When it was time for Rima to return to London, it was hard for her to leave her dead mother in California. But on the other side of the world were her two sons, one in London and one in Jordan, both married, and one already a father. A photo she showed me of her first grandson brought to her lips the only smile she was able to muster during the grueling day of her mother's funeral.

Today the cemetery has the appearance of a multicultural quilt. I notice Chinese Americans buried next to African Americans, Hispanics next to Polynesians, a Japanese wife alongside her Jewish husband.

The faces of three different women with names and epitaphs reflecting very different backgrounds rest within a few feet of one another. "Esfir Rabinowich / 1905–2001 / Always loved / Always remembered" appears on a large black polished stone, carved in the asymmetrical style I have come to recognize as popular among recent Russian immigrants. "Pele naise / vao tuputupu / fusimaholi / 1923–1996" is pictured in a colored porcelain circle, with the familiar lines from St. Paul, in both English and Tongan, inscribed above her head: "I have fought the good fight / I have finished the race / I have kept the faith" (2 Timothy 4:7). The youthful white face of "Hagemann / Betty Edna / Mother of five / 1926–1981" smiles out from a porcelain oval above the words "When you see a poppy think of me." A poppy, the California state flower, accompanies the inscription.

A Russian Orthodox cross with two horizontal bars and one diagonal bar towers over rows of smaller crosses, each with only one horizontal bar.

A rosary dangles over the headstone of Jose S. Melgoza (1942–1989), whose youthful Latino face is immortalized in porcelain. The epitaph below it reads: "Mi señor es mi luz y salvacion" (My Lord is my light and salvation).

A cloth butterfly on a stick shades the flat stone of Richard Dwayne La'quion Nash, six years old. His bright eyes and wide smile shine up from his photo, flanked on each side by the dates of his short life: "Sunrise / Jan. 28, 1992–Sunset / Feb. 6, 1998." I wonder if the four miniature toy cars lined up in a row were the last toys he had played with, in keeping with an old African American tradition.

My mother's cemetery in Palo Alto has been my touchstone over these past few years. The changes I see there, I look for elsewhere. Ethnic migrations similar to those in California are found throughout the nation: tombstones for Chinese in Chicago, for Russians in Pennsylvania, for Latinos in New York, for Middle Easterners in Michigan. The newer tombstones stand out from the older markers in several ways. First, there is the language. Chinese and Japanese characters, which appeared on

American tombstones in the nineteenth century, are relative newcomers, but not so new as the Arabic or Cyrillic alphabet, or Vietnamese and Tongan inscriptions. They call attention to themselves in those parts of older ecumenical cemeteries that are still open to burials, usually on the margins.

But in addition to the languages, there are styles one comes to recognize as ethnically distinct. The recent Russian immigrants are the avant-garde in their choice of asymmetrical shapes, their use of dramatic contrast between highly polished stone and rough-hewn granite, and portraits of the deceased scanned onto the stone.

One arresting marker that catches my eye each time I enter Alta Mesa is the double headstone for Irina Libova and Vladimir Smirnov. Under her name is the date of birth, October 28, 1976; under his, October 8, 1970. She smiles directly out from a large, color porcelain photo. He has a more stolid look. This unconventional stone, with the right-hand edge sliced off and the left-hand edge carved so as to suggest a rough mountain, is explicated by the words at the bottom indicating the young couple's date and place of death: December 28, 1999, Pico de Orizaba. Pico de Orizaba is a fantastic snowcapped Mexican mountain, the third highest in North America. With an elevation reaching to over 18,000 feet, it attracts hardy climbers from all over the world. There Irina Libova and Vladimir Smirnov, two youthful adventurers, came to a tragic end. But the stone is not mournful. Two centrally carved shooting stars seem to suggest that their indomitable spirit still lives.

Native American Cemeteries in Our Times We began this book with a consideration of pre-Columbian burial mounds, and it seems appropriate to end with a small sample of contemporary Native American gravesites. While the "mighty mounds" are long gone, many Native Americans living on and off reservations have managed to preserve aspects of their heritage connected to traditional death rites. These vary from one Indian nation to the next, yet all are attempts to honor or placate the dead, who are believed to live on as spirits. Over time, many — perhaps most — Indians have been able to retain their vision of an afterworld within the framework of Christianity.

Near the town of Gunlock, Utah, a reservation cemetery belonging to the Shivwit band of Paiute Indians offers a good example of how one tribe has combined indigenous customs with mainstream burial practices. The cemetery is situated in a gulley between wedge-shaped hills that shade from brown to russet during the course of a day. All the graves are shaped in the form of mounds extending the length of the body underneath — as small as two feet for a baby and as large as six or seven feet for an adult. These dirt mounds are not covered over with grass or any other greenery, and many of them are surrounded by oval borders of rocks. Miniature mounds, we thought, recalling the lofty ones of an earlier age.

The graves in the oldest section are marked by whitewashed sandstones, each bearing in black paint the name of the deceased, and sometimes the year of death. They have a stark beauty that contrasts with the more modern sections studded with a variety of handmade and professional markers. Some of these bear Christian symbols — for instance, wooden crosses, angels, or the Mormon temple. Many of the stones are also inscribed with Indian imagery: tepees, feathers, drums, eagles, deer, longhorn bulls, a warrior astride a horse. One of the most prominent, that of Douglas Lavan Martineau (1932–2000), has a dramatic eagle stretched across two edges of the front and carvings of petroglyphs on the back, with this epitaph: "Our Dad / A Lifetime of dedication in search of / truth and knowledge of people long forgotten."

Martineau's highly polished dark headstone and a few others of this ilk bring sophisticated money and high tech into the graveyard. But most of the markers are testimonials to lives of limited means and less worldly accomplishments. Some of the deceased are remembered only by their popular names, without benefit of a surname: "Monkey Man," "Unicorn," "Little Jim," "Tantos," "Mustache."

Since World War II and especially during the Korean and Vietnam wars, a number of Shivwits served in the military — facts proudly recalled on their tombstones. Some were killed in battle, sacrificing their lives like so many other servicemen and servicewomen whose claim to American soil is of more recent vintage. Of these, one marker stood out from all the rest (plate 61) — a white painted helmet hanging on a large white cross over the grave of:

CRAWFORD SNOW
UTAH
CPL. US ARMY
VIETNAM PH
AUG 10 1944–MAY 14 1967

This modest Shivwit cemetery in the backcountry of Utah has a dry southwestern flavor unlike those in more verdant parts of the nation, but wherever they are located, Native American cemeteries share certain historical similarities. From the mid-nineteenth till the mid-twentieth century, most grave markers were handmade from wood or local stone, if the graves were marked at all. After World War II, and especially during the last thirty-five years, commercial stones became more common and gave Indian cemeteries a more mainstream appearance. But simultaneously, a renewed sense of ethnic identity related to the 1960s civil rights movements, including the founding of the American Indian movement in 1968, pulled in the opposite direction. Not surprisingly, today's tombstones often feature age-old Indian images as well as Christian symbols.

Two small cemeteries on the Onondaga Reservation in upstate New York south of Syracuse follow this historical pattern. The oldest, mostly illegible, stones from the nineteenth century have no elements that would identify them as specifically Native American, whereas a number of strikingly original sand-blasted stones from the past four decades have both Christian and tribal emblems. Some of these are decorated with symbols of the Onondaga clans: wolf, deer, eel, beaver, and — most common — the turtle.

The pink granite tombstone for "Arthur N. Thomas / Dec. 31, 1932–July 29, 1984" has a cross with flowers at the top of the marker and a turtle seen sideways at the bottom, with the words "turtle clan" above and below.

More typically, on other headstones the turtle is presented in a stylized form, as if one had an aerial view and could see the turtle's head, tail, and legs from above. One handsome wooden marker has nothing more than a large turtle icon below the name Emy Mae Jones.

A turtle clan symbol also adorns the headstone for Louie Papineau, whereas a small eel designates the clan of his wife, Alice Agnes Papineau. It is traditionally taboo to marry someone of the same clan. Their son Jerald Papineau, otherwise known as Guy Hue Dia or "Flying Sky," also has an eel on his stone, reflecting the Onondaga's matrilineal social structure.

In addition to animal motifs, tribal names, and nicknames, a few tombstones carry representations of the game of lacrosse, played by Native Americans in various versions and under different names for countless centuries. When French explorers first saw it played, they baptized it *la crosse* after their own *jeu de la crosse,* a form of field hockey. Lacrosse died out in the northern United States by the mid-nineteenth century, but was revived in upstate New York during the 1860s by the Onondaga tribe. It began to be popular in Canada, in metropolitan New York, and at several eastern colleges, with Native Americans often pitted against white players. Among Onondaga males, lacrosse is not only a sport but also an activity with cultural significance and even religious meanings. The richly carved pink granite stone for Kenton W. Stout (1965–1985) carries images of a lacrosse ball, an automobile, and a boy playing lacrosse. The young man, dead at twenty, is clearly remembered by his family with pride in his athleticism.

A burial for Lyman "Nick" Whiterock (1936–2006) in Owyhee, Nevada, on the Duck Valley Shoshone Indian Reservation was attended by approximately three hundred people, mostly Native Americans with a few Euro-Americans. Bill Wright, an honorary pallbearer, had a special relationship to the deceased, since Nick had cowboyed on Bill's ranch for many years, as had Nick's two deceased brothers. According to Bill's report, the events before, during, and after Nick's interment were a medley of Christian, Indian, and U.S. military rituals.

First there was a ceremony in a large community hall on the reservation, with Nick's casket onstage surrounded by his pictures and many flowers. Because Nick had completed two tours of duty, one with the Marines and the other with the Eighty-second Airborne, and had been active in the Veterans of Foreign Wars, a military guard stood on each side of his casket. A Christian minister delivered a formal eulogy. Nick's first cousin and Bill Wright told stories recalling Nick's life. During the service, an Indian group standing behind the pulpit sang songs and hymns that had been Nick's favorites.

After the indoor ceremony, the casket was loaded into a car and driven to a remote, windswept site in the sagebrush surrounded by volcanic hills. There in the reservation cemetery, another Christian service took place, followed by the military guard unit's twenty-one-gun salute. The casket was lowered into a big hole to the sound of drums and Native American chanting, which were part of a long Indian ceremony. Flowers pinned to the pallbearers' lapels were thrown on top of the casket. Then bags of Nick's belongings — his favorite clothes, the boots he rode in — were also thrown into the hole. In response to my later question, Bill noted — perhaps for the first time — that no women had participated in either the indoor onstage ceremony or the outdoor burial. They had been there but remained in the background.

Afterward, back at the reservation in a barrackslike building, the women served food and expressed their feelings to the other mourners. Nick's widow, Adrianne, crippled and on crutches, remembered how he had always told her "to lift up" her head. This is what a cowboy has to do with a horse if he wants to stay on it.

The Cemetery Preservation Movement Since the 1970s, when Native Americans and other groups began to reclaim their ethnic identities, mainstream America has paid increasing attention to its historic cemeteries. At a time when many were neglected and even abandoned, various individuals and organizations responded to the preservationist call. In some instances, people in search of their ancestors have saved family cemeteries from obliteration; in others, religious and secular groups have taken the lead in restoring local burial grounds through projects requiring hundreds of hours of volunteer work. The Boy Scouts, in particular, have been active for years in restoration projects that entail cleaning, patching, and resetting stones. In addition, the Veterans' Administration Headstone Program provides stones free of charge for eligible veterans whose graves in both military and nonmilitary cemeteries are currently

unmarked or whose stones have been stolen, defaced, or incorrectly inscribed in the first place (plate 62). In Brooklyn's Green-Wood Cemetery
alone, more than twelve hundred new markers were provided as part of a
project undertaken by volunteers in search of all the Civil War dead interred there.

A few private organizations facilitate preservation efforts. One of the
most impressive is the Chicora Foundation in Columbia, South Carolina,
established in 1983 to restore cemeteries, especially those in the Southeast. Its work includes (1) surveying burial grounds; (2) mapping the location of graves, even those which are unmarked; (3) identifying and in-
ventorying both Euro-American and Afro-Americans plots; (4) providing
conservation treatment for stone, brick, and ironwork; and (5) preparing
nominations for the National Register of Historic Cemeteries. Numerous
cemeteries, mainly in the Carolinas and Georgia, have benefited from
their expertise.

Another flank of preservationists seeks to copy tombstone inscriptions for archival purposes. Most significant, the USGenWeb Tombstone
Transcription Project is a vast Internet operation that enlists volunteers to
record tombstone inscriptions from all fifty states, providing a database
that is open to everyone.

Others impassioned by the beauty and historic value of ceramic memorial portraits are photographing them before they lose their luster
or fall prey to vandals and thieves. Ronald William Horne hopes that
his book *Forgotten Faces,* a collection of photos from two Colma, California, cemeteries, will be the first of "a virtual encyclopedia" documenting
American immigration.

At this very moment, an army of preservationists is at work throughout the country with the aim of saving cemeteries from physical decay,
while other individuals document the inscriptions on tombstones before
further deterioration sets in. We cemetery buffs know that the story of our
country is written in stone in countless graveyards, from north to south
and east to west, and we do not want to lose these singular archives.

Tombstones wage a constant battle against the elements — against
wind and storm and rampant foliage. We have seen markers burned by
fire, blackened and unreadable; plaster and brick torn away from tombs

by a furious hurricane; fieldstone markers hidden and cracked by rambling vines; and marble headstones melting from the onslaught of snow and rain. When Thomas Hardy wrote his poetic line "Down their carved names the rain-drop ploughs," he was well aware that rain erodes beloved names but unaware that acid rain would considerably hasten the process.

Our trips to the Hana coast of Maui in 2005 and 2006 provided dramatic evidence of how quickly a situation can deteriorate. The first year we were awed by the beauty of old tombstones piled up in a Japanese cemetery on a promontory above the ocean. The second year, those same elegant stones lay on the beach below, washed by the tide and doomed to disappear (plate 63).

Green Burials Perhaps the most significant cemetery development to emerge at the beginning of the twenty-first century is the green burial movement. Green burials bring together land conservationists and advocates of "natural" burial in a joint effort to preserve the landscape. Already a staple of funereal options in the United Kingdom, where they make up more than 10 percent of interments, green or natural burials are relatively new in the United States. The thirty-two-acre Ramsey Creek Preserve, which opened in 1998 in rural Westminster, South Carolina, is acknowledged as the nation's first green cemetery. A second one, the 350-acre Glendale Memorial Nature Preserve on the Florida Panhandle, was founded in 2002. The ninety-three-acre Greensprings Natural Cemetery on the eastern fringe of New York's Finger Lakes boasts eight thousand additional acres of protected forest on three of its sides. Fernwood in Marin County, California, which dates from the nineteenth century and abuts the Golden Gate Natural Recreation Area, has set aside part of its thirty-two acres for natural burials. Other cemeteries in Oregon, Washington, Texas, and Colorado are also promoting the green burial movement throughout the West. As of 2004, even Arlington National Cemetery offers a green option for any qualifying veteran "through burial of his cremated remains in a biodegradable box in a section of the cemetery without grave markers."

Today's green burial enthusiasts, with their impassioned sense of purpose, recall early-twentieth-century cremation advocates. In both in-

stances, the desire to embrace radically new procedures is linked to a neg-
ative assessment of conventional practices, deemed overly commercial-
ized, spiritually decadent, and environmentally incorrect. In particular,
proponents of green burial decry the use of embalming chemicals and
metal caskets designed to prevent the body from decomposing. Glendale
Memorial makes its case by citing the statistics of toxic elements buried
each year along with the bodies: 827,060 gallons of embalming fluid, caskets containing 90,272 tons of steel and 2,700 tons of copper and bronze,
and vaults requiring 1,636,000 tons of reinforced concrete and 14,000
tons of steel. In their place, green burials use only biodegradable substances: cotton, wool, wood, silk, mulberry leaves, and recycled materials
such as paper.

In addition, green burials usually cost less than traditional burials,
which today average $6,000 and often rise to $10,000. Prices in green
cemeteries range from the modest fees at Greensprings ($500 for a plot,
plus $350 to dig the grave) to those at the upper end of the scale antici-
pated by the Prairie Wilderness Cemetery in Greely, Colorado ($4,000 for
a whole-body burial, $1,000 for the burial of ashes). Supplements, such
as planting a tree above the grave or installing a stone marker (when permitted), can increase the costs accordingly. Not all green cemeteries feel
comfortable with cremation. Greensprings calls attention to cremation's
environmental downside. The process requires large amounts of energy
and emits both sulfur dioxide and trace metals from the body (for instance, mercury from teeth fillings) "while preventing nutrients in bodies
from enriching the land." There is a fervent sense in green circles that we
owe the land our unembalmed bodies, that an unimpeded return to the
earth is natural or, as one person put it, a "part of the circle of life." Another expressed the same idea more nakedly: "the idea that I could become worm food is an honor."

Green burials are part of a much larger social development that began
with home births and hospice care and other efforts to make living and
dying more authentic, without the cumbersome trappings of modern
technology and the pressures of commercialization. In joining forces
with environmentalists, supporters of green burial have placed ecological
needs above the desire for personal commemoration. They project them-

selves into the future through preservation of a special piece of land, hoping that it will hold meaning for generations to come. Some speak of their spiritual connection to the earth as a sacred trust, just as more traditional religious believers speak of their relationship to the divine.

Last Words This book has focused on cemeteries as markers of religious and ethnic diversity because America has been from the start a multicultural endeavor, where individuals of different religions, races, and national ancestry have lived together and died together. Whereas Americans have shown a long-standing preference for being buried with people of their own cultural background, the recent increase in ecumenical graveyards is a sign of our ability to come together in an elemental way.

Yet it is impossible to ignore the poles of privilege that separate the well-off from the poor, in death as in life. Those with means are buried in pleasant, carefully tended garden cemeteries under monuments of granite and marble. Those without means often lie in unkempt plots under cement or makeshift markers that tend to disappear over time. Cemeteries are stark reminders of America's economic inequalities that persevere beyond the grave.

Wherever one lives in the United States, there are cemeteries — some thriving, some neglected, some in the process of being restored, many forgotten. Although they have existed on this continent for at least four hundred years, their future is uncertain. Perhaps, because viable space grows ever scarcer and cremation is on the increase, the cemetery is beginning what will prove to be a long decline. Perhaps future generations will look upon them as mere artifacts, quaint repositories of the past (plate 64). And some will puzzle over these lines of Emily Dickinson, for whom the grave was a familiar companion.

> The Earth lays back these tired lives
> In her mysterious Drawers.

NOTES

PREFACE

xi *To borrow words from:* James Agee and Walker Evans, *Let Us Now Praise Famous Men* (Boston: Houghton Mifflin, 2001), [1941], xi.

I. CLAIMING THE LAND

1 *"Are they here":* "The Prairies," *Poems of William Cullen Bryant* (London: Humphrey Milford, Oxford University Press, 1914), 119.

2 *The current chief's divine status:* D. J. Hally, "Platform Mound Construction and Instability of Mississippian Chiefdoms," in J. F. Scarry, ed., *Political Structure and Change in the Pre-historic South-eastern United States* (Gainesville: University Press of Florida, 1996), 92–127.

3 *"In the olden days":* Nancy Hunter Warren, "New Mexico Village Camposantos," *Markers* 6 (1987): 115.
"Our men were destroyed": George Percy, "Observations by Master George Percy, 1607," in Lyon G. Tyler, ed., *Narratives of Early Virginia, 1606–1625* (New York: Barnes & Noble, 1959), 21.

4 *"scarce able to bury the dead":* "A True Relation," in Philip L. Barbour, ed., *The Complete Works of Captain John Smith (1580–1631)* (Chapel Hill: University of North Carolina Press, 1986), vol. 1, 33.

5 *Excavations conducted in:* Elizabeth A. Crowell and Norman Vardney Mackie III, "The Funerary Monuments and Burial Patterns of Colonial Tidewater Virginia, 1607–1776," *Markers* 7 (1990): 107.

6 *"In two or three months"*: William Bradford, *Of Plymouth Plantation 1620–1647* (New York: Modern Library, 1967), 77.

They did such a good job: Nathaniel Philbrick, *Mayflower* (New York: Viking, 2006), 90.

7 *"We supposed there were many"*: William Bradford and Edward Winslow, *Mourt's Relation or Journal of the Plantation at Plymouth* (New York: Garrett Press, Inc., 1969), 20.

"a great burying place": Ibid., 49.

"If they die": William Penn, "Description of Pennsylvania, 1683, XX," *Old South Leaflets* (Boston: Directors of the Old South Work, Old South Meeting House, n.d.), vol. 7, 384.

This is a rare instance: Terry Jordan, who has studied this practice in southeastern Texas graveyards, also suspects African origins behind the custom of scraping and mounding graves. See Terry G. Jordan, *Texas Graveyards: A Cultural Legacy* (Austin: University of Texas Press, 1982), 16–19. See also Gregory Jeane, "Rural Southern Gravestones: Sacred Artifacts in the Upland South Folk Cemetery," *Markers* 4 (1987): 55–84.

8 *Burying a family member:* This idea is brilliantly developed in Robert Pogue Harrison, *The Dominion of the Dead* (Chicago: University of Chicago Press, 2003).

9 *"He wanted somebody to die"*: William Saroyan, "Madness in the Family," in *Madness in the Family: Stories by William Saroyan* (New York: New Directions Publishing Company, 1988), 3–4.

"Where do you bury?": Elizabeth Spencer, Introduction, in Eudora Welty, *Country Churchyards* (Jackson: University of Mississippi, 2000).

2. MARKING THE GRAVE

10 *"who have placelessly perished"*: Herman Melville, *Moby-Dick* (New York: Oxford University Press, 1999), 38.

11 *"who do not know"*: Margaret Mitchell, *Gone With the Wind* (New York: Macmillan, 1936), 736.

"It was very meaningful": *New York Times*, August 29, 2006.

And some radical religious groups: David Hackett Fischer, *Albion's Seed: Four British Folkways in America* (New York: Oxford University Press, 1989), 521.

12 *Although British colonies:* Elizabeth A. Crowell and Norman Vardney Mackie III, "The Funerary Monuments and Burial Patterns of Colonial Tidewater Virginia, 1607–1776," *Markers* 7 (1990): 116.

Another marker from 1653: Boston's Historic Burying Grounds Initiative, "Eliot Burying Ground," Ibid., 68.

14 *"As runs the Glass"*: Cited in Peter Benes, *The Masks of Orthodoxy* (Amherst: University of Massachusetts Press, 1977), 33.

14 *A striking version:* Boston Museum of Fine Arts, *New England Begins: The Seventeenth Century* (Boston: Museum of Fine Arts, 1982), vol. 2, plate no. 327.

15 *Imported from England:* Hugh DeSamper, *Bruton Parish Church: Its Spiritual and Historical Legacy* (Williamsburg, VA: Bruton Parish Church), 12; and Susan H. Godson, ed., *A Guide to the Memorials of Bruton Parish Church* (Williamsburg, VA: Bruton Parish Church, 2006), 26–27.

   From the 1740s onward: Laurel Gabel, "An Analysis of 9,188 Boston-area Gravestones," *AGS Quarterly,* 30, no. 1 (Winter and Spring 2006): 5.

   This wave of religious enthusiasm: Peter Benes has shown how changes on gravestones in Plymouth County, Massachusetts, conformed "typologically and chronologically" to the progress of the revival. Benes, *Masks of Orthodoxy,* 159.

19 *The Lamson family carvers:* Ralph L. Tucker, "Lamson Family Carvers," *Markers* 10 (1993): 186.

20 *Among the most obvious:* These and some of the other New England markers mentioned in this chapter can be seen on the Internet in the Farber Gravestone Collection.

   In 1893, the first memorial: Ronald William Horne, *Forgotten Faces: A Window into Our Immigrant Past* (San Francisco: Personal Genesis Publishing, 2004), 64.

   "Imperishable Limoges porcelain portraits": Lisa Montanarelli, "A History of Photographic Tombstones," in ibid., 22.

21 *They had been hidden:* Thomas Bridgman, *Memorials of the Dead in Boston; Containing Exact Transcriptions of Inscriptions on the Sepulchral Monuments in the King's Chapel Burial Ground* (Boston: Benjamin B. Mussey and Co., 1853), 15 and 34n.

24 *"Sepulchres should bee made":* John Weever, *Ancient Funerall Monuments* (London: 1631), 10, cited by Crowell and Mackie III, "Funerary Monuments," 115. See also Allan I. Ludwig, *Graven Images: New England Stonecarvings and Its Symbols, 1650–1815* (London: Wesleyan University Press, 1999), 55.

25 *Colonel Richard Cole:* Philip Alexander Bruce, *Social Life of Virginia in the Seventeenth Century* (New York: Frederick Ungar Publishing Co., 1964), 109.

   As for the "middling sort": Godson, ed., *Memorials of Bruton Parish Church,* xiii–xiv.

   This pattern suggests: Benes, *Masks of Orthodoxy,* 49–50.

   "three volleys of shot": Bruce, *Social Life of Virginia,* 219.

26 *For instance, at one Virginia funeral:* Ibid., 221.

   At another funeral: Ibid., 220.

   "no drinking immoderately": Ibid., 221.

27 *"virtual warrens of vaults":* David Charles Sloane, *The Last Great Necessity: Cemeteries in American History* (Baltimore: Johns Hopkins University Press, 1991), 23.

3. SOLIDARITY IN THE CEMETERY

28 *solitaire* and *solidaire*: Albert Camus, "Jonas," in *L'Exil et le Royaume* (Paris: Gallimard, 1957), 176. Carol Cosman translates these two words as "independent" and "interdependent" in the most recent English publication of *Exile and the Kingdom* (New York: Vintage, 2006), 123.

"Even if it should not be": Algimantas Kezys, S. J., ed., *A Lithuanian Cemetery: St. Casimir Lithuanian Cemetery in Chicago, Ill.* (Chicago: Lithuanian Photo Library and Loyola University Press, 1976), 50.

29 *Before 1840, Jews:* Susan Wilson, *Garden of Memories: A Guide to Historic Forest Hills* (Boston: Forest Hills Educational Trust, n.d.), 22.

"because the name of Calvary": Bishop Francis Mora from 1898 Diocesan Catholic Directory, cited in Msgr. Francis J. Weber, *Requiescant in Pace: The Story of Catholic Cemeteries in the Archdiocese of Los Angeles* (Mission Hills, CA: Saint Francis Historical Society, 2003), 1.

30 *"those who are not baptized"*: Ibid., 3–4.

33 *While Orthodox Jews believe:* Earl A. Grollman, ed., *Concerning Death: A Practical Guide for the Living* (Boston: Beacon Press, 1974), 129.

34 *Published many years:* Frances Anne Kemble, *Journal of a Residence on a Georgian Plantation*, ed. John A. Scott (New York: Knopf, 1961), 146–48.

36 *An inspiring project:* China Galland, *Love Cemetery: Unburying the Secret History of Slaves* (San Francisco: HarperSanFrancisco, 2007).

38 *Today, the estimated Muslim population:* Jane I. Smith, "Patterns of Muslim Immigration," http://usinfo.state.gov/products/pubs/muslimlife/immigrat.htm.

39 *"If it were not for our non-Muslim partners"*: *Detroit News*, June 15, 2006.

40 *the person in the grave:* This paragraph is a summary of Ira M. Lapidus, "The Meaning of Death in Islam," in Howard M. Spiro, Mary G. McCrea Curnen, and Lee Palmer, eds., *Facing Death: Where Culture, Religion, and Medicine Meet* (New Haven: Yale University Press, 1998), 150–53.

"This strengthens the relationships": "Muslim Funeral Guide for Residents of the San Francisco Bay Area," typescript.

41 *An eight-foot cemetery wall:* Steve Prothero, Web Exclusive: "Religious Diversity," episode no. 534, April 25, 2002.

4. DISTANCING THE DEAD

43 *"It is believed that this cemetery"*: Timothy Dwight, *Travels in New England and New York*, vol.1 (Cambridge, MA: Belknap Press of Harvard University Press, 1969), 138.

"It is always desirable": Ibid., 137.

44 *"Nature's teachings"*: "Thanatopsis," *Poems of William Cullen Bryant* (London: Humphrey Milford, Oxford University Press, 1914), 11–13.

45 *With a population that:* Blanche Linden-Ward, *Silent City on a Hill: Landscapes of Memory and Boston's Mount Auburn Cemetery* (Columbus: Ohio State University Press, 1989), 8. For Mount Auburn history, see also Shary Page Berg, *Mount Auburn Cemetery Master Plan*, vol. 2, *Historic Landscape Report* (Cambridge, MA: The Halvorson Company, Inc., 1993).

46 *"It is the duty of the living"*: Joseph Story, cited in Jacob Bigelow, *A History of Mt. Auburn Cemetery* (Cambridge, MA: Applewood Books, 1988), 144.

47 *If, as Simon Schama:* Simon Schama, *Landscape and Memory* (New York: Alfred A. Knopf, 1995), 571–78.

48 *The first national meeting of undertakers:* Gary Laderman, *Rest in Peace: A Cultural History of Death and the Funeral Home in Twentieth-Century America* (New York: Oxford University Press, 2003), 5.

49 *"It was almost four o'clock"*: Thomas Wolfe, *Look Homeward, Angel* (New York: Scribner, 2004), 464–65.
   "We dressed and sang hymns": John Vernelson, "Razing the Dead," www.scpronet.com/point/9604/p08.html.

50 *"competed for corpses"*: Michael Sledge, *Soldier Dead: How We Recover, Identify, Bury, and Honor Our Military Fallen* (New York: Columbia University Press, 2005), 219.

5. DEATH'S-HEADS AND FUNERAL GLOVES: BOSTON, MASSACHUSETTS

53 *The 611 remaining gravestones:* Laurel Gabel, "An Analysis of 9,188 Boston-Area Gravestones," *AGS Quarterly* 30, no. 1 (Winter and Spring 2006): 4.

54 *There were probably wooden:* David Stannard, *The Puritan Way of Death: A Study in Religion, Culture, and Social Change* (New York: Oxford University Press, 1977), 116.
   Between his two wives: Charles Chauncey Wells and Suzanne Austin Wells, *Preachers, Patriots & Plain Folks: Boston's Burying Ground Guide to King's Chapel, Granary and Central Cemeteries* (Oak Park, IL: Chauncey Park Press, 2004), 42.
   "At burials, nothing is read": cited in Stannard, *Puritan Way of Death*, 109.

55 *"love and respects"*: Nathaniel B. Shurtleff, ed., *The Records of the Colony of Massachusetts Bay in New England*, vol. 3 (Boston: William White, 1853–54), 162.

56 *"By a singular caprice"*: Thomas Bridgman, *Memorials of the Dead in Boston; Containing Exact Transcriptions of Inscriptions on the Sepulchral Monuments in the King's Chapel Burial Ground* (Boston: Benjamin B. Mussey and Co., 1853), 17.

57 *"honest man of color"*: From a sign posted on the cemetery fence.

58 *Headstones that are attributed to him:* For photos, see *New England Begins: The Seventeenth Century*, vol. 2 (Boston: Museum of Fine Arts, 1982), 323.
   Joseph Lamson's own tombstone: For photo, see Robert L. Tucker, "The Lamson Family Gravestone Carvers of Charlestown and Malden, Massachusetts," *Markers* 10 (1993): 169.

59 *"David, son to":* Robert J. Dunkle and Ann S. Lainhart, *Inscriptions and Records of the Old Cemeteries of Boston* (Boston: New England Historic Genealogical Society, 2000), 157.
   One hundred and twenty years ago: Charles Chauncey Wells, *Copp's Hill Burying Ground Guide* (Oak Park, IL: Chauncey Park Press, 1998), 41.

60 *"be deposited in the same Tomb":* Stannard, *Puritan Way of Death*, 161.

61 *"On Wed. morning last":* Wells, *Copp's Hill*, 73.

62 *"by reason of his cows":* Ibid., 78.
   One of the oldest and most impressive: A photo of this tombstone can be found in *New England Begins*, 317.

63 *We know from many:* For a southern example, see the diary of William Byrd on the death of his infant son in 1710 in William Byrd, *Secret Diary of William Byrd*, Louis B. Wright and Marion Tinling, eds. (Richmond, Va.: The Dietz Press, 1941), 188–92.
   "I order'd little Sarah": Cited by Judith S. Graham in *Puritan Family Life: The Diary of Samuel Sewall* (Boston: Northeastern University Press, 2000), 3.
   "It was from God": Ibid., 105.

64 *"Omission of Duty towards them":* Ibid.
   "I give to my sister": New England Begins, 316.

65 *The Reverend Andrew Eliot:* Stannard, *Puritan Way of Death*, 111–13.
   The spoons given: Examples can be found in the Essex Institute in Salem, Massachusetts; the Winterthur Museum in Delaware; and the Cleveland Art Museum.

66 *Nevertheless, when the wife:* James J. Farrell, *Inventing the American Way of Death, 1830–1920* (Philadelphia: Temple University Press, 1980), 94.
   "so many religious denominations": Edith Gelles, author of *Abigail and John Adams* (New York: Morrow, 2008), personal letter, June 2007.

6. "GONE ARE THE LIVING, BUT THE DEAD REMAIN": NEWPORT, RHODE ISLAND

72 *The Coggeshall burial ground:* Vincent F. Luti, *Mallet and Chisel: Gravestone Carvers of Newport, Rhode Island, in the Eighteenth Century* (Boston: New England Historical Genealogical Society, 2002), 1.

72 *Mary Coggeshall's inscription:* Photo in ibid., 2.
Family burial grounds: New York Times, April 29, 2007.

77 *For instance, boys were often given:* I am indebted to Keith W. Stokes for information about Newport's early African American community.

78 *Photos of these:* Ann and Dickran Tashjian, "The Afro-American Section of Newport, Rhode Island's Common Burying Ground," in Richard E. Meyer, ed., *Cemeteries and Gravemarkers: Voices of American Culture* (Ann Arbor: UMI Research Press, 1989), 163–96.

79 *"one day rubing [sic] stones":* Luti, *Mallet and Chisel*, 298.
"free and at Liberty": Ibid., 299.
"Our Darling Pompey": Tashjian in Meyer, *Cemeteries and Gravemarkers*, 191, from the manuscript preserved in the Rhode Island Historical Society.

80 *In addition to the slave population:* See www.colonialcemetery.com/index2 .htm.
"walking ahead of the hearse": Tashjian in Meyer, *Cemeteries and Gravemarkers*, 192.

7. CEMETERIES AS REAL ESTATE: NEW YORK CITY

82 *"nearly ceased":* David Charles Sloane, *The Last Great Necessity: Cemeteries in American History* (Baltimore: Johns Hopkins University Press, 1991), 67.

83 *Finding their remnants:* Carolee Inskeep, *The Graveyard Shift: A Family Historian's Guide to New York City Cemeteries* (Orem, UT: Ancestry Publishing, 2000).

85 *In 1682 in Flatbush:* Margaret M. Coffin, *Death in Early America: The History and Folklore of Customs and Superstitions of Early Medicine, Funerals, Burials, and Mourning* (New York: Thomas Nelson, Inc., 1976), 70.

86 *Other Dutch inscriptions:* Alice Morse Earle, "Death Ritual in Colonial New York," reprinted from *Colonial Days in Old New York* (New York: Charles Scribner's Sons, 1896) in Charles O. Jackson, ed., *Passing* (Westport, CT: Greenwood Press, 1977), 40–41.

88 *"a little hook of land":* Malcolm H. Stern, "Portuguese Sephardim in the Americas," in Martin A. Cohen and Abraham J. Peck, eds., *Sephardim in the Americas: Studies in Culture and History* (Tuscaloosa: University of Alabama Press, 1993), 157.

89 *A Hebrew inscription appeared:* David and Tamara De Sola Pool, *An Old Faith in the New World: Portrait of Shearith Israel, 1654–1954* (New York: Columbia University Press, 1955), 310.
Since its opening: Sloane, *The Last Great Necessity*, 83.

90 *"the Angola slaves":* Esther Singleton, *Dutch New York* (New York: Benjamin Blom, 1968), 5.

91 *Soon, however, African Americans:* "African Burial Ground National Monument," *African Burial Ground News* 4, no. 4 (Summer 2006): 5.

"No Negro shall be buried": Roi Ottley and William J. Weatherby, eds., *The Negro in New York* (New York: New York Public Library, 1967), 17.

Indeed, one for young adults: Joyce Hansen and Gary McGowan, *Breaking Ground, Breaking Silence: The Story of New York's African Burial Ground* (New York: Henry Holt and Company, 1998); and Warren R. Perry, Jean Howson, and Barbara A. Bianco, eds., *The New York African Burial Ground Archaeology Report,* prepared by Howard University, February 2006, www.african-burialground .gov/ABG-Final Reports.htm.

93 *Contrary to its liberal image:* Brent Staples, "A Convenient Amnesia about Slavery," editorial, *New York Times,* December 15, 2005.

94 *"at least a fourth Part":* William Livingston, "Of the Extravagance of Our Funerals," in Jackson, ed., *Passing,* 44. On New York funerals, see also Earle, *Colonial Days,* 298–304; and Singleton, *Dutch New York,* 252–63.

While such legislation: Sloane, *The Last Great Necessity,* 27–28.

"there shall be a solemn procession": James Hardie, A. M., *The Description of the City of New York* (New York: Samuel Marks, 1827), 127–28.

95 *For thirty days:* Ron Chernow, *Alexander Hamilton* (New York: Penguin Press, 2004), 710.

It appears that: Sloane, *The Last Great Necessity,* 20.

8. PLAIN AND FANCY: PHILADELPHIA AND LANCASTER COUNTY

99 *The Quakers even:* David Hackett Fischer, *Albion's Seed: Four British Folkways in America* (New York: Oxford University Press, 1989), 426–27, 520–21.

"for a meeting house": Written on a sign inside the cemetery.

Eventually the graveyard: Allan M. Heller, *Philadelphia Area Cemeteries* (Atglen, PA: Schiffer, 2005), 35.

100 *When he died, at the age of eighty-four:* Jean K. Wolf, *Lives of the Silent Stones in the Christ Church Burial Ground* (Philadelphia: Christ Church Preservation Trust, 2003), 10.

101 *"Philadelphia should have a rural cemetery":* Thomas H. Keels, *Philadelphia Graveyards and Cemeteries* (Charleston: Arcadia, 2003), 21.

102 *"shaded with pines":* Quoted in Margaret M. Coffin, *Death in Early America: The History and Folklore of Customs and Superstitions of Early Medicine, Funerals, Burials, and Mourning* (New York: Thomas Nelson, Inc., 1976), 31–32.

The Laurel Hill managers: David Charles Sloane, *The Last Great Necessity: Cemeteries in American History* (Baltimore: Johns Hopkins University Press, 1991), 83.

9. THE SOUTHERN WAY OF DEATH: SOUTH CAROLINA AND GEORGIA

113 *And it is impossible:* John Berendt, *Midnight in the Garden of Good and Evil: A Savannah Story* (New York: Random House, 1994).

By comparison: David Hackett Fischer, *Albion's Seed: Four British Folkways in America* (New York and Oxford: Oxford University Press, 1989), 52, 112.

114 *A Confederate cemetery in Franklin:* Robert Hicks, *The Widow of the South* (New York: Warner Books, 2005).

116 *"any seven or more persons":* "The Fundamental Constitutions of Carolina, 1669, XCVII," *Old South Leaflets* (Boston: Directors of the Old South Work, Old South Meeting House, n. d.), vol. 7,409.

The stones for Martha Peronneau: Diana Williams Combs, *Early Gravestone Art in George and South Carolina* (Athens, GA: University of Georgia Press), 11.

117 *Here, on the tomb of an Episcopal priest:* Pamela D. Gabriel and Ruth M. Miller, *Touring the Tombstones: St. Michael's Protestant and Episcopal Church* (pdgabriel @yahoo.com, 2005), 7.

118 *"our cemetery may hence forth":* Pamela D. Gabriel and Ruth M. Miller, *Touring the Tombstones: Unitarian Church* (pdgabriel@yahoo.com), 2.

119 *"for the use of Jews":* Thomas J. Tobias, revised by Solomon Breibart, *Tombstones That Tell Stories* (Charleston: Kahal Kadosh Beth Elohim, 2000), 2.

122 *"blowing in the wind hair":* Alphonso Brown, "The Brown Fellowship Society," (http://www.gullahtours.com/befellows.html), Internet article.

123 *"planters, politicians, military leaders":* Web article, www.scocr.org/Links/mag noliacemetery.htm.

125 *This custom:* Robert Farris Thompson, *Flash of the Spirit: African and Afro-American Art and Philosophy* (New York: Random House, 1983), 132–35.

"Dis wuz a common ting": Savannah Unit, Georgia Writers' Project, Work Projects Administration, *Drums and Shadows: Survival Studies Among the Georgia Coastal Negroes* (Garden City, NY: Anchor Books, 1972), 54.

"the spirit don't stay in the grave": Ibid., 57.

126 *"the King of Terrors":* Samuel Willard, *A Compleat Body of Divinity* (Boston: n.p.,1 726), 234, cited in Allan Ludwig, *Graven Images: New England Stonecarving and Its Symbols, 1650–1815* (Hanover, CT: Wesleyan University Press, 1999), 82.

127 *Africans from the Congo-Angolan region:* Leland Ferguson, *Uncommon Ground: Archaeology and Early African America, 1650–1800* (Washington, D.C.: Smithsonian Institution Press, 1992), 116.

129 *"An intense black man":* Robert Farris Thompson, "Siras Bowens of Sunbury, Georgia: A Tidewater Artist in the Afro-American Visual Tradition," *Massachusetts Review* (Spring 1977): 491.

129 *"These were wooden images"*: Savannah Unit, *Drums and Shadows*, 109.

"*a monument in the transatlantic tradition"*: Thompson, "Siras Bowens," 498.

130 *"Yuh break duh dishes"*: Savannah Unit, *Drums and Shadows*, 122.

"*Sometimes we played"*: Caroline Couper Lovell, *The Light of Other Days* (Macon, GA: Mercer University Press, 1995), 36.

132 *"We hab membuhs"*: Savannah Unit, *Drums and Shadows*, 48.

133 "*duh spirit'll jis wanduh"*: Ibid., 73.

"*idyllic City of the Dead"*: Lovell, *Light of Other Days*, 24.

134 "*so beautiful that"*: John Muir, *A Thousand-Mile Walk to the Gulf* (San Francisco: Sierra Books, 1991), 39–42.

"*The dead are very much"*: Berendt, *Midnight*, 31.

10. NEW ORLEANS: WHERE IT'S BETTER TO BE BURIED ABOVE GROUND

140 *"In early days"*: cited by Robert Florence and Mason Florence, *New Orleans Cemeteries: Life in the Cities of the Dead* (New Orleans: Batture Press, 1997), 11–12.

141 "*like not having Christmas"*: Eve Troeh, radio essay, Nov. 2, 2005, NPR.

Because many New Orleans tombs: Entitled Opinions, radio program, Feb. 28, 2006, KZSU FM 90.

It was first celebrated: Joan B. Garvey and Mary Lou Widmer, *Beautiful Crescent* (New Orleans: Garner Press, Inc., 1982), 122.

145 *The Samuel J. Peters Junior High School:* Florence and Florence, *New Orleans Cemeteries*, 80–81.

147 "*When I was a child"*: John Gregory Brown, *Decorations in a Ruined Cemetery* (Boston: Houghton Mifflin, 1994), 18.

"*gradually force the body"*: Ibid., 223.

150 *But if the older jazz funeral:* Ellis L. Marsalis Jr., Introduction, Leo Touchet and Vernal Bagneris, *Rejoice When You Die: The New Orleans Jazz Funerals* (Baton Rouge: Louisiana State University Press, 1998).

11. RITUALS OF REMEMBRANCE: ST. LOUIS AND THE BOONSLICK

153 *In Conshohocken,:* The information about St. Matthew's Roman Catholic Church cemetery was provided by Donna E. Walcovy.

marker at the Miami City Cemetery: The information about the Miami City Cemetery was provided by Mike Mitchell.

In that Italians are expected: John Matturi, "Windows in the Garden: Italian-American Memorialization and the American Cemetery," in Richard E. Meyer, ed., *Ethnicity and the American Cemetery* (Bowling Green, OH: Bowling Green State University Popular Press, 1993), 23–25.

159 *"He lies buried"*: Letter of Alexander Wilson to Alexander Lawson, Natchez, Mississippi Territory, May 28, 1811, *Port Folio* 7, no. 1 (January 1812).
In life: Connie Nisinger, www.findagrave.com.

160 *"ordered his monument"*: Mark Twain, *Life on the Mississippi* (New York: Oxford University Press, 1996), 499.
"confiscated the ancient mariner's": Ibid., 498.

161 *Falling Angels*: Tracy Chevalier, *Falling Angels* (New York: Dutton, 2001).
Especially after 1850: Elisabeth L. Roark, "Embodying Immortality: Angels in America's Rural Garden Cemeteries," *Markers* 24 (2007): 66.

163 *Researcher Ann Morris*: Ann Morris, "Sacred Green Space: A Survey of Cemeteries in St. Louis County," typescript, June 2000.
This cemetery has been documented: Keith Rawlings, *Gone but not Forgotten: Quinette Cemetery, a Slave Burial Ground, Est. 1866* (Kirkwood, MO: Youth in Action, Inc., 2003).

165 *We were drawn there*: Maryellen Harshbarger McVicker, "Reflections of Change: Death and Cemeteries in the Boonslick Region of Missouri," www.mo-river
.net/history/boonslick/index.htm.

12. ETHNICITY, RELIGION, AND CLASS IN UNDERGROUND CHICAGO

171 But paradoxically: Matt Hucke and Ursula Bielski, *Graveyards of Chicago: The People, History, Art and Lore of Cook County Cemeteries* (Chicago: Lake Claremont Press, 1999), 188.
Even though the murderers: William Bradford Huie, "The Shocking Story of Approved Killing in Mississippi," *Look* magazine 20, no. 2 (Jan. 29, 1956): 46–48, 50.

172 *Those early Irish*: Hucke and Bielski, *Graveyards of Chicago*, 184–87.

179 *The combination of solid*: Barbara Lanctot, *A Walk Through Graceland Cemetery* (Chicago: Chicago Architecture Foundation, 2004), 37–39.

181 *"almost any of the communities"*: "Serving the Catholic Community since 1837," on the Internet at www.CathCemChgo.org.

183 *"Today, having arrived in America"*: Birute Pukeleviciute, "Angelus Domini," in *A Lithuanian Cemetery: St. Casimir Lithuanian Cemetery in Chicago, Ill.* (Chicago: Lithuanian Photo Library and Loyola University Press, 1976), 176.

187 *"Let us remember that"*: Evelyn Krenek Fergle et al., *Introduction to Bohemian National Cemetery Crematorium/Columbarium* (Chicago: Bohemian National Cemetery, 2005), cover page.

189 *Helen A. Sclair*: Helen A. Sclair, "Ethnic Cemeteries: Underground Rites," in Melvin G. Holli and Peter d'A. Jones, eds., *Ethnic Chicago* (Grand Rapids, MI: William B. Eerdmans Publishing Company, 1995), 635.

13. CELEBRATING THE DEAD IN POLYGLOT TEXAS

191 *"Our children are growing"*: Carl Guenther, *An Immigrant Miller Picks Texas: The Letters of Carl Hilmar Guenther*, trans. Regina Beckmann Hurst and Walter D. Kamphoefner (San Antonio: Maverick Publishing Company, 2001), 80.

192 *The site chosen:* Maria Watson Pfeiffer, typescript copy of her study of San Antonio's cemeteries, 2.

"If a member is sick": Ibid., 8.

194 *"... the poor child"*: Mary A. Maverick, *Memoirs of Mary A. Maverick*, Rena Maverick Green, ed. (Lincoln: University of Nebraska Press, 1989), 93–94.

197 *"a French town with a German flavor"*: Julia Nott Waugh, *Castro-Ville and Henry Castro, Empresario* (Castroville, TX: Castro Colonies Heritage Association, 1994), 1.

199 *"My friends, you have justified"*: Ibid., 26.

These are both cast iron and wrought iron: For comparison with wrought-iron crosses in North Dakota cemeteries, see Timothy J. Kloberdanz, "Unser Lieber Gottesacker" (Our Dear God's Acre): An Iron-Cross Cemetery on the Northern Great Plains," *Markers* 22 (2005): 160–81. See also John Gary Brown, *Soul in the Stone: Cemetery Art from America's Heartland* (Lawrence: University Press of Kansas, 1994), 39–41.

201 *"To see engraved on the tombs"*: Janine Erny, *... et parmi les pionniers du Far West il y avait des Alsaciens* (Aubenas: Le Verger Editeur, 1999), 324. My translation.

202 *Even a royal edict:* Terry G. Jordan, *Texas Graveyards: A Cultural Legacy* (Austin: University of Texas Press, 1982), 66.

Established in 1731: Lewis F. Fisher, *The Spanish Missions of San Antonio* (San Antonio: Maverick Publishing Company, 1998), 79–80.

206 *"This is Mexican defiance of death"*: Sergei Eisenstein, "Day of the Dead," in Carole Naggar and Fred Ritchin, eds., *Mexico: Through Foreign Eyes* (New York: W. W. Norton, 1993), 154.

14. CALIFORNIA: MISSIONARIES, MINERS, MOGULS, AND MOVIE STARS

208 *The church was part of:* Kent G. Lightfoot, *Indians, Missionaries, and Merchants: The Legacy of Colonial Encounters* (Berkeley: University of California Press, 2004), 56.

A report written in 1797: Robert H. Jackson and Edward Castillo, *Indians, Franciscans, and Spanish Colonization: The Impact of the Mission System on California Indians* (Albuquerque: University of New Mexico Press, 1995), 44.

208 *Venereal disease:* James A. Sandos, *Converting California: Indians and Franciscans in the Missions* (New Haven: Yale University Press, 2004), 127.

Funeral songs would urge: Malcolm Margolin, ed., *The Way We Lived: California Indian Stories, Songs, and Reminiscences* (Berkeley: Heyday Books, 1993), 81.

Lightfoot, *Indians, Missionaries, and Merchants,* 64.

"to the beautiful trail above": Ibid., 82.

210 *"The grounds have long since":* O. F. M., Maynard Geiger, *Mission Santa Barbara 1782–1965* (Santa Barbara: Heritage Printers, 1965), 26.

211 *The sawmill in the mountains:* Alan H. Patera, *Coloma: First Town of the Mountains* (Lake Grove, OR: Western Places, 1998), 6; and Sylvia Anne Sheafer, *Gold Country* (Carlsbad, CA: Journal Publications, 2001), 10, 42.

212 He had intended: Lynette Mizell, ed., *Coloma Cemeteries* (Coloma, CA: Gold Discovery Park Association, 1997), 23.

213 *Born in Canada:* Ibid., 24.

214 *"Hannah Seater":* Ibid., 23.

A few "Negro" residents: Ibid., 22.

215 *"fallen women":* Ibid., 29.

Louis Kloepfer: Ibid., 28.

223 *Where are the graves:* Sucheng Chan, *Asian Californians* (San Francisco: MTL/ Boyd and Fraser, 1991), 29.

In 1890: Ibid., 84–85.

"The first thing to be removed": Charles Caldwell Dobie, *San Francisco's Chinatown* (New York: D. Appleton-Century, 1936), 67.

224 *Its boundaries:* "Chinese Funerary Burners: A Census," www.uidaho.edu/special-collections/papers/burners.htm.

The ritual burning: Roderick Cave, *Chinese Paper Offerings* (Hong Kong: Oxford University Press, 1998), 65–68.

However esoteric: Sue Fawn Chung and Priscilla Wegars, eds., *Chinese American Death Rituals: Respecting the Ancestors* (Lanham, MD: AltaMira Press, 2005), and www.uidaho.edu/special-collections/cemintro.htm.

228 Riots broke out: Gary Laderman, *Rest in Peace: A Cultural History of Death and the Funeral Home in Twentieth-Century America* (New York: Oxford University Press, 2003), 37.

15. WHO OWNS THE BONES? SITES AND RITES IN HAWAII

233 *These controversies:* Kenneth R. Conklin, "NAGPRA in Hawai'i — The cases of Honokahau and Mokapu," 2003, accessible at www.angelfire.com/hi2/hawaiiansovereignty/nagpramokapuhonokahua.html.

234 *"When I was seventeen years old"*: Kahu Charles Kauluwehi Maxwell Sr., "Protection of the Iwi na Kapuna (Bones of Our Ancestors)," December 2001, accessible at www.moolelo.com/naiwi.html.

235 *"secretly exhuming the body"*: "Hearing before the Select Committee on Indian Affairs," May 14, 1990 (Washington, D.C.: U.S. Government Printing Office), 401–2.

"Sometimes a person": David Malo, *Hawaiian Antiquities,* trans. Nathaniel B. Emerson (Honolulu: Bishop Museum Press, 1951), 96–99.

236 *"in cardboard boxes"*: "Hearing," 410.

237 *" . . . the King came on board"*: Sydney Parkinson, *A Journal of a Voyage to the South Seas, in His Majesty's Ship, the Endeavour* (London: Charles Dilly and James Phillips, 1784), 336–37.

246 *An elegant reproduction:* For photos, see Nanette Napoleon Purnell, *Oahu Cemetery: Burial Ground & Historic Site* (Honolulu: O'ahu Cemetery Association, 1998), 28–29, 104.

249 *The sadness of closure:* Nanette Napoleon Purnell, "Oriental and Polynesian Cemetery Traditions in the Hawaiian Islands," in Richard E. Meyer, *Ethnicity and the American Cemetery* (Bowling Green, OH: Bowling Green State University Popular Press, 1993), 193–99.

252 *"If they become too Americanized"*: *Honolulu Advertiser,* April 4, 2005.

16. NATIONAL MILITARY CEMETERIES

256 *By the end of the war:* Richard West Sellars, "Pilgrim Places: Civil War Battlefields, Historic Preservation, and America's First National Military Parks, 1863–1900," *CRM: The Journal of Heritage Stewardship* 2, no. 1 (Winter 2005): 14.

260 *"which had been ploughed up"*: Cited in William A. Blair, *Cities of the Dead: Contesting the Memory of the Civil War in the South, 1865–1914* (Chapel Hill: University of North Carolina Press, 2004), 96.

Not until President William McKinley: Michelle A. Krowl, "'In the Spirit of Fraternity': The United States Government and the Burial of Confederate Dead at Arlington National Cemetery, 1864–1914," *Virginia Magazine of History and Biography* 111, no. 2 (2003): 151–86.

262 *"the removal of the remains"*: Blair, *Cities of the Dead,* 176.

Arlington superintendent: John Woestendiek, "On Behalf of a Grateful Country . . . ," *Baltimore Sun,* September 14, 2003.

264 *The site of Custer's Last Stand:* See Bob Reece, "Interment of the Custer Dead," www.friendslittlebighorn.com/dusttodust.htm.

270 *A minister from:* *Honolulu Advertiser,* July 23, 2005.

270 *The Veterans' Administration:* Scott Bauer, "Wiccan Veterans Get Stone Grave Markers with Etched Pentacle," *San Francisco Chronicle,* May 28, 2007.

17. OLD AND NEW FASHIONS IN DEATH

272 *But city planners:* Stephen Prothero, *Purified by Fire: A History of Cremation in America* (Berkeley: University of California Press, 2001).
Today people choose cremation: "Ashes to Ashes," *USA Today,* February 22, 2007.
In 2004: Cremation Association of North America, as cited in the *San Francisco Chronicle,* June 6, 2007.

274 *"new aesthetic of death":* Patricia Leigh Brown, "In Death as in Life, a Personalized Space," *New York Times,* January 18, 2007.

275 *"We're rebranding ourselves":* Ibid., May 25, 2007.
"entertaining education programs": *Around the Parks,* Forest Lawn Memorial-Parks and Mortuaries, Fall/Winter 2006.

276 *A leader:* W. Dean Eastman, "Tiptoeing through the Tombstones," *Common Place* 2, no. 2 (January 2002); www.common-place.org/vol-02/no-02/school.

278 *This did not stop one family:* Anthony Ramirez, "She Loved Life. (And Bourbon. And Bawdy Jokes.); New Eulogies, at Odds with Church Tradition," *New York Times,* November 1, 2004.
During the past two decades: Marilyn Johnson, *The Dead Beat* (New York: Harper-Collins, 2006).

279 *Some of the twenty-two thousand funeral homes:* *New York Times,* July 20, 2006.

280 *"What people did in life":* Melanie Sidwell, "Modern Gravestones," *San Diego Union Tribune,* September 16, 2004.

281 *A recent patent:* Issued to Robert Barrows of Burlingame, California, for "Video Enhanced Gravemarkers," www.videoenhancedgravemarker.com.
These video tombstones: "'Talking Tombstone' Lets the Dead Tell Their Tales," www.STLtoday.com, February 27, 2007.

282 *Because cremains:* "Granite's Global Competition," *New York Times,* October 25, 2006.
Sadly, stonecutting establishments: For photos from Vermont's Hope Cemetery, see Douglas Keister, *Stories in Stone: A Field Guide to Cemetery Symbolism and Iconography* (Salt Lake City: Gibbs Smith, 2004), 231, 271–72.
So far, this commercialization: www.gravestonestudies.org.

283 *Animal burials in a segregated part:* Darryl Enriquez, "Cemeteries for People Making Room for Pets," www.jsonline.com, February 25, 2007.

291 *Two small cemeteries:* For my knowledge of the Onondaga cemeteries, I am indebted to Nicole Angeloro for her unpublished paper "Twenty-eight Winters

and One Summer: Ethnic Identity and the Grave Markers of the Onondaga Nation."

294 *In Brooklyn's Green-Wood Cemetery:* Glenn Collins, "More Than 1,200 New Gravestones, and Countless Civil War Sacrifices," *New York Times,* May 28, 2007.

"a virtual encyclopedia": Ronald William Horne, *Forgotten Faces: A Window into Our Immigrant Past* (San Francisco: Personal Genesis Publishing, 2004), 186.

295 *When Thomas Hardy wrote:* Hardy's poem "During Wind and Rain" was brought to my attention by Stanford English professor John Felstiner.

Perhaps the most significant: See Mark Harris, *Grave Matters: A Journey Through the Funeral Industry to a Natural Way of Burial* (New York: Scribner, 2007).

"through burial of": Private First Class Justin Nieto, "Return to Nature in Arlington," Arlington National Cemetery website, January 23, 2004.

296 *"while preventing nutrients":* William Kates, "'Green' Burials Growing in Popularity," Associated Press, July 3, 2006.

"part of the circle of life": Ibid.

"the idea that": Mark Pothier, "For Some, a Casket Just Isn't Natural," *Boston Globe,* April 25, 2005.

297 *"The Earth lays back":* Emily Dickinson, *The Complete Poems of Emily Dickinson,* Thomas H. Johnson, ed. (Boston: Little, Brown and Company, 1960), 202.

ACKNOWLEDGMENTS

In this book, I cannot possibly do justice to the extensive research undertaken by innumerable archaeologists, anthropologists, sociologists, historians, philosophers, folklorists, literary scholars, and art historians who have contributed to the growing body of scholarship on cemeteries. I am especially indebted to the work of Richard E. Meyer, David Charles Sloane, and David E. Stannard. For anyone interested in learning more, the Association for Gravestone Studies, on the Web at www .gravestonestudies.org, is a good place to begin.

In addition to published material, the Internet now has a huge collection of data providing information about thousands of American burial sites. Foremost among these, the Farber Gravestone Collection offers a rich array of 13,500 photos taken from 9,000 gravestones.

Stanford University professor Robert Pogue Harrison's brilliant opus *The Dominion of the Dead* provided inspiration for my first two chapters, and his encouragement helped me along the way. Other Stanford colleagues who gave me the benefit of their expertise include Susan Groag Bell and Edith Gelles from the Michelle Clayman Institute for Gender Research; Rabbi Patricia Karlin-Neumann; and Professors Albert and Barbara Gelpi, Van Harvey, and Arnold Rampersad. Stanford undergraduate Julia Brown served as the perfect research assistant.

Professor Bram Dijkstra of the University of California at San Diego offered counsel at an early stage of the manuscript, Professor Cynthia Epstein of the Graduate Center at NYU gave me advice on sociological issues, and Emeritus Professor Ira Lapidus of the University of California at Berkeley reviewed my writing on Muslim practices. The author and translator Stina Katchadourian; the fiction writer Theresa Brown; my son Benjamin Yalom; and my good friend Larry Hatlett sensitively critiqued parts of the manuscript. As always, my husband, Irvin Yalom, was my most demanding reader.

Generous specialists at local sites included historian Maryellen McVicker of Boonville, Missouri, who not only took us to the cemeteries of central Missouri but also put us up at her house. Keith W. Stokes, the executive director of the Chamber of Commerce in Newport, Rhode Island, tramped through the snow to show us that city's historic Common Burial Ground. Two authorities on old cemeteries, Solomon Breibert and Ruth Miller, helped make our stay in Charleston particularly fruitful. In San Antonio, Rosa Catacolos, director of Gemini Inc., made sure that we experienced a vibrant celebration of the Days of the Dead in the Centro Cultural Aztlán; Maria Watson Pfeiffer graciously gave us the typescript of her study of San Antonio's cemeteries; and tour guide Kathleen Wicoff squired us to several historical sites and subsequently critiqued the Texas chapter. Nanette Napoleon Purnell, author of a fine book on the Oahu Cemetery, explained Hawaii's multicultural burial rituals at various sites.

Personal assistance via telephone and Internet was provided by many organizations and individuals, among them Bob Reese from Montana, who guided me long-distance through the Custer National Military Cemetery; Bill Wright from Nevada, who offered his personal account of a Shoshone Indian funeral; and Rabbi Joshua Segal of New Hampshire, who shared his work on the Touro Jewish Cemetery in Newport.

I am deeply grateful to my friend and agent, Sandra Dijkstra, and to my editor at Houghton Mifflin, Deanne Urmy, both of whom believed in this unlikely project from the start and helped us keep faith till the sweet end.

SELECTED BIBLIOGRAPHY

Benes, Peter. *The Masks of Orthodoxy: Folk Gravestone Carving in Plymouth County, Massachusetts, 1689–1805.* Amherst: University of Massachusetts Press, 1977.

Blair, William A. *Cities of the Dead: Contesting the Memory of the Civil War in the South, 1865–1914.* Chapel Hill: University of North Carolina Press, 2004.

Bridgman, Thomas. *Memorials of the Dead in Boston; Containing Exact Transcriptions of Inscriptions on the Sepulchral Monuments in the King's Chapel Burial Ground.* Boston: Benjamin B. Mussey and Co., 1853.

Brown, John Gary. *Soul in the Stone: Cemetery Art from America's Heartland.* Lawrence: University Press of Kansas, 1994.

Chung, Sue Fawn, and Priscilla Wegars, eds. *Chinese American Death Rituals: Respecting the Ancestors.* Lanham, MD: AltaMira Press, 2005.

Coffin, Margaret M. *Death in Early America: The History and Folklore of Customs and Superstitions of Early Medicine, Funerals, Burials, and Mourning.* New York: Thomas Nelson, Inc., 1976.

Combs, Diana Williams. *Early Gravestone Art in Georgia and South Carolina.* Athens: University of Georgia Press, 1986.

Deetz, James. *In Small Things Forgotten: An Archeology of Early American Life.* New York: Anchor Books, 1996.

Earle, Alice Morse. *Colonial Days in Old New York.* New York: Charles Scribner's Sons, 1896. See especially chapter 14.

Farrell, James J. *Inventing the American Way of Death, 1830–1920.* Philadelphia: Temple University Press, 1980.

Fischer, David Hackett. *Albion's Seed: Four British Folkways in America.* New York: Oxford University Press, 1989.

Florence, Robert, and Mason Florence. *New Orleans Cemeteries: Life in the Cities of the Dead*. New Orleans: Batture Press, 1997.

Forbes, Harriet Merrifield. *Gravestones of Early New England, and the Men Who Made Them, 1653–1800*. Boston: Houghton Mifflin, 1927.

Galland, China. *Love Cemetery: Unburying the Secret History of Slaves*. San Francisco: HarperSanFrancisco, 2007.

Godson, Susan H., ed. *A Guide to the Memorials of Bruton Parish Church*. Williamsburg, VA: Bruton Parish Church, 2006.

Goodman, Fred. *The Secret City: Woodlawn Cemetery and the Buried History of New York*. New York: Broadway Books, 2004.

Grollman, Earl A., ed. *Concerning Death: A Practical Guide for the Living*. Boston: Beacon Press, 1974.

Hansen, Joyce, and Gary McGowan. *Breaking Ground, Breaking Silence: The Story of New York's African Burial Ground*. New York: Henry Holt, 1998.

Harris, Mark. *Grave Matters: A Journey Through the Modern Funeral Industry to a Natural Way of Burial*. New York: Scribner, 2007.

Harrison, Robert Pogue. *The Dominion of the Dead*. Chicago: University of Chicago Press, 2003.

Horne, Ronald William. *Forgotten Faces: A Window into Our Immigrant Past*. San Francisco: Personal Genesis Publishing, 2004.

Hucke, Matt, and Ursula Bielski. *Graveyards of Chicago: The People, History, Art and Lore of Cook County Cemeteries*. Chicago: Lake Claremont Press, 1999.

Inskeep, Carolee. *The Graveyard Shift: A Family Historian's Guide to New York City Cemeteries*. Orem, UT: Ancestry Publishing, 2000.

Jackson, Charles. O., ed. *Passing: The Vision of Death in America*. Westport, CT: Greenwood Press, 1977.

Jackson, Kenneth T., and Camilo José Vergara. *Silent Cities*. New York: Princeton Architectural Press, 1989.

Jordan, Terry G. *Texas Graveyards: A Cultural Legacy*. Austin: University of Texas Press, 1982.

Keister, Douglas. *Stories in Stone: A Field Guide to Cemetery Symbolism and Iconography*. Salt Lake City: Gibbs Smith, 2004.

Kezys, Algimantas, S. J., ed. *A Lithuanian Cemetery: St. Casimir Lithuanian Cemetery in Chicago, Ill.* Chicago: Lithuanian Photo Library and Loyola University Press, 1976.

Laderman, Gary. *Rest in Peace: A Cultural History of Death and the Funeral Home in Twentieth-Century America*. New York: Oxford University Press, 2003.

Lambert, David Allen. *A Guide to Massachusetts Cemeteries*. Boston: New England Genealogical Society, 2002.

Lanctot, Barbara. *A Walk Through Graceland Cemetery*. Chicago: Chicago Architecture Foundation, 1988.

Linden-Ward, Blanche. *Silent City on a Hill: Landscapes of Memory and Boston's Mount Auburn Cemetery*. Columbus: Ohio State University Press, 1989 (revised University of Massachusetts Press, 2007).

Ludwig, Allan. *Graven Images: New England Stonecarving and Its Symbols, 1650–1815*. Hanover, CT: Wesleyan University Press, 1999.

Luti, Vincent F. *Mallet and Chisel: Gravestone Carvers of Newport, Rhode Island, in the Eighteenth Century*. Boston: New England Historic Genealogical Society, 2002.

Lynch, Thomas. *The Undertaking: Life Studies from the Dismal Trade*. New York: W. W. Norton, 1997.

Marion, John Francis. *Famous and Curious Cemeteries: A Pictorial, Historical, and Anecdotal View of American and European Cemeteries and the Famous and Infamous People Who Are Buried There*. New York: Crown Publishers, 1977.

Markers: The Journal of the Association for Gravestone Studies. Lanham, MD: University Press of America, 1984–present.

Meyer, Richard E., ed. *Cemeteries and Gravemarkers: Voices of American Culture*. Ann Arbor: UMI Research Press, 1989.

———. *Ethnicity and the American Cemetery*. Bowling Green, OH: Bowling Green State University Popular Press, 1993.

Mitford, Jessica. *The American Way of Death*. New York: Simon and Schuster, 1963.

Mizell, Lynette, ed. *Coloma Cemeteries*. Coloma, CA: Gold Discovery Park Association, 1997.

Morris, Susan. *A Traveler's Guide to Pioneer Jewish Cemeteries of the California Gold Rush*. Berkeley, CA: Judah L. Magnes Museum, 1996.

Native American Grave and Burial Protection Act. Washington, DC: U.S. Government Printing Office, 1990.

Neff, John R. *Honoring the Civil War Dead: Commemoration and the Problem of Reconciliation*. Lawrence: University Press of Kansas, 2005.

Prothero, Stephen. *Purified by Fire: A History of Cremation in America*. Berkeley: University of California Press, 2001.

Purnell, Nanette Napoleon. *O'ahu Cemetery: Burial Ground & Historic Site*. Honolulu: O'ahu Cemetery Association, 1998.

Ragon, Michel. *The Space of Death: A Study of Funerary Architecture, Decoration, and Urbanism*. Translated by Alan Sheridan. Charlottesville: University Press of Virginia, 1983.

Rawlings, Keith. *Gone but Not Forgotten: Quinette Cemetery, a Slave Burial Ground, Est. 1866*. Kirkwood, MO: Youth in Action, Inc., 2003.

Ridlen, Susanne S. *Tree-stump Tombstones*. Kokomo, IN: Old Richardville Publications, 1999.

Rosen, Fred. *Cremation in America*. Amherst, NY: Prometheus Books, 2004.

Savannah Unit, Georgia Writers' Project, Work Projects Administration. *Drums and*

Shadows: Survival Studies Among the Georgia Coastal Negroes. Garden City, NY: Anchor Books, 1972.

Shorto, Russell. *The Island at the Center of the World: The Epic Story of Dutch Manhattan and the Forgotten Colony That Shaped America.* New York: Doubleday, 2004.

Singleton, Esther. *Dutch New York.* New York: Benjamin Blom, 1968. See especially chapter 11.

Sledge, Michael. *Soldier Dead: How We Recover, Identify, Bury, and Honor Our Military Fallen.* New York: Columbia University Press, 2005.

Sloane, David Charles. *The Last Great Necessity: Cemeteries in American History.* Baltimore: Johns Hopkins University Press, 1991.

Solomon, Jack, and Olivia Solomon. *Gone Home: Southern Folk Gravestone Art.* Montgomery, AL: New South Books, 2004.

Stannard, David. *The Puritan Way of Death: A Study in Religion, Culture, and Social Change.* New York: Oxford University Press, 1977.

————, ed. *Death in America.* Philadelphia: University of Pennsylvania Press, 1975.

Strangstad, Lynette. *A Graveyard Preservation Primer.* Lanham, MD: Rowman and Littlefield, 1995.

Tashjian, Dickran, and Ann Tashjian. *Memorials for Children of Change: The Art of Early New England Stonecarving.* Middletown, CT: Wesleyan University Press, 1974.

Thompson, Robert Farris. *Flash of the Spirit: African and Afro-American Art and Philosophy.* New York: Random House, 1983.

Veit, Richard. *Digging New Jersey's Past: Historical Archeology in the Garden State.* New Brunswick, NJ: Rutgers University Press, 2002. See especially chapter 5.

Vlach, John Michael. *The Afro-American Tradition in Decorative Arts.* Athens: University of Georgia Press, 1990.

Wasserman, Emily. *Gravestone Designs, Rubbings, and Photographs from Early New York and New Jersey.* New York: Dover, 1972.

Weber, Francis J. *Requiescant in Pace: The Story of Catholic Cemeteries in the Archdiocese of Los Angeles.* Mission Hills, CA: Saint Francis Historical Society, 2003.

Wells, Charles Chauncey. *Boston's Copp's Hill Burying Ground Guide.* Oak Park, IL: Chauncey Park Press, 1998.

————, and Suzanne Austin Wells. *Preachers, Patriots, & Plain Folks: Boston's Burying Ground Guide to King's Chapel, Granary and Central Cemeteries.* Oak Park, IL: Chauncey Park Press, 2004.

Welty, Eudora. *Country Churchyards.* Jackson: University of Mississippi, 2000.

Wolf, Jean K. *Lives of the Silent Stones in the Christ Church Burial Ground: 50 Family Profiles.* Philadelphia: Christ Church Preservation Trust, 2003.

INDEX